BETWEEN DREAMS AND GHOSTS

Stanford Studies *in* Middle Eastern
and Islamic Societies *and* Cultures

BETWEEN DREAMS AND GHOSTS

Indian Migration and Middle Eastern Oil

Andrea Wright

STANFORD UNIVERSITY PRESS
Stanford, California

Stanford University Press
Stanford, California

Printed in the United States of America on acid-free, archival-quality paper

Library of Congress Cataloging-in-Publication Data

Names: Wright, Andrea (Professor), author.
Title: Between dreams and ghosts : Indian migration and Middle Eastern oil
 / Andrea Wright.
Other titles: Stanford studies in Middle Eastern and Islamic societies and
 cultures.
Description: Stanford, California : Stanford University Press, 2021. |
 Series: Stanford studies in Middle Eastern and Islamic societies and
 cultures | Includes bibliographical references and index.
Identifiers: LCCN 2021013027 (print) | LCCN 2021013028 (ebook) | ISBN
 9781503629516 (cloth) | ISBN 9781503630109 (paperback) | ISBN
 9781503630116 (ebook)
Subjects: LCSH: Foreign workers, East Indian—Persian Gulf States. |
 Petroleum workers—Persian Gulf States. | East Indians—Persian Gulf
 States. | Petroleum industry and trade—Social aspects—Persian Gulf
 States. | Persian Gulf States—Emigration and immigration—Social
 aspects. | India—Emigration and immigration—Social aspects.
Classification: LCC HD8662 .W75 2021 (print) | LCC HD8662 (ebook) | DDC
 331.6/2540536—dc23
LC record available at https://lccn.loc.gov/2021013027
LC ebook record available at https://lccn.loc.gov/2021013028

Cover photo: Kuwait City, Kuwait. Andrea Wright
Cover design: Rob Ehle

For Evelyn

Contents

Acknowledgments

WRITING THIS BOOK, I HAVE ACCRUED DEBTS TO INDIVIDUALS around the world. As I write these acknowledgments and reflect on this project from when I began to think of it in 2006 to now, in 2021, I am humbled and honored by the gifts given to me along the way—gifts that include time, energy, joy and sorrow, critical readings, and ghost stories. I am thankful to the individuals in India and the Gulf who shared their daily lives with me, including Arjun, Deepak, Jimmy, Pandeya, Mr. Bashar, Rani, Alex, Scott, Henry, Mr. Sahil, Shabana, Asma, Yogesh, Mr. Ramchandra, Padma, Mr. Hussain, Mr. Shah, and so many others. I wish I were able to thank you without a pseudonym, and I hope you find this text insightful and informative. I thank the Indian associations in the United Arab Emirates that welcomed me to their events and whose members invited me to their homes as though I was family. I would never have gotten my project started without the help of an association based in Mumbai, and I am indebted to the kindness the workers at this organization for introducing me to migrants and recruiting agents. I also thank the recruiting agents who gave me access to their businesses, the energy companies that allowed me to interrupt their daily activities and spend time with their workers, and government workers who shared their daily work. I appreciate all of your openness, your help throughout the process, and, most of all, your friendship, and I hope my deep respect for you comes through in this work.

This project changed quite a bit as I conducted research, wrote, and rewrote. I am grateful to a number of people for their intellectual contributions during this process. In particular, I thank David William Cohen for his mentorship, close reading, and discussions regarding the power and politics of knowledge; Juan Cole for his encouragement to think about the Middle East and South Asia together; Matthew Hull for his critical insights; and Farina Mir for her detailed feedback and encouragement to think about larger historiographic arguments. Conversations, readings, and questions at both the University of Chicago and the University of Michigan helped me develop this project, and I thank Dipesh Chakrabarty, Fernando Coronil, Geoff Eley, Paul Johnson, John Kelly, Conrad Kottak, Alaina Lemon, Claudio Lomnitz, Barbara Metcalf, Eric Mueggler, Stephan Palmié, and Julie Skurski. I thank Bali Sahotra for his feedback very early in this process and Andrew Shryock for his encouragement to explore this topic. I also thank Diana Denney and Kathleen King, who provided so much support for me at the University of Michigan.

I thank the institutions that gave me a home base outside the United States during portions of my research. In India, Aligarh Muslim University was an excellent host, and Ali R. Fatihi provided valuable guidance. In the UAE, the Dubai School of Government provided me with institutional affiliation that included a lively community of scholars, and staff helped me easily negotiate bureaucratic spaces. Over the course of my research and writing, I was provided support from the Fulbright-Hays Doctoral Dissertation Research Award; William & Mary; and the University of Michigan, including the Doctoral Program in Anthropology and History, the Center for South Asian Studies, the Rackham Graduate School, and the Ross School of Business. I am thankful to *Cultural Anthropology* for permission to republish a revised and expanded version of "Making Kin from Gold," and Amsterdam University Press for permission to reprint portions of "The Immoral Traffic in Women."

Solid foundations in multiple languages were central to this project. I thank Maxim Romanov for his private instruction in Arabic and the Arabic teachers at the Center for Maghrib Studies in Tunis, Tunisia, for their tutelage. I am thankful for my Urdu teachers in the United States and Lucknow, India, including Fahmida Bano, Fauzia Farooqui, Wafadar Hussain, Sheba Iftikhar, Ahtesham Khan, Zeba Parveen, and Ajay Shukla. These teachers not only taught me Urdu but helped foster my love of the language. Syed Ali's excellent instruction at the University of Michigan and his patience and encouragement helped refine my language skills. I am heavily indebted to him not only for language instruction but also his consistent engagement with this work.

Friends, mentors, and colleagues read drafts, commented, and listened to me brainstorm, and they have contributed in countless ways to this work. Early versions of this book profited from the engagement of Danna Agmon, William Benton, Daniel Birchok, Robert Chidester, Heloise Finch, Emanuela Grama, Rebecca Grapevine, Federico Helfgott Seier, Jordan Kraemer, Azfar Moin, Janam Mukherjee, Latika Neelakantan, Rajanpreet Nigam, Neha Paliwal, David Pedersen, Esteban Rozo, Behzad Sarmadi, Stephen Sparks, and Junko Teruyama. More recent iterations of this book have also benefited from comments and insights from Fahad Bishara, Joel Beinin, Neilesh Bose, Lawrence Cohen, Namita Dharia, Md. Azmeary Ferdoush, Nelida Fuccaro, Mary Hegland, Luke Heslop, Zakir Hussain, Reece Jones, Gabriele Koch, Natalie Koch, Julia Kowalski, Larisa Kurtovic, Mandana Limbert, Lisa Mitchell, Heather Paxson, Doug Rogers, Rania Sweis, Faedah Totah, Neha Vora, Anand Yang, and the anonymous reviewers at Stanford University Press. In addition, feedback from members of Brunel University London's anthropology department, members of MADCAP (Movement and Directions in Capitalism) at the University of Virginia, the Institute for South Asia Studies at UC Berkeley, participants in the Life Worlds of Oil workshop, the Gulf Studies Symposiums, and the AIIS Dissertation to Book workshop have all enriched this book.

At William & Mary, my colleagues, including Francis Tanglao Aguas, Adela Amaral, Michael Blakey, Michael Cronin, Jonathan Glasser, Tomoko Hamada, Martin Gallivan, Hiroshi Kitamura, Jennifer Bickham Mendez, Claire Pamment, Anne Rasmussen, Tomoyuki Sasaki, Stephen Sheehi, and Chitralekha Zutshi, have generously provided feedback and support. William Fisher's thoughtful insights and close readings were very helpful as I finished this book. I am thankful to Brad Weiss for his consistent engagement, mentorship, and encouragement. I also owe a debt of gratitude to R. Benedito Ferrao, Monica Seger, and Michelle Lelièvre for their scholarly engagements, advice, and frienship. In addition, at W&M, I am thankful for help from Joni Carlson, Marisa LeForge, Kerry Murphy, and Monika Van Tassel to support this work. At Stanford University Press, I am grateful to Kate Wahl for her comments and support, and I thank Caroline McKusick and others who have contributed to the publication of this book.

This book has benefited from the sustained engagement of Hoda Bandeh-Ahmadi, Alexandre Beliaev, Chandra Bhimull, David Boyk, Katherine Hendy, Elizabeth Kelley, and Purvi Mehta. Your friendships sustain me, and your brilliance inspires me. Finally, I am immensely appreciative of the encouragement and support of Evelyn, Alice Wright, Paula Wright, Carol McIntire, Karen McIntire, the Golems, Peter Glamb, Dante Rance, Jojo & the Kick-Its, Neda Burapavong, Allie Rasmus, Meghan Pluimer, Bob Goffin, Darek Wycislo, Tom Dodson, and David Oliver.

Introduction

BEYOND SCARCITY AND SURPLUS

DURING A THIRTY-HOUR TRAIN RIDE FROM MUMBAI, A COSMOPOL-
itan city on the Arabian Sea, to Uttar Pradesh, in northeastern India, Deepak and
I played card games and gambled small amounts of money on these games.[1] In a
break between our games, Deepak turned to me and, switching from joking to a
more serious tone, described the significance of this trip to him. We were traveling to his home state—not far from where his parents, before their deaths, had
owned a small farm. Deepak himself first left Uttar Pradesh when he found a job
in the Gulf through a recruiting agent who visited the area over a decade ago. He
had worked for six years in the Gulf and then four years at recruiting agencies in
Mumbai. With this experience, Deepak found a job that now allowed him to bring,
he said, "a chance" for other young men to *sapna saakaar karo* (live the dream).

When I met him, Deepak worked as an employee at a recruiting agency I
call Mancom. Mancom is based in Mumbai, and it operates as an intermediary
between oil and gas corporations outside India that want to hire Indian workers
and Indian workers who want to work abroad. Deepak was one of three individuals
who worked full time at Mancom recruiting manual laborers for oil projects in
the Arabian/Persian Gulf.[2] Many migrant laborers to the Gulf come from Indian
states like Uttar Pradesh, where the per capita income is half the national average.
Based on experience, Deepak expected that in Uttar Pradesh, he would be able to

hire, at a pay rate lower than many Indians will accept, the hundreds of workers the energy contractor required.[3]

The following day, I met Deepak at the interview site and found hundreds of men waiting to be interviewed. At first, my appearance sparked murmurs. I heard some men near me begin to speculate that I must work for an oil company. Why else, they asked aloud, would a *gori*, or White woman, be in the area?[4] Quickly trying to quell this story, I explained that I was only a researcher who wanted to learn about migration and write a book. As I repeated to prospective migrants that I had no ties to companies in the Gulf, most returned their attention to the area where Deepak gathered applicants' information, sorted applicants into categories, and watched applicants demonstrate their strength by carrying heavy loads across the yard.

One young Muslim man, Ahmed, continued to stand with me and ask questions about my life and my research. Ahmed lived on a farm with his parents, his brothers, his brothers' wives, his nieces and nephews, and his sister. As we spoke, he explained that there were few jobs in the area and that the farm did not produce enough food to meet his family's needs. They were heavily in debt to a local moneylender who charged high interest rates. In addition, Ahmed's eldest sister, Naheed, needed to get married, but the family did not have enough resources to provide the funds for her to do so. Ahmed's parents wanted him to go to the Gulf to earn money, help support the family, and contribute to his sister's marriage. Many of Ahmed's friends already worked in the Gulf, and he saw it as his duty, as a son and brother, to work abroad. He reflected, "My friends have gone. I also must go." After his interview, he and I walked through his village. He pointed to his neighbor's new *pucca* house, a house made of bricks,[5] and a tractor parked in front. The neighbors bought their house and tractor after two sons began working in the Gulf, and Ahmed did not want to be "left behind" as those from his village who migrated improved their living situations. As we continued our conversation, Ahmed told me, "My dream is to fly on an airplane."

Today, there are approximately 8.5 million Indians living in Bahrain, Kuwait, Oman, Qatar, Saudi Arabia, and the United Arab Emirates (UAE).[6] These countries have large nonnational populations, and noncitizens make up the majority of their workforces.[7] Indians work at all levels of the Gulf economy, from CEOs to laborers, but the majority of them hold unskilled or semiskilled positions. Unskilled and semiskilled are two categories that the Indian government used historically and still uses today to classify workers. The term *unskilled workers* most often refers to manual laborers. *Semiskilled workers* have some technical training or experience and their positions include pipe fitters, steel binders, electricians, plumbers, bar benders, pressmen, masons, welders, and drivers.[8]

Many young Indian men like Ahmed dream of migrating to the Gulf, but once there, they find the work physically and emotionally difficult. Working on oil projects or in factories that manufacture parts used on oil projects often requires physically exhausting work and long hours. Most men work outside, and the summer temperatures regularly exceed 110 degrees Fahrenheit. In addition, labor laws favor employers, and workers are legally forbidden to unionize or strike for better working conditions. Some workers in the Gulf face even greater challenges, including not being paid for their labor, not being able to return home when they choose, physical abuse, and injury or death while on the job.

Aware of the challenges that Indian migrants to the Gulf experience, the Indian government regulates emigration for those who have not completed the first two years of secondary school (i.e., completed ten years of schooling). Building on colonial laws and in response to contemporary instances of worker abuse in the Gulf, Indians who have not completed the first two years of secondary school, commonly referred to as 10th pass, must receive permission from the Indian government in order to emigrate to the Gulf for work. As prospective migrants seek government permission, they work with recruiting agencies that act as intermediaries between workers and oil companies. Once a worker finds a job in the Gulf, he goes alone for an allotted time, usually one to two years. After their work contract ends, migrants return to their homes, where they often rest for a few months before attempting to find another job in the Gulf.

THE SCALES OF OIL PRODUCTION

The size of the global oil and gas industry is enormous.[9] The first time I attended the Abu Dhabi International Petroleum Exhibition and Conference, I wandered through the vendors set up in the conference halls only to be literally stopped in my tracks because I needed to walk around giant machine parts that were ten feet in diameter or chains that were made of links where each link was wider in diameter than I am and almost as long as my arm.[10] Oil consumption is also incredibly large: the world consumes, on average, 99.67 million barrels per day of oil.[11] The labor used to produce this oil is counted annually in the thousands of millions of hours worked.[12]

In contrast to the overwhelming size of the industry, oil is often approached on the premise of its scarcity—a self-evident fact that is reinforced every time a newspaper headline speculates on the end of oil.[13] It is measured in light of depletion, that is, by how much oil each country is estimated to have remaining and accessible.[14] In news reports, crises in large oil-producing states such as Iran, Iraq, and Venezuela are viewed as lessening the supply of oil on the market and driving up prices.[15] Given the dominance of this approach to oil, it makes sense, then, that labor, a key part in transforming oil from nature to resource, or something lying underground to a commodity, would also get caught up in the discourse of scarcity and surplus.[16]

Surplus and scarcity carry such discursive strength that it seems self-evident that they are the reasons for Indians migrating to work on the Gulf's oil projects. Notably, popular media and government officials argue that the Gulf has a surplus of oil wealth but a scarcity of labor. In contrast, India is described as having a surplus of labor but a scarcity of wealth. Indeed, many recruiting agents described their work in such terms. In conversation, Mr. Shah, a recruiting agent based in Mumbai, said, "India is the world capital of world labor resources. Ten lakh [people] go, but never shorted of labor manpower here."[17] A close friend of Mr. Shah and fellow recruiting agent agreed with Mr. Shah's characterization of Indian migration. Adding that he "sends 80 percent [of the Indian workers he facilitates jobs for] to Saudi Arabia, because it is the biggest producer of oil, so naturally requirement [of numbers of workers] is high." These short descriptions of Indian migration to the Gulf emphasize financial reasons for migration.

The narrative power of scarcity and surplus to engage with and explain Indian labor migration is not limited to use in the present: bureaucrats working in the Indian government after the country's independence from the British in 1947 also saw labor migration as a consequence of these forces. One bureaucrat argued that given concerns over the increase in India's population, a program that encouraged or subsidized emigration would be an ideal solution.[18] In the 1950s, Indian bureaucrats also argued that Indians migrated in response to internal pressures in India, such as lack of jobs. Unemployment was strongly felt in the Indian oil industry, and there were no positions within India for those with oil worker skills.[19] Others pointed out that jobs in the Gulf were lucrative for Indians, and emigrants saved more during one contract period in the Gulf than they could hope to save "in a lifetime of work" in India.[20] In articulating scarcity and surplus as the underlying force of labor migration to the Gulf, the Indian government, recruiting agents, and oil company managers often conceptualize migrants as entrepreneurs—rational actors who are making calculated decisions.

If we view the oil industry from a global or state-centered perspective, these scales distort labor to make the process appear frictionless.[21] But if we attend to the process of Indian migration to the Gulf, we find that this process destabilizes and questions the normalization of neoliberal imaginings. Neoliberalism, here, refers to the increasing privatization and liberalization of markets.[22] Such economic shifts have an impact on labor. As people migrate in response to changing economic circumstances, temporary labor becomes increasingly the norm, and workers are not represented by unions or political parties.[23] In this book, neoliberalism is not an abstract concept that shapes migration; it emerges in the signing of contracts, cultivating entrepreneurial citizens, managing labor, envisioning the future, and fighting for one's rights. Thus, an ethnographic perspective on labor in the oil industry questions the frictionless role of labor and demonstrates how precarious labor complicates the commodity chain.[24]

In addition, if we consider migration with an ethnographic lens and focus on the everyday lives of migrants and their families, then we find much is lost in using supply and demand, surplus and scarcity to explain labor in the Gulf's oil industry. Indeed, as anthropologists of migration have shown in a diversity of contexts, such frameworks ignore many structural inequalities and lived realities.[25]

A couple of years later, I met Ahmed again—this time in Abu Dhabi, UAE, where he was working. He described his arc from India to the Gulf: "The problem with India is [I] cannot save much, [it is] not raining well, I do farming, so [no rain] is a big effect. [Also] in India, it is like you go here and there and you spend [money]; here [in the UAE] you just go back to your room, so you can save." For many poor Indians, the oil fields of the Gulf are one of the few international destinations where men who do not have formal education are able to find lucrative employment. But Ahmed's choice to migrate was also informed by his dreams, familial obligations, and friends' activities. In addition, multiple parties, including recruiting agency employees, government bureaucrats, and oil company managers, also participated in his migration.[26]

Social practices and structural inequalities clearly motivate migration, and migration also influences social practices. Thus, while economic necessity informs Indian migration to the Gulf, ethnographic research demonstrates that migration is not a simple economic calculus. Rather, migration is a process that brings together diverse individuals to form communities. This process is deeply informed by participants' dreams for the future, as well as the historical context in which they situate their activities. Through examining migration with this ethnographic lens, it becomes apparent that invoking surplus and scarcity to explain Indian labor migration rhetorically produces economies with systems of values that make labor cheap and oil expensive.

NETWORKS IN THE ARABIAN SEA

Labor in the oil industry is challenging to study ethnographically. In part, this is due to the scale of the industry.[27] Labor relations are also hidden from public view through managerial practices and government decisions, and many migrant laborers working in the Gulf live in camps that are a distance from urban centers. These camps are just one of the many contemporary management practices built on earlier management practices developed to limit worker actions. In addition to difficulties meeting workers, researchers often face legal and social barriers as they attempt to gain access to oil companies, recruiting agents, and migrant laborers.[28]

Ignorant of these challenges, I moved to Mumbai in 2009 to begin fieldwork on Indian migration to the Gulf. When I arrived, I began to call recruiting agencies that were running advertisements in newspapers. After my calls were rejected or I was hung up on, I started to physically show up at agencies, only to have doors literally shut on my face. Trying to find something to do, I contacted an *anjuman* (association) for Muslims from the state of Bihar who work in Mumbai. This association was formed by wealthy Muslims from the state who hoped to provide religious and financial services to poor Bihari Muslims who came to work in the many home factories in Mumbai's Dharavi neighborhood. Assistance was seen as an urgent necessity because Bihar is one of India's poorest states and Muslims face discrimination throughout India.

On my first visit to the association, I climbed a set of stairs where a goat was tied between the landings. The meeting was a few days before Eid al-Fitr, and the goat's meat was distributed later that week to Bihari laborers for their holiday meals. As I walked into his office, I was greeted by the head of the association, a *mullah*, or religious leader, who aspired to open an Islamic banking system that would provide loans at no interest. After discussing his (and the goat's) upcoming Eid plans, I told him about my research. He replied that he himself was not involved in Gulf migration. While he could not help me with that, he said, he could introduce me to members of the anjuman. I eagerly accepted, happy to have something to do.

With the head of the anjuman's introduction, I spent time in home factories, where men worked stitching clothes or suitcases. My days were occupied drinking tea with factory owners, chatting with employees during their lunch breaks, and meeting community leaders. I continued to mention my interest in Gulf migration, but everyone I met told me they knew nothing about this topic. Finally, over a month later, a member of the anjuman's board of directors, who knew of my interest in Gulf migration, introduced me to Mr. Shah, a recruiting agent based in Mumbai. A Muslim originally from the state of Bihar, Mr. Shah was a regular donor to education programs run by the association. I called him, and he agreed to meet me the following week. As I exited an elevator and entered Mr. Shah's office, located in modern office building in a stylish neighborhood of Mumbai, I felt far from the home factories I had just left.

Mr. Shah welcomed me to his office and spent many days telling me about the migration process. He also introduced me to a number of other recruiting agents in the city, and it was through him that I was able to begin my research in the relatively insular world of recruiting agents. Importantly for my research, Mr. Shah introduced me to Mr. Sahil, the owner of Mancom, the company where I conducted the bulk of my ethnographic research with recruiting agents. While watching interviews organized by Mancom employees and at other recruiting agencies, I also met oil company managers working in the Gulf. When I arrived in the United Arab Emirates for research, I contacted the managers I met through Mancom and other recruiting agencies, and a few allowed me to visit their oil project sites. Beginning fieldwork was not easy, and even after Mr. Shah provided an introduction, many recruiting agents, as well as government officials and oil company managers, still met me with skepticism. Later, some of them said they were worried when we first met that I was really a journalist, writing an exposé on Indian migration to the Gulf.

As I met with recruiting agents and observed job interviews, I realized that recruiting agency offices were highly gendered spaces: most of the owners and employees of the recruiting agencies were men. At Mancom, a medium-sized recruiting agency, two senior workers, both women, handled the recruitment of skilled workers and professionals. At another recruiting agency, Fauzia, the daughter of the owner of the agency, helped her father manage the business. In general, however, I was almost always the only woman present. Recruiting agents explained to me that the reason their employees are all men is that subagents and unskilled or semiskilled laborers are "rough" or "uneducated" and therefore inappropriate for women to work with. Similarly, at most oil projects in the Gulf, I was almost always the only woman present.[29]

My research with oil company managers and recruiting agents, along with Indian government officials, recruiting agency employees, and migrants, taught me that migration is a social process.[30] Migrants travel to work in the oil industry and are often employed by large, multinational corporations. Their migration is regulated by governments that are explicitly implementing neoliberal reforms. This process highlights that the oil industry in the Gulf was and continues to be structured by a disarticulated process—one that is not determined solely by the needs of an industry and is not centrally coordinated. Indeed, it is an active goal of companies to disarticulate the process. Today, as in the past, many large oil companies do not want to hire their own laborers, thereby absolving themselves of direct responsibility for worker welfare. Instead, these companies work with subcontractors who in turn work with agents based in India to find workers there. This form of disarticulation combines with laborers' own selective affinities. As I seek to illustrate, given the ways in which labor circulates in the Arabian Sea, workers are central to, but not necessarily bound by, the oil industry and state. My analysis deprioritizes industrial needs. Instead, it focuses on how workers move, noting both the constraints on and possibilities of that movement.

As I conducted archival work and listened to oral histories, I developed an appreciation of the endurance of institutions that move labor and the historic depth of the multiple groups that participate in moving labor from India to the Gulf's oil projects. [31] Participants build networks as they circulate in the Arabian Sea, and communities are formed through the process of migration.[32] These communities at times include laborers and other Indian migrants to the Gulf; small business owners in India; Indian bureaucrats; *khalījīs*, or Gulf Arabs; and oil company managers.

Through analyzing contemporary labor policies within multiple genealogies, we find that government officials and company managers built on colonial labor mobilities in order to staff oil projects. Workers also informed the process of labor migration. Historically, from the strikes by Indians in the oil fields to the restructuring of emigration laws, Indian laborers and lawmakers have attempted to exert control over labor conditions at Gulf oil projects. Likewise, the strikes and political activities of khalījī workers have also been influential moments in the shaping labor policies in the Gulf. These moments were further affected by the activities of merchants, oil companies, and the British administration in the Gulf.

Today, the result of all these combined factors can be seen in the contemporary *kafala*, or sponsorship, system in which workers have limited means to negotiate their working conditions.[33]

In exploring oil production as a social process, historical and contemporary affiliations and circulations emerge as central features of contemporary migration. Many migrants stress the importance of local affiliations and build networks that rely on their natal village. These affiliations represent a highly localized aspect of social lives that workers often maintain as they move from their natal villages to the Gulf.[34] These relationships inform the specificity of oil production in the Arabian Sea. In turn, migration and oil have and continue to influence regimes of citizenship, politics, and family life in India and the Gulf. In considering the formation of communities by circulation, I attend to migrants' and their networks' dynamic capacities to form and reform communities, states, and regions. A focus on the process of migration destabilizes a focus on both the individual and the nation-state in favor of examining transnational networks of diverse actors.[35] Thus, the order of oil production in the Arabian Sea is brought into being by the relationships developed by actors.

THE POETICS OF DREAMS AND GHOSTS

My interest in Indian migration to the Gulf began in 2006 when I was living in Lucknow, the capital of Uttar Pradesh. In the fall of that year, I took a trip to Beirut, Lebanon, that required a long layover in Dubai, UAE. Unfamiliar with the city, I decided to use the time to visit the Mall of the Emirates, as one of my Urdu teachers in Lucknow had asked for a picture of the ski slope inside the mall. Outside the airport, I followed the signs for local transportation and found a line of waiting taxis. Entering a taxi, I asked the driver, in Arabic, to take me to the mall. In response, he shook his head and indicated that he did not speak Arabic. As I watched the taxi's meter tick upward, I asked the driver, in English, to take me to the mall. Once again, he shook his head, telling me, this time in English, that he could not understand my English. After repeating my request in English and Arabic again, I was unsure of how to proceed, and I began to feel nervous. At the time, I was on a modest fellowship for language study in India. My stipend was paid in rupees and calculated for Lucknow's low cost of living. The taxi driver and I stared at each other, the meter continued to climb, and I could see my monthly stipend for food and other necessities rapidly disappearing as each minute increased the cost of the taxi ride. Finally, I repeated my request to the taxi driver, but this time in Hindi, hoping that he would understand.

As I finished my sentence, the driver looked taken aback. "Madame," he asked, "how do you know Hindi?" I replied that I lived in Lucknow and studied Urdu and Hindi at a school there. My answer further surprised him, and he exclaimed that he was from a village near Lucknow. He then began to call his friends who worked in Dubai but were also from Uttar Pradesh. He told them that he had a White woman in his taxi—an American White woman who was now living in India and could speak Hindi. During the calls, I spoke Hindi when asked so as to prove to the driver's friends the validity of his claims. Eventually we decided that I would not go to the mall, and instead, I went to a tea stall where I met a group of men, all from villages in Uttar Pradesh who worked in Dubai as taxi drivers. Thus, my long layover shifted from looking at a ski slope in the desert to a day spent talking with Indian taxi drivers, learning about their lives, and hearing their reasons for working in the Gulf. It also shifted my focus from how communities are formed within India to how communities are formed as people move from India to the Gulf and back again.

Before that day, I was not aware of the large number of Indians working in the Gulf, but I quickly became interested in the approximately 1 million Indian men who travel annually to work as laborers in the Gulf. When I returned to Lucknow after my trip, I visited with some of the families of the taxi drivers I met that day and listened to the experiences of individuals whose children, husband, and/or fathers work in the Gulf. Often families reflected on the physical absence of their sons or husbands. Many also pointed to gifts brought home by migrants and items purchased with money sent by migrants, indicating ways in which the person, despite living far away, remained a presence in their daily lives. These gifts were sent because of affection and duty, and prospective migrants are warned, often through ghost stories, that forgetting one's familial obligations could lead to death or disaster.[36]

As I conducted research, I learned that *dreams* and *ghosts* are terms that migrants themselves invoke to explain and situate their migration. Throughout this book, I examine the poetics of ghosts and dreams and how they are used by migrants, as well as by other participants in labor migration to the Gulf.[37] I find that future visions often emerge in dreams: dreams of modernity, material comfort, and expanding capitalist frontiers. These dreams build on past narratives, which my interlocutors most often discuss as traditions, obligations, or histories. Ghosts appear as reminders of the past; they shape contemporary practices and disrupt the present.[38]

Ghosts and dreams thus work as entry points for understanding contemporary capitalism, states, and labor. Often migrants invoke poetics to describe situations such as losing one's small farm (dispossession) or working on oil projects far from their homes (alienation). These poetics emerge at times in unexpected metaphors, such as describing a rig as a Hindu temple or describing gold as a substance, like blood, that shapes kinship relations. Migrants use poetics to resist, critique, or refuse state and corporate power, and in doing so, they provide alternative perspectives on social relations and the future.[39] Other poetics are also invoked by my interlocutors, including recruiting agents' reference to mangoes and migrants and oil company managers' describing oil as the devil. An ethnographic view of Indian labor migration and the poetics invoked provide insight into migration's temporal contexts—ways people make sense of their everyday lives and temporally locate themselves between the past and the future.

My analysis of the poetics that my interlocuters use builds on anthro/historical work that critically interrogates both disciplinary boundaries and the politics of knowledge production. The insights provided by this perspective contribute in many ways to this book; I examine the formation of categories, ideas, and processes in order to understand how the practices of those involved in labor migration changed over time and consider the weight of previous practices, categories, and ideas in the present.[40] In order to do this, I put ethnographic research into dialogue with archival research, oral histories, and social media. These sources lend perspectives on the history of Indian labor migration to the Gulf and emphasize the multiplicity of ways in which migrants, agents, and oil company managers engaged with and shaped migration in the past. What emerges are the enduring power of institutions and ideologies, even as the words used to describe them change. In addition, anthro/history helps move laborers to the center of my research and decenters state narratives.[41] This approach illuminates how laws and practices that are often defined as precapitalist are actually formed in conjunction with contemporary state and corporate policies. It also demonstrates how capitalism incorporates noncapitalist social relations and values into its reproduction and how diverse actors expand and develop capitalism.[42]

BOOK OUTLINE

This book follows the process of migration—from villages to oil projects and back again—and all parties involved in this process—from migrants to corporations. In Part I, I look at how individuals migrate. I consider how the process of migration allow us to see how corporate practices, government policies, and international discourses have an impact on specific localities and communities. In turn, an ethnographic approach to migration highlights how migrants shape the institutionalization of these policies and practices. Chapter 1 examines how colonial laws and colonial capitalism shaped Indian migration historically. It then considers the Indian government's contemporary attempts to liberalize emigration and the ways in which liberalization reinforces colonial assumptions concerning rights and liberties. The result is that Indian citizens are unevenly affected by emigration regulations. In Chapter 2, I explore how recruiting agents and Indian government officials understand emigration regulations to not only protect vulnerable workers but to also protect India's brand image abroad. In Indian business and government engagement with India's brand, migrant labor is differentiated from other export commodities because migrants are seen as uniquely able to transform themselves into higher-quality commodities through training in Indian entrepreneurship. Chapter 3 then looks at how migrants, low-level government bureaucrats, recruiting agency employees (most of whom, like Deepak, previously worked in the Gulf), and oil company managers create networks. As they do so, prospective migrants often work in the spaces between government and business policies, mining moments of disjuncture for opportunities to elude or expedite formal channels. In these spaces, migrants both inform and negotiate the processes that are meant to structure their movement.

As migrants travel, they, like Ahmed, describe their migration as a way to "live the dream" and "be a good son." Ghost stories circulate among migrants regarding those who fail to fulfill their obligations. In this context of dreams and ghosts, workers are making sense of their migration through situating it as meaningful to their families, their communities, and their country. In Part II, I consider two contexts in which migrants and their families explain the importance of migration. Chapter 4 examines the relationship between kinship and labor migration. In particular, it looks at how migrating to the Gulf offers men the possibility of buying gold for their daughters' or sisters' weddings, thereby fulfilling their familial obligations and enacting their masculinity. Chapter 5 looks at migrants' approaches to modernity and the future. In this analysis, migrants use European and American company practices to critique contemporary Indian development plans—plans that exclude minority communities from membership in the nation and its future. Migrants are critical also of American and European practices, and they argue for a future that values obligations and connections, not only with other people, but also with the environment.

Part III attends to the experiences of migrants and demonstrates the ways in which colonial capitalism, imperialism, and corporate practices structure the contemporary racialized labor hierarchies that are prevalent in the Gulf. It examines how historic and contemporary practices used to manage labor migration produce and reinforce these hierarchies and workers' limited rights. This analysis argues that the poor working conditions that workers experience in the Gulf cannot be simply attributed to Gulf Arab traditions or the negative impact of oil rents on states. Chapter 6 demonstrates that current labor conditions are shaped by oil company management techniques and international discourses that tie oil to national security, and the chapter focuses on the role of labor camps as a management tool as well as a space of precarity. In Chapter 7, I examine how contracting between companies allows companies to displace corporate risk, usually onto the most vulnerable. Safety protocols, in particular, are used to facilitate both contracting and to displace corporate liability. Safety is also actively engaged with by workers, and they reframe safety as part of their own moral order. The Conclusion examines how returned workers focus on corporate or state obligations as they plan community activism in their attempts to hold state and corporate actors accountable, and it explores stories that workers tell in which ghosts emerge when employers treat employees poorly or when employers do not fulfill their contractual obligations.

Part I

OF MANGOES AND MEN

AROUND MANCOM'S OFFICE BUILDING, MANGO TREES PROVIDE shade and a respite from the surrounding noise and crowds of Mumbai's northern suburb. The junior employees of the office and I often spent our lunchtime trying to pick mangoes without the building guards noticing and chasing us off. We ate the mangoes when they were green, or unripe, with salt and enjoyed their tart flavor. Later in the year, when the mangoes were ripe on the tree, we enjoyed the sweet fruit as a dessert after lunch. Not far from Mancom's offices was the recruiting agency of Mr. Hussain, a recruiting agent I had been introduced to at a meeting between recruiting agents and the Ministry of Overseas Indian Affairs. Mr. Hussain is a young man who had studied in London and now spent half of his year in Dubai, United Arab Emirates (UAE), and the other half in Mumbai. Articulate, outgoing, and engaging, Mr. Hussain immediately invited me to visit his office when I met him. At his office, there were no mango trees; it was located on the third floor of an anonymous office building in Mumbai. Much smaller than Mancom, Mr. Hussain's company needed only a few rooms to hold its entire staff. Although it was small, this office had a long-standing connection with the Gulf, and Mr. Hussain's work as a recruiting agent followed in the footsteps of his father and grandfather. When describing his family history to me, he made a slippage between mangoes and migrants that illustrated to me how the conceptual and material apparatuses that used to facilitate trade are now used to structure labor migration to the Gulf.

Mr. Hussain's family began shipping goods to the Arabic-speaking Gulf in the late British colonial period. His grandfather was a customs agent in Mumbai, and he went on hajj in the early 1940s. While he was in Mecca, Mr. Hussain's grandfather stayed at a guesthouse where he met people from Oman. During their conversations, a family from Oman asked him if he could supply "textiles, construction material, steel pipes, carpets, mangoes, basically everything," and Mr. Hussain's grandfather agreed. This meeting proved to be the beginning of a lucrative trading company that focused on exporting materials and fruit from India to the Trucial States (today the UAE) and Oman. Mr. Hussain's father continued this business, and he increased the export of mangoes from India to the Gulf. In the late 1970s, the family "started exporting people" but continued to export goods, especially mangoes. This changed in the 1990s, when the family found that exporting goods had become less lucrative and they began to "export more and more" workers to the Gulf.

Mr. Hussain was not the only recruiting agent who was involved with trade before entering the recruitment business. Mancom's owner, Mr. Sahil, is a Hindu from Gujarat who took over Mancom when his father retired. As I spoke with Mr. Sahil's father one day, he described how his father and his father's father had traded with the Gulf, estimating that the family has been practicing this trade since at least the late 1800s. Another recruiting agent, Mr. Shah, has been in the recruiting agency business since 1975. Before this time, he had worked as a secretary for a Gulf consulate in Mumbai, where he made many contacts with Gulf-based companies. Explaining how he became a recruiting agent, Mr. Shah said, "It came natural to deal with Middle East countries, and I got the idea that I should be an exporter [of goods] and manpower." For Mr. Shah, government employment and trading opportunities provided an entry into business in the Arabian Sea.

Other recruiting agents stressed the importance of religious networks in their choice to be recruiting agents. Mr. Hussain's father began his export business while on hajj, and other recruiting agents told me they also began their businesses through connections they made on hajj. One of the most respected recruiting agents in Mumbai, Ashraf Saab,[1] began "shipping workers and pilgrims" in 1964. Before 1964, when he was a young lawyer working in Mumbai, Ashraf Saab was hired for legal consulting by the Government of India's Hajj Committee. Through this position and subsequent trips to Saudi Arabia, Ashraf Saab established strong business connections in Saudi Arabia that helped him become the only official booker for a Saudi transportation company in India. When I met him, Ashraf Saab's company was booking many Indian Muslims' tickets for travel during hajj; in 2011, for example, his company booked travel for 85,000 people going on hajj. In addition to facilitating religious pilgrimage, his company is also one of the biggest recruiting agencies in Mumbai. He specializes in recruiting laborers to work on oil projects in Saudi Arabia. In his experience, the organizational structures of religious pilgrimage and labor migration overlap closely.

Recruiting agents describe their work to me as "catching" a man and then "exporting" him. This language of commerce, in conjunction with shift from exporting goods to labor, or, in Mr. Hussain's terms, from mangoes to men, highlights the commodification of labor that occurs as rural farmers take jobs in the Gulf. The view of migrants as commodities is reinforced by the marketization of labor in a field in which people are hired from multiple countries. This marketization, often envisioned by both government officials and recruiting agents as a competition among nation-states, further reinforces the categorization of migrants as an export commodity.

While recruiting agency activities are often rooted in histories of trade and religious pilgrimage, oil company practices have roots in British colonial capitalism and geostrategic competition. Indian laborers began working at Gulf oil projects in 1908 with the discovery of oil in Persia (today Iran). Oil became increasingly important to the British after Winston Churchill, in 1911, decided to use oil to power the British navy, which not only revitalized the navy but also increased Britain's dependence on oil.[2] Hoping to maintain and extend Britain's control of Gulf oil, the British government obtained oil concessions with the rulers of the Gulf countries. These concessions specified that if oil was found within their territories, the rulers would not give concessions to foreigners except those approved by the British government.[3] These oil concessions built on earlier treaties signed between the Gulf rulers and the British. The British pursued these earlier treaties in the late nineteenth and early twentieth centuries as a means to provide a buffer zone between British India and the Ottoman Empire.[4] Administratively, the Arabic-speaking Gulf was overseen from the Bombay Presidency in India. The benefits of the trucial system were not limited to protecting India, and the system also secured British trade routes.[5] These treaties gave the British an advantage when the Gulf rose to prominence for its potential oil reserves.

Of course, the British were not the only ones interested in developing the Gulf's oil fields. In addition to Russia's influence in Persia, American companies were vying to develop oil projects there. The British government tried to prevent American companies from participating in the Gulf oil industry outside Saudi Arabia and also sought to curb American influence in all of the oil companies working in the Gulf. One way the British administration did this was by insisting that British subjects, including persons from British India, staff oil companies. This staffing policy was possible given the already strong presence of Indians in the Gulf. In addition, many of the British managers of oil companies had begun their careers in British India before moving across the Arabian Sea. The British approved oil agreements only with the stipulation that the companies would hire large numbers of locals and British subjects. As a consequence, the British Political Resident in the Gulf had considerable control over the recruitment of employment. In addition to restricting the numbers of Americans working in the Gulf, the British also limited the numbers of skilled Persians and Iraqis working there, for fear of political upheaval. This was particularly important in the mid-twentieth century when oil projects were the site of political unrest and imperial competition. During the 1960s, strikes by *khalījī*, or Gulf Arab, workers proved costly, and officials and oil company managers characterized these strikes as threats to both state and corporate security. In response, oil companies decided to preferentially hire South Asian workers whom they believed were more loyal to the British. They could also be fired without political or economic consequences.[6]

Throughout the twentieth century, oil companies wanted cheap and easily replaceable labor, and, in the early twentieth century, the British government used the same system that was used to move Indian indentured workers to plantations in the British Empire.[7] Today, this system continues, but moves increasingly to poor areas of India to find the large numbers of workers who are willing to leave their families for one or two years at a time for relatively low pay. To hire these workers, recruiting agents play a central role in the migration of unskilled and semiskilled laborers. Recruiting agents help migrants negotiate the governmental policies that restrict the movement of unskilled or semiskilled workers to the Gulf and provide links between multinational companies and Indian labor, thereby mediating between migrants and companies and between migrants and the government.

The logic of colonial labor mobilities continues to inform labor migration, but as Mr. Hussain's family history demonstrates, migration is also shaped by religious, trade, and localized networks. The poetics of mangoes and men points to the role of history and bureaucratic process in the production of labor migration. Emigration processes often deploy the same structures used to move goods, reinforcing the global market's view that they are both commodities. Migrants, government bureaucrats, recruiting agents and their employees, and oil company managers are all actively involved in migration. They also develop, maintain, and navigate emigration restrictions and their accompanying bureaucratic hurdles.

Chapter 1

PROTECTING VULNERABLE CITIZENS

BASED IN MUMBAI, INDIA, MANCOM SPECIALIZES IN RECRUITING workers for oil and gas projects in the Gulf. A medium-sized recruiting agency, most of Mancom's employees had previously worked in the Gulf. One of Mancom's top-performing employees was Mr. Anthony, a Christian from southern India who had spent his adult life working as a manager at an oil project. Because of his ability to speak Arabic, Mr. Anthony often translated for Gulf managers, who were most comfortable speaking Arabic. One day, I watched as Mr. Anthony worked with two Kuwaiti managers who were in the office to hire employees for a temporary labor agency that supplies day laborers for oil and gas construction projects. As I sat with them, pairs of interviewees were ushered into the rooms by one of the handful of young men who worked as a "peon" or "office boy" at Mancom. In the meeting, the two Kuwaiti managers looked at the interviewees' résumés and asked questions, in Arabic, concerning the interviewees' experience and skills. Mr. Anthony translated from Arabic to Hindi for the interviewees and then translated their responses back into Arabic for the prospective employers. In interviews such as these, Mr. Anthony often took the opportunity to expand interviewees' answers and highlight the unique skills or experience of the interviewees. He would also prompt the interviewees when they had trouble answering questions. Mr. Anthony had a vested interest in the Kuwaiti managers hiring workers at Mancom as his job performance was directly tied to how many workers he placed with companies.

In addition, he wanted to be sure the interviewees were happy with the quality of the candidates at Mancom, because Gulf-based companies, such as this one, often hire hundreds of workers at a time. A company may work with multiple recruiting agencies to fill these positions quickly, and Mancom wanted to supply as many of these workers as possible. Because Mancom could legally charge each worker INR 20,000 (approximately US$437 in 2010) for finding the worker employment, each potential person hired increased the company's profits.

After interviewing two men, Azaad and Munsif, who met their qualifications, the Kuwaiti managers handed contracts, written in both Arabic and English, to the interviewees. Mr. Anthony, holding a copy of the contract, translated into Hindi the contract's terms and highlighted what he considered to be the most important parts of it, particularly their salaries and the length of their employment. As Mr. Anthony spoke, the interviewees nodded in agreement. A manager then asked Mr. Anthony, in Arabic, "Hal yifhamuna?" (Do they understand [the contract]?). I had spoken with the managers earlier that day, and, in that conversation, they had shared with me that they were in Mumbai because "aleummal alhnwd hum al'arkhas" ([Indian] workers are the cheapest). They also told me that their company is small, and, as a result, they knew that the pay is not as high as people might find at similar jobs in the Gulf. These issues were not mentioned to the interviewees, and Mr. Anthony simply turned to the interviewees and asked, in Hindi, "Aap samajhe?" ([Do] you understand?). Azaad and Munsif, aware of the close to one hundred men waiting in the halls and courtyard of Mancom for an interview and eager for their first jobs in the Gulf, nodded their heads to reassure the managers that they understood and agreed.

Later that day, I spoke with Azaad and Munsif, and they said they were happy to have found jobs in the Gulf. Azaad explained that he and Munsif were both from Bihar, one of India's most economically depressed states, where they had worked as farmers. They had attended only a few years of school, and, they said, they were not "strong" in reading Hindi. Furthermore, they knew neither English nor Arabic. They had moved to Mumbai a few years before they were hired by the Kuwaiti company. In Mumbai, they worked in a home factory in Dharavi, a neighborhood in Mumbai. At this factory, they, along with fifteen other Muslim men from Bihar, worked long hours, six days a week, manufacturing goods. At night, the men climbed to the platform above the workshop to sleep. Pay largely depends on a man's speed and experience, and Azaad reported he usually earned around INR 5000 per month (approximately US$111 in 2010 or US$4 per day of work). This amount, Azaad told me, was twice what he earned working in his village in Bihar.

When I asked him how he found his work in Dharavi, Azaad told me, "Jobs are found through networks of others, and this is how." Most of the workers came from the same district in Bihar as the owner of the factory. Azaad continued, explaining that in Bihar, "there is no employment, no industry, no mills and this year there is drought and this year many people will come" to Mumbai searching for work and relying on friends to find jobs. Munsif interjected, estimating there are two lakhs, or 200,000, Biharis living in Mumbai and 90 percent of these Biharis are Muslim. When I asked him why so many Bihari Muslims live in Mumbai, Munsif said the reasons were related to education access and discrimination against Muslims. "More Muslims than Hindus are illiterate," Munsif said. In addition, he told me he believes that Hindus are preferentially chosen for government jobs, which are still considered some of the best ones in Bihar.

As I spoke with Azaad and Munsif about their new job, I told them about the parts of their contract that I felt had not been well explained in the interview. These concerns included the conversion of Kuwaiti dinars to Indian rupees and that food and housing would be deducted from their paychecks. I also told them that the contract stipulated that if they decided to leave the position before the contract ended, they would be required to reimburse their employer the cost of their plane tickets and recruitment fees. These factors did not dim Azaad's and Munsif's eagerness to take the job in the Gulf, and they told me it was their "dream" to work there.

By signing contracts, Azaad and Munsif indicated that they understood and freely consented to the terms of their contracts.[1] However, from the perspective of the Indian government, Indian citizens who want to migrate to the Gulf but who have not matriculated, or gone through tenth grade, are not fully able to consent to their contracts due to their limited education. The government categorizes these men as "vulnerable," and Azaad and Munsif, because that they had not matriculated and were going to jobs in Kuwait, fell into this category. In order to protect vulnerable citizens, the Indian government regulates emigration. For those who require emigration permission, the government approves worker contracts, oversees recruiting agents, and confirms that migrants are traveling to legitimate jobs with reputable companies.

Indian emigration regulations draw explicitly from colonial policies developed to move labor through the British Empire in the nineteenth century. Emigration policies are also affected by bureaucratic engagements with citizenship and con-temporary intrastate activities, such as anti-trafficking initiatives. This chapter explores contemporary emigration regulations, their histories, and how the state's responsibility to its citizens is debated and expressed in regard to these regula-tions. Through exploring the history of colonial labor mobilities as well as postco-lonial debates on the duties of the state to its citizens, this chapter demonstrates how the bureaucratic apparatuses developed to facilitate colonial labor mobilities continue to be used. In attending to how colonial practices inform contemporary state policies, tensions between vulnerable citizens and rational citizens emerge as a central factor for emigration regulation.

The trope of vulnerability emerges from British colonial approaches to India. Within postcolonial contexts such as India, the state often simultaneously im-plements (neo)liberalizing policies, such as smaller government structures and privatization of social services, with a focus on the state's role in development.[2] This form of governmentality rests on the idea that not all individuals are able to "represent themselves as rights-bearing citizens."[3] While situated within such a context of neoliberal governance, the categorization of vulnerable peoples and its gendered implications also draws on a colonial logic that assumes some people are still "unfit for liberty."[4] Indian nationalist thought and postcolonial policies travel "along channels excavated by colonial discourse."[5] One consequence of this is that nationalist discourse used the power structures and methods of producing knowledge defined by the British in which peasants of India were robbed of their agency and subjectivity.[6] However, Indian government employees and recruiting agents do not simply replicate colonial practices, but rework these practices within the contemporary moment.

EMIGRATION REGULATIONS

Indian emigration regulations require that recruiting agents submit large amounts of paperwork before being able to find workers for companies abroad. During my first interview with Mr. Shah, a recruiting agent, he outlined the steps that he took when hiring workers for jobs in the Gulf. Here, I share the steps he told me that day with additional insights I gleaned from watching this process at multiple companies. First, a recruiting agent receives an order from a client detailing the requirements, or number of workers and desired skill sets. Next, he gets the following documents from the company: power of attorney, the letter of demand, the contracts, visa copies (or a block visa for Saudi Arabia), and a contract regarding placement fees. This paperwork provides the agent with the authority to recruit workers for the company.

After the paperwork is in place, an agent mobilizes possible recruits. This may be done through working with a database maintained by the company or advertising in local papers; for skilled or professional positions, online websites may be used. The agent then screens CVs and makes a short list of possible workers who match the company's requirements. At larger offices like Mancom, pre-interviews are conducted in order to screen candidates. Once the candidates have been screened, the agent draws up an interview schedule. If there are many possible candidates in Mumbai, then interviews may be held there. This is not always the case, however, and sometimes it is necessary to travel to other parts of India in order to recruit workers. Most often the company sends a representative to be present at the interviews, but sometimes the recruiting agent conducts interviews for the client.

Once workers have been hired, all workers, including skilled and professional workers, need to have their degrees and certificates verified, go through medical screening, and obtain visas. After this, passports are put forward for visa endorsement with the country to which the migrant is traveling. Some countries, like Kuwait, require that round-trip airline tickets be included. Once the visa has been endorsed, migrants who are categorized as vulnerable must receive clearance from the local Protector of Emigrants office, usually referred to as the POE. In order to receive this clearance, the recruiting agent must submit the documents to the local Protector of Emigrants office. As Mr. Shah described this process, he emphasized his role in facilitating migrants' negotiation of bureaucratic processes and helping companies certify the skills of their potential employees.

Today, emigration regulations are laid out in the Emigration Act of 1983. Central to this act is the oversight of emigration for Indians who have not matriculated. When a man who has not matriculated wishes to migrate for work to one of seventeen countries, including all of the countries of the Arabic-speaking Gulf, he must receive permission from the Indian government prior to his departure from India.[7] Indian women face even greater restrictions, and the migration of women who have not matriculated is often discursively conflated with either sex work or trafficking. According to the Emigration Act of 1983, it is not legal for an uneducated woman under 30 years of age to migrate to the Gulf for work.[8]

Those who fall into the category of "vulnerable" have passports that are marked with the words "Emigration Check Required" (often referred to by the

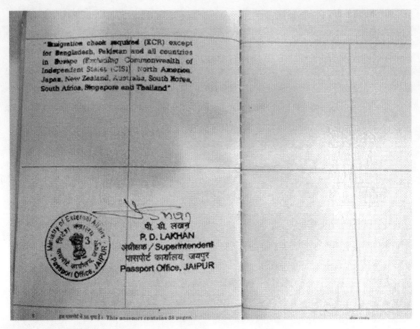

FIGURE 1. ECR Passport, 2010.
Source: Author.

abbreviation ECR). When I began my research, the category of those who required emigration clearance had a stamp in their passports that read "Emigration Check Required" (Figure 1). Today, "Emigration Check Required" is printed at the top of the biographical section of the passport (Figure 2). When an individual with "Emigration Check Required" in their passport attempts to leave India and travel for work to the countries for which the Emigration Act applies, passport control officials check to ensure that approval has been given by a Protector of Emigrants office. When the paperwork is approved, a stamp is placed in the passport near the visa for the country of destination. A person who does not have the proper documentation will be stopped by immigration control at the airport or port and may not leave. During most of my research, those who did not require an emigration check were given a stamp of "ECNR" or "Emigration Check Not Required." Today the policy is to leave this blank for Emigration Check Not Required, making Emigration Check Required the marked category.[9]

During my fieldwork in India, in 2009, the Ministry of Overseas Indian Affairs (MOIA) oversaw Indian emigration. This ministry was created in 2004 in order to provide services to Indians abroad and to supervise the Protector of Emigrants

FIGURE 2. ECR Passport, 2015.
Source: Author.

offices.[10] The government employees involved in regulating emigration whom I spoke with often said regulations are necessary to ensure that workers are not taken advantage of by companies or illicit agents. Thus, the Ministry of Overseas Indian Affairs regulated recruiting agents, approved contracts, and attempted to ensure migrants were not hired by "blacklisted" companies—those that have abused, not paid, or abandoned workers in the past.[11] Emigration oversight by government officials is also meant to protect Indians from traveling to dangerous locations.[12]

A key office in the ministry is the Protector General of Emigrants, based in New Delhi, which manages local Protector of Emigrants offices. At local offices, recruiting agents submit contracts for review in order to ensure that the terms do not violate the standards established by the government. One way they do this is through ensuring wages meet the minimum established by the government. For example, in 2009, the minimum wage was INR 7,400 to INR 12,450 per month, depending on the country (approximately US$156 to US$263), and the minimum wage for housemaids was INR 13,700 per month in the United Arab Emirates (approximately US$289).[13] If a contract does not offer this level of compensation, the company is not allowed to hire Indian workers with Emigration Check Required passports. Not only do local Protector of Emigrants offices regulate the beginning of the process, but after a worker has been hired, recruiting agents take the approved and signed contracts, the worker's passport, and other required documentation to the local Protector of Emigrants office to receive emigration permission for the worker.

In 2008, the average daily number of people receiving permission from the Indian government to migrate was 3,430. Of these people, recruiting agents facilitated 3,275 clearances, or over 95 percent of the necessary clearances.[14] Emigration requirements help entrench the necessity of recruiting agents for both companies and prospective workers. Companies that want to hire Indian labor are required to complete large amounts of paperwork and negotiate multiple government offices. This amount of paperwork and the uneven application of policies at different government offices is enough to discourage almost all companies from attempting to hire workers without a recruiting agent. From the perspective of prospective migrants, navigating government offices and receiving emigration clearance is challenging, and most people who migrate work with a recruiting agency, especially the first time a worker goes abroad. As a result, recruiting agencies like Mancom play a central role in the migration of Indians to work in oil projects based in the Gulf, and, as such, serve as organizers of labor circulation.

Gender, class, and religion unevenly affect who is required to receive permission to emigrate, and Indians from the poorest states and those from lower castes and non-Muslims are more likely to be categorized as "vulnerable" and in need of government permission. For example, Indian Muslims like Azaad and Munsif tend to have attended fewer years of school than members of other religious groups. While 65 percent of all Indians are literate, less than 60 percent of Muslims in India are literate, and in rural areas, this figure is closer to 50 percent.[15] percent. Additionally, whereas 26 percent of Indians over 17 years of age have matriculated, only 17 percent of Indian Muslims have done so. Women too are unevenly affected, and only 13 percent of all women have matriculated.[16] Women also require more emigration documentation than men to emigrate, and this means that women are dependent on their male relatives during the emigration process. For example, while men need a "No Objection Certificate" signed by a police officer in their district, women with Emigration Check Required Passports must have their "No Objection Certificate" also signed by their husbands or fathers. In addition, bureaucrats working in the Protector of Emigrants offices must ensure that if a woman is traveling to work as a maid, the household that hires her has been vouched for by an Indian national.[17]

THE HISTORY OF INDIAN LABOR MIGRATION

At a meeting between recruiting agents and government employees, I met Dr. A Didar Singh, the Secretary of the Ministry of Overseas Indian Affairs, from December 2009 until November 2011. When I showed up at his office a few months later, he took the time to explain the emigration process from his perspective. During our meeting, he stressed that the Indian government does not wish to interfere with migration and "only wants to protect the most vulnerable of workers." This is important, he continued, because "the Emigration Check Requirement applies," to countries like the Gulf states, which "are countries with high requirements of low skill person and labor regulations are not as strong as some other more developed countries. And the majority of emigrants are low-skill, low-education persons from India." As he continued to explain the ministry's role in emigration regulation, he expressed a central tension: it is the right of citizens in the national era to decide whether to migrate, without interference from the government. Simultaneously, vulnerable Indians must also be protected.

Dr. Singh stressed the historic context in which emigration regulations were created and how historic factors endure into the present. Indeed, I heard him narrate the history of Indian emigration the first time I met him, at a meeting between recruiting agents and representatives of the ministry. At that meeting, he explained to those present how he understood the historical role of agents and the governmental oversight of emigration:

> The POE [Protector of Emigrants] is the oldest office in [the Government of] India, except the spice trade. Since the slave trade was banned in 1824, the British set up the system of Protector General of Emigrants and there were registered agents based in the presidencies. They offered employment abroad. This was called indentured labor, but it is the same as today and it is a replacement to the slave trade. The experience you [recruiting agents] have no one else has and we expect this industry to be number one.

Dr. Singh's history of emigration describes a change in labor extraction from slavery in precolonial India to indentured labor during the colonial period to contemporary free labor migration. His narrative exemplifies the Indian government's perspective and is a historical narrative I often hear from government employees working to regulate emigration. For the government bureaucrats with whom I spoke, this understanding of migration's long history is encouraged by the endurance of institutions and laws from the colonial period to the present.

For Dr. Singh, the narratives of Indian slavery, indentured labor, and contemporary labor migration mapped onto political structures and geographic places. Slavery was a pre-British colonial phenomenon and indentured labor a British colonial practice to move labor from India to the rest of the British Empire. These labor circulations followed the contours of the colonial world. In historically situating Indian emigration within a global discourse with colonial roots of oppression, Dr. Singh gestured toward the colonial legacy of contemporary emigration policies. His framework focuses on the dignity of India and Indians, and many of the government's procedures and attitudes are ideally meant to protect this dignity by protecting vulnerable Indians, even if these ends are not always realized.

Enduring Legacies of Colonial Infrastructure

Dr. Singh's narrative points to how the concept of vulnerable populations and the laws and policies that govern the migration of Indians to the Gulf are strikingly similar to the policies the British colonial government in India instituted to govern indentured labor migration in the nineteenth century. Beginning in the 1830s, the British Raj enacted emigration policies as a means to manage the movement of indentured laborers out of India. Indentured labor was important to providing labor throughout the British colonies after the 1807 Slave Trade Act, the 1833 Slavery Abolition Act, and the eventual banning of slavery in territories held by the British East India Company in 1843. From the 1830s onward, India was one of the largest sources of indentured labor in the world.[18] As the indentured labor system was implemented, concerns arose if indentured laborers were "freely" selling their labor. Both British government officials and the British public worried that the people who were hiring indentured laborers were not honest about the working conditions laborers would face. In addition, it was believed that extreme poverty restricted individuals' options; for example, during times of famine, there was a marked increase in the number of people going to work as indentured workers. Finally, once indentured workers left India, they often had constraints on their ability to return at the end of their contracts, and it was not uncommon for plantation owners to refuse to pay for workers' return to India.

In an attempt to ensure that indentured labor was not a new form of slavery, the British colonial government in India institutionalized the Protector of Emigrants structure, which had two key duties. First, the Protector of Emigrants was to ensure that migrants were not coerced, were healthy, and were treated fairly in their destination country.[19] Second, the offices also oversaw recruiting agents who facilitated the emigration of Indians as indentured laborers throughout the British Empire.[20] These duties remain the same today.

During the nineteenth century, agents were often British businessmen based in port cities who worked with Indian subagents operating in the interior of India. These subagents, also called native recruiters, were thought to mislead and lure or kidnap "naive natives" into indenture contracts and to target desperate women.[21] The Protector of Emigrants system was enacted with an underlying assumption that more laws would result in better conditions for indentured laborers, but this was not necessarily the case; for example, colonial planters and metropole capitalists argued there were labor shortages after the abolition of slavery and pressured British Parliament to relax labor policies. As Madhavi Kale's work demonstrates, by the 1840s, few protections for "freed peoples' rights and liberties" remained. In this context, indenture was an "imperial labor reallocation strategy" and "a site where hierarchies of empire were enunciated, contested and inscribed."[22]

In 1917, due to pressure from Indian nationalists, indentured labor from India ended. At this time, the British colonial authorities rewrote the emigration laws, and in 1922, the Government of India, under the advisement of Sir G. L. Corbett, a British member of the Indian Civil Service, passed the Emigration Act of 1922, which replaced the Emigration Act of 1908. It was thought in 1922 that a new emigration act was necessary because the 1908 Act dealt primarily with indentured labor, and since the Defense of India Rules, emigration with the intention of laboring for hire was illegal.[23] This act continued to use the Protector of Emigrants system developed to move indentured labor. Also, like earlier emigration acts, consent and freedom were key concerns of the act's authors.

In her investigation into the connections among colonialism, slavery, liberalism, and trade, Lisa Lowe finds that the colonial logics of labor were shaped by colonial subjugation, liberal philosophy, and racialized divisions of humanity. Central to colonial governance and the management of labor were the contradictory tensions between the liberal ideology of "free" labor and the racial categorizations that characterized some people as "unfit for liberty."[24] With the 1807 Slave Trade Act, "the category of 'freedom' was central to the development of what we could call a modern racial governmentality in which a political, economic, and social hierarchies ranging from 'free' to 'unfree' was deployed in the management of diverse labors of metropolitan and colonized people."[25] Liberal ideologies and racialized hierarchies worked in conjunction with the techniques and technologies developed to regulate colonial migration. In the case of indentured labor from India, these colonial techniques and technologies informed contemporary understandings of individual liberty, citizenship, and state sovereignty.[26] The state also operated in conjunction with colonial capitalist expansions. Within this context of Indian indenture, greater emphasis was placed on the ease of facilitating labor mobilities rather than regulating the conditions of labor.[27] As Radhika Mongia demonstrates, the signing of contracts came to signify "the definitive element of 'freedom.'"[28]

In order to regulate emigration, the Emigration Act of 1922 outlined three types of emigrants. This categorization was similar to the Emigration Act of 1908, but the categories in 1922 were defined more broadly. According to the Emigration Act of 1922, the first type of emigrants included unskilled workers or laborers, such as agriculturalists, porters, and rickshaw pullers. These workers were prohibited from emigrating to any country that was not approved by Parliament.[29] The second type of emigrants were skilled workers "of a comparatively low order and status, belonging to classes of persons who by reason of their ignorance, were likely to be imposed upon or by reason of the number in which they emigrate were likely to create political or economic problems in the country of immigration." This category included domestics, artisans, clerks, shop assistants, entertainers, and food servers.[30] The third category of emigrants was reserved for professionals, such as businessmen, doctors, lawyers, and students. These professionals were assumed to have a "higher degree of intelligence or knowledge" and were thus left outside the scope of the 1922 act and not required to obtain "No Objection Certificates."[31] Women and minors faced additional impediments to emigration. Classified together, both were prohibited from emigrating unless the Protector of Emigrants, upon "examination" of the potential emigrant, was "satisfied that he/ she can take care of himself/herself in the country of employment."[32] These laws reduced the ability of women, children, and unskilled workers to migrate using the discourse of protecting vulnerable groups.

The Emigration Act of 1922 also limited unskilled emigration to countries approved by the Government of India. In the original implementation of the act, emigration was controlled only when workers were emigrating overseas to work for hire and when they were assisted in their departure. Those who emigrated on their own did not need to follow the outlines of the Emigration Act because emigrating on one's own reflected a form of initiative that ought not be discouraged. This deregulation of unaided unskilled labor migration was overturned in 1938 by the Indian legislature, and all unskilled emigrants were deemed to be within the scope of the Emigration Act.[33] As the following section describes, after India's independence in 1947, competing viewpoints of citizens as either free or vulnerable continued to animate emigration regulations.

Protecting Citizens Abroad

With the independence of India and Pakistan in 1947, India's new status provided an important framework and context for rethinking emigration policies. As bureaucrats debated emigration regulations, they often expressed two conflicting goals: they did not want to impede the freedom of citizens but simultaneously argued that protecting citizens was a central obligation of the state. For the nascent Indian state, and today, the question of how an individual's rights are best ensured by the government was, and continues to be, a pressing issue. The methods the Indian government developed to oversee emigration of workers to the Gulf in the early years of Indian independence bridge two paradoxical understandings of citizenship. In one, citizens are vulnerable, and in the other, they are rational liberal actors. This division became important as the Indian state sought to determine what its duties were to its citizens abroad. As questions regarding the nature of the state and citizenship were being debated, bureaucratic practices were developed to oversee emigration, many of which remain in play today.

The rights of citizens to emigrate and, in particular, an individual's ability to consent to contracts and to make their own choices are sometimes viewed to be in tension with the government's duties to protect its citizens.[34] The necessity of states to protect rights is central to much political theory. Hannah Arendt takes on such a question in her discussion of stateless peoples, who, having no state to "represent or protect them," were unable to effectively access rights.[35] In her analysis, she argues that individuals must belong to a nation-state in order to access rights and connects the ability of citizens to access rights with state sovereignty.[36] Through debates on emigration to the Gulf, the implementation of policies, and the negotiation of worker contracts, bureaucrats in India defined the state's obligations to its citizens and debated the implications of citizens working abroad for national sovereignty.[37]

When deciding how to legislate emigration in the postcolonial Indian state, Indian bureaucrats referred to the Emigration Act of 1922 and its reasoning to inform their own actions. In the late 1940s and early 1950s, many Indian government employees argued that in order to best implement the Emigration Act of 1922, they needed to not only know the text of the act but also to understand its underlying principles. In discussions concerning the act, bureaucrats regularly referred back to the writings of Sir G. L. Corbett, a main adviser in the drafting of the act. In the development of the act, bureaucrats noted, Corbett suggested that it prohibit emigration to countries where Indians did not enjoy the same rights as other classes of British subjects. It was feared that any imposition of an inferior status on Indians living and working in another country would foster constant political trouble. Conversely, Corbett suggested that emigration to countries where rights were given to Indians should be permitted and encouraged. Corbett reasoned that emigration to such countries would solve problems related to India's growing population, provide economic opportunities, and "give Indians a wider outlook on the world in general."[38]

As they debated these underlying principles, postcolonial officials made clear that their purpose was not to "enlarge [the act's] scope or change its basic structure."[39] Despite agreeing on the act's principles, after independence, government officials found implementation of the legislation to be difficult. This difficulty arose from balancing the rights of individual citizens and the duties of the state. In the mid-1950s, Indian bureaucrats working for the Ministry of External Affairs reflected on the reasons behind the 1922 act. They discerned two ideologies behind the legislation. First, from Corbett's note written in 1921,

> It would be wrong to endeavour to hamper or control free emigration. It would be unjustifiable interference with the liberty of the subject. No nation controls free emigration. Free emigration presupposes a certain amount of intelligence, money and enterprise, and in cases of this kind, the individual should be left to decide for himself.[40]

Government officials interpreted this quote as highlighting and prioritizing the rights of citizens to emigrate and the need for the government to respect its citizens' freedom. According to bureaucrats at the Ministry of External Affairs, which oversaw emigration at that time, this notion of liberty for citizens also had to be balanced with the responsibilities of the government. In a speech attributed to Sir George Barn on the occasion of introducing the Emigration Act of 1922, the difference between skilled and unskilled workers was articulated:

> It is the unskilled workers who require the greatest measure of help and protection from the Government and the Bill endeavors to give it to them. The skilled worker is in a very different position to the unskilled worker. He is much more capable of looking after his own interests and, consequently requires less help and protection from the Government. At the same time we feel that the emigration of skilled workers should be under some measure of control, and that the Government should give him some measure of protection.[41]

Bureaucrats used this quote to think through the differing levels of agency available to migrants based on their job type. The differences between unskilled and skilled work meant that the government had different responsibilities for each group. In contrasting these two arguments, Indian bureaucrats laid out the two poles of the debate on emigration—one in which the paradoxical nature of citizens as both free and vulnerable was reinforced.

Often in the early 1950s, Indian politicians and bureaucrats were sharply divided on the government's role in regulating emigration. Some expressed concerns over the increase in India's population and suggested that a program that encouraged or subsidized emigration would be an ideal solution.[42] Others suggested that it was better for Indians to remain in India than face discrimination abroad. This perspective often drew connections between colonialism and Indian emigration. One official wrote:

> It would appear that in the present context of world affairs it is just as well that people of India in particular should not venture abroad, if only the reason that her experience of emigration problem ranging over a century and more has been one doleful saga of exploitation by the colonial powers to begin with, and of the denial of legitimate rights of emigrants in more recent times.[43]

Arguments such as these equated the exploitation of emigrants to the exploitation of the country under British colonialism. A central feature of the arguments for restricting and controlling emigration was the changed circumstances of India after independence.[44]

Women's migration was also debated and legislated in this moment, but women were not seen as potential labor migrants to the Gulf. As India and Pakistan made the transition from one to two states, the Indian government was challenged to define who was a citizen of India and who was a citizen of Pakistan. Even before the Indian constitution was passed on January 26, 1950, citizenship provisions were brought into force. As shown in Vazira Zamindar's work on Partition, these citizenship provisions linked "birth, residence, migration, and citizenship"; a "'domicile' and birth 'in the territory of India'" were needed for a person to be a citizen of India. This derived from colonial law of coverture in which the domiciles of children under age 18 are dependent on their fathers, and the domiciles of women are dependent on their husbands. By following the legal doctrine of coverture and defining citizenship by domicile and birth, women's citizenship became contingent on their husbands.[45] Coverture also meant that Indian women were not envisioned as potential individual emigrants by the early Indian state.

The close association of women, the home, and the nation meant that women needed to be located within a family if they were to claim rights. The state also took on a familial role with the goal of protecting Indian women. When women did emigrate, the assumptions were—and continue to be today—that they were either moving with their husbands or participating in "immoral activity." This was exemplified in a series of complaints brought to the Indian government regarding the "immoral traffic in women" in the 1950s and 1960s. In 1950, the Indian government ratified the International Convention for the Suppression of the Traffic of Persons and of the Exploitation of the Prostitution of Others. In 1956, the government passed the Suppression of Immoral Traffic in Women and Girls Act, which lays out the legal penalties for the trafficking of women and girls.[46] Such practices conflated working women's emigration, trafficking, and sex work. Today, women who have Emigration Check Required passports must meet different requirements than men to emigrate for work, and questions concerning their morality often emerges in these discussions.[47]

Oil Companies and the State

As bureaucrats debated emigration regulations, they became increasingly focused on the emigration of Indian men to work in the Gulf. In the second half of the twentieth century, the migration of Indian men to the Gulf was rapidly growing. In the early 1950s, officials at the Ministry of External Affairs said that after Malaya, the Gulf was the most important area to which Indians were migrating.[48] By 1952, the Protector of Emigrants office in Bombay, the main office granting emigration clearances to the Gulf, was busier than ever before, with increased requests for emigration clearances and an increased number of cases in which workers had attempted to emigrate illegally.[49] In 1953, the government estimated that 6,000 to 7,000 Indians were traveling to the Gulf annually, and officials estimated that migrants were remitting around INR 2.5 million (US$525,210 in 1953) every year.[50]

Oil companies became one of the largest employers of Indian workers only a few years after independence. As a result of the large numbers of Indian workers they hired and the close connections between oil companies and the British government, oil companies wielded large amounts of political influence and played a key role in shaping Indian emigration policies. As more oil companies became established in the Gulf and hired increasing numbers of Indian workers, methods of recruiting Indians solidified into standardized practices. Some contractors recruited in India directly. In Bombay in 1952, there were 670 authorized recruiting agents. The government, building on laws established in 1930, oversaw these agents to ensure that workers were not charged for the cost of recruitment. Smaller recruiting agents were required to deposit an amount equal to one and one-half times the single fare for a migrant, and more established agents were able to deposit a lump sum with the Protector of Emigrants to ensure workers were recruited fairly and not stuck in a foreign country.[51] Some larger oil companies and contractors recruited directly for themselves, and British Petroleum's India branch acted as an agent for both oil companies and "territories" in the Gulf under British administration.[52] This method of recruitment relied on colonial practices, oil companies' influence, the politics of oil production, and the temporary nature of emigration. India's status as a new state meant that bureaucrats working for the government were faced with the question of which colonial emigration regulations ought to be continued in the postcolonial state.

Increased emigration to the Gulf and the unique character of this migration opened up debates in the Indian government regarding the Emigration Act of 1922, the act's interpretation, and its implementation. In the early 1950s, bureaucrats were concerned about the scope of emigration regulations and critically examined which emigrants were covered by the act. Bureaucratic debates related primarily to the types of workers being hired by oil companies and how those workers were then treated. For bureaucrats, these issues directly related to debates on the nature of Indian citizenship and the role of the state. Importantly, as a new nation,

Indian bureaucrats wanted to differentiate contemporary Indians abroad from earlier indentured laborers. In exerting controls over emigration, they worked to protect citizen rights, maintain India's reputation internationally, and exert the sovereignty of India to control its borders.

Many Indian officials felt it was necessary to push for the rights of Indian workers abroad, and as a result, the Indian government directly negotiated worker contracts. Some bureaucrats argued that Europeans and Americans were better educated, drew higher salaries, and had better positions in oil companies. Therefore, these employees were able to fight for their rights, even if those rights were not explicitly stated in their contract. According to Indian government officials, most Indians abroad were not "sufficiently well educated, occupy comparatively only minor and inferior categories of service and do not have such a social and official status as to provide them with sufficient guarantees (unwritten) to be able to take care of their interests."[53] Through writing and negotiating contracts with oil companies, the government tried to ensure Indians' rights. In writing these contracts, a logic of Indian bureaucratization was applied to oil company practices and a conceptualization of a vulnerable Indian emigrant emerged. This vision of the vulnerable Indian continues to inform the logic of emigration regulations.

THE COST OF REGULATION

Colonial logics and contemporary neoliberalizing policies manage labor mobilities through differentiating some laborers as vulnerable. This construction of difference not only informs the process of migration but also serves to generate additional revenue for some wealthy elites. Colonial labor mobilities certainly increased profits to plantation owners and rested on a logic of dispossession, the commodification of labor, control of mobility, and risk displacement.

Today, labor moves through international markets and, once again, generates wealth for elites.[54] Some of this wealth is connected to optimizing oil company profits through reducing expenses. Wealth is also generated as workers acquire permission for emigration from the government and in the enforcement of emigration regulations. This wealth is legitimated through a view of "vulnerable" Indians as different—as not fully able to comprehend and consent to the terms of their contracts.[55] The consequence is that Indians who require emigration permission must accrue debt to pay for their emigration.

According to Indian emigration regulations, recruiting agents can charge a migrant INR 20,000. But workers often end up paying much more, and to find jobs most workers with whom I spoke borrowed between INR 70,000 and INR 120,000 (approximately US$1,531 to US$2,624 in 2010). This is a huge amount of money for many families, as most migrants who require emigration clearance told me their family farms are smaller than an acre in size and that their job options are either to migrate or to work locally as casual laborers. Casual laborers earn, on average, between US$2 and US$3 per day.[56] Thus, to get the funds needed to navigate the migration process, prospective labor migrants borrow money, usually at high interest rates from moneylenders and use their small landholdings as collateral.[57] Why workers pay so much is debated by recruiting agents and government officials: recruiting agents blame the government and the government blames recruiting agents.[58]

Protector of Emigrants offices have a history of abusing power and unevenly applying the rules related to migration. This history is well publicized in Indian newspapers and the subject of much gossip by migrants and recruiting agencies. In 2010, the Indian Central Bureau of Investigation (CBI) estimated that for many years, workers in Protector of Emigrants offices had been illegally collecting INR 64 crore, or over US$12 million, every year from migrants seeking emigration clearance.[59] When Indian scholars discuss these illegal activities, they often describe it as a "nexus formed between erring government officials and recruiting agents."[60] This nexus means that Indians hoping to work in the Gulf often need to borrow large amounts of money at high interest rates from moneylenders in order to emigrate.

Recruiting agency employees often pay a portion of the fees to government officials to have legitimate applications approved so that a worker who requires emigration clearance may receive this permission. One recruiting agency employee told me, "It costs INR 200 (US$4) for the POE to process a legit visa and they charge INR 2,000 (US$44) or more, usually INR 7,000 (US$153), to process illegal ones."[61] Such fees were recognized by all recruiting agents with whom I spoke. When explaining the reasons for these fees, Mr. Kumar, a recruiting agent, said, "This is because these people make policy for their own vested interest and things have been difficult under [the Ministry of Overseas Indian Affairs]." When I asked for further elaboration, Mr. Kumar explained to me that "this needless policy helps them by allowing officials to take bribes. Here [are] two examples. First, when I do an interview in an area [my] office [is] not located in, then I must give bribe. Second, same problem with the visas. Like for a carpenter, I must give bribe." Another recruiting agent, Mr. Zakir, agreed with Mr. Kumar that government workers were making money and blamed it on popular perceptions of recruiting agents. "In the eyes of government and also many people, RAs [recruiting agents] are bad or cheats because they are taking money from the people who are going abroad. So, the ministry thinks, 'Why not take my share as well?'"

Mr. Zakir and Mr. Kumar used words such as *corruption* and *bribes* to critique government employees' morals.[62] This also allowed recruiting agents to attempt to legitimate their activities by saying they were forced to operate in illegal ways due to bureaucrats. In addition, the choice of the word "corruption" and accompanying reports of this corruption work to signify the activity of these bureaucrats who oversee emigration as exceptional. The label of "exceptional" maintains the legitimacy of the state through an individualization of immoral practices. It also creates the impression of state control and complete oversight as opposed to fragmentary understandings of Indian migration.[63]

In contrast, government officials blame recruiting agents, a topic that is often repeated in the Indian news. For example, a common way of characterizing recruiting agents is as "racketeers" who are "sending unskilled workers abroad for a life of misery."[64] Indeed, the stereotype of the recruiting agent as illicit actors is so prevalent that my neighbors and acquaintances in India were surprised that I would spend time with such undesirable people. One consequence of such stereotypes is that recruiting agents at times feared being mistaken for human traffickers.

In 2009, some government attempts to curb trafficking were worrisome for Indian recruiting agents. At that time, recruiting agents were particularly concerned about the Government of Punjab's proposed Prevention of Human Trafficking Act, 2008. They read the proposed legislation as placing the blame for illegal human trafficking on recruiting agents. In particular, recruiting agents pointed to a section of the bill that they saw as conflating recruiting agents who are registered with the government and people who pose as agents and operate illegally:

Innocent/illiterate/gullible persons fall in the trap of unscrupulous persons who allure and induce such persons with false promises to send them abroad by charging heavy amount of money. But thereafter these persons are exploited by these elements for their illegal monetary gains by giving them false assurances for arranging their visas to foreign countries in general and advanced countries like Canada, USA, UK etc. [in] particular.[65]

Such legislation was particularly unsettling, as recruiting agents were aware of the negative coverage they received in the media, where their work was seen to profit from poor Indians' precarious circumstances. Recruiting agents were upset and felt the law framed them as traffickers.[66] Given that agents facilitate the migration of vulnerable Indians for financial gain, they objected to the expansive definitions of "smuggling" and "trafficking" in the act. Not only are these terms vaguely defined in the Punjabi Act, but they are also loosely mobilized in popular discourse. In response to this proposed act, recruiting agents argued to bureaucrats in the Ministry of Overseas Indian Affairs that the proposed act by the Punjabi state contradicted the Emigration Act in place at the federal level. If implemented, recruiting agents feared the vague wording of the proposed state law would be used to imprison or levy large fines against agents.

CONCLUSION

Many former colonial states continue to use colonial laws and logics in governance, but these often are forced to change as economic policies and international aid require bureaucrats to meet international standards. For example, in Pakistan, the World Bank's Enhanced HIV and AIDS Control Funding created competition between the private sector, nongovernmental organizations, and the government. The result was that Pakistani bureaucracy shifted toward looking more corporate, with an emphasis on bureaucrats acting as efficient entrepreneurs and away from a civil service orientation to their job.[67] As in Pakistan, in some areas of governance in India, bureaucrats feel they are forced to balance new perspectives stemming from neoliberal reforms with previous perspectives held by the civil service. According to ministry employees, liberalizing means decreasing restrictions. While in many contexts the continuation of colonial policies feels in tension with changing governance practices under neoliberalization, bureaucrats with whom I worked found the colonial logic of emigration restrictions to be in line with new trends in neoliberal governmental practices. Indeed, Dr. Singh's history of Indian emigration and current bureaucratic perspectives seem to hold both neoliberal changes and colonial practices in conversation.

Government officials increasingly weigh obligations to protect citizens with pressure to liberalize the government. In 2010, one official working in the Ministry of Overseas Indian Affairs described how he understood changes to India's emi-gration regulations: "We have liberalized the migration regime because we wanted only people who are really vulnerable, less educated, and unable to take care of themselves [to have to receive clearance]. Those who are reasonably educated can take care of themselves, so why restrict?" This bureaucrat described to me how moves to "liberalize migration" include changing the education standard for Emigration Check Not Required or ECNR passports: "[The requirement] used to be 10 +2 years of school but was changed in 2006 to 10th pass." In addition, he told me, the ministry decreased the number of countries for which those who have Emigration Check Required passports must obtain emigration permission. This effort to "liberalize" migration continues today. The 2014 Indian elections allowed the Bharatiya Janata Party (BJP) to form a majority government. Following this election, the Ministry of External Affairs began to oversee the Ministry of Overseas Indian Affairs, and in 2016, the ministries were merged. The merger was seen as a means of keeping the BJP's campaign promise of "minimizing govern-ment and maximizing governance"[68] and points to the increasing liberalization of governance in India.

This liberalization of governance is understood to exist as Indians continue to migrate globally and Indian labor competes in a global marketplace. While colonial logics and labor mobilization infrastructure continue, bureaucrats are able to balance the protection of vulnerable Indians through a lens that sees Indian labor in a global market of competition. Today, labor migrants are seen not only vulnerable, but also representative of India's brand.

Chapter 2

CULTIVATING ENTREPRENEURS

DR. SINGH, THE SECRETARY OF THE MINISTRY OF OVERSEAS INDIAN Affairs, stood at the front of a room in the ministry's offices in New Delhi and described to his staff the importance of regulating emigration. "The contours of globalization will be determined by migration." Pausing, he asked, "What is globalization? It is just another word for migration." Other employees of the ministry nodded to indicate their agreement with Dr. Singh's assessment of Indians on a global stage. As we left the meeting, an employee of the ministry explained to me that he saw regulating emigration as a "service to the nation." It would not look good, he explained, if the "wrong types" of Indians traveled abroad: "We do not want people to think we are a nation of beggars." This perspective was common, and bureaucrats often told me that poor Indians must be assured of jobs prior to emigrating so they would not end up "begging on the streets," thereby reflecting negatively on India. According to these officials, migrants to the Gulf are the most likely to end up as beggars because there is no strong oversight of companies and large numbers of uneducated Indians from rural areas migrate, only to find themselves stranded, uncared for, or unemployed. Government bureaucrats contrast poor Indians working in the Gulf with what they described as the "ideal Indian abroad": an Indian who migrates to America and is "rich, skilled, and educated."

Migrants' importance to India and Indian globalization are celebrated through events such as Pravasi Bharatiya Divas (Non-Resident Indian Day), which began

43

in 2000 as a way to recognize the achievements and contributions of Indians abroad. In January 2019, India's prime minister, Narendra Modi, opened the annual celebration at a convention, titled that year, *naye bhaarat ke nirmaan mein bhaarateey pravaasiyon kee bhoomika* (Role of Indian Diaspora in Building New India). As he welcomed Non Resident Indians (NRIs) to his home constituency in Varanasi, Prime Minister Modi, speaking in Hindi with a few English words interspersed, addressed Indians working abroad: "aap ko bhaarat ka brand ambassadors . . . bhaarat kee kshamataon aur kshamataon" (You are India's brand ambassadors . . . [and symbols of] India's capacities and capabilities). The Indian government's interest in the brand image of India reflects the ways in which the language of business and marketing are used to inform migration policies and practices. Prime Minister Modi's emphasis on capacities and capabilities also invokes a future built on India's greatest resource: its citizens' potential.

Similar to government officials, recruiting agents frequently reflect on the relationship between India's brand and Indian migrants. Larger recruiting agency owners who facilitate migration to oil and gas projects also see Indian migrants as reflective of their own companies' brand. In an interview with Mr. Kumar, the owner of a recruiting agent based in Mumbai that is similar in size to Mancom, he described the close connections between migrants, India's brand, and his own company's reputation: "When people show up [for interviews], they come so scrubby, but I want them to look professional and the minute the client sees them, I want him to want those guys. Brand. It's all about creating a brand as the best." In this conversation, Mr. Kumar's description of interviewees for laboring positions articulates two key points. First, individuals who are applying to work as laborers in the Gulf are not automatically good representatives of India's and his company's brand. Second, migrants can be taught to be good brand representatives.

Indian companies and government officials became increasingly interested in branding India in a global market in the 1990s, and migrants are considered part of India's brand. In discussions of how to brand Indian labor, "Indianness" becomes a "position in a globalized field" or marketplace.[1] The emphasis is on representing what is constructed as uniquely Indian,[2] and uniquely Indian characteristics involve the "revitalization of ideas of devotion to God, familial piety, and domestic consumption."[3] In the case of Indian migrant workers to the Gulf, recruiting agents and government officials often describe Indian workers to be in competition with workers from Bangladesh, Nepal, Pakistan, and the Philippines. This chapter explores how managing migration becomes a disciplinary project of cultivating entrepreneurial migrants so as to improve the quality of India's brand and thus to compete globally.

Unlike other commodities, migrants are seen as uniquely able to transform themselves into higher-quality commodities through training in Indian entrepreneurship. This logic of entrepreneurship is pervasive, and, according to many recruiting agents, migrants must be entrepreneurial in order to be good representatives of India's brand. This implies that migrants should both bear the brand of India and be brand makers themselves. As self-reliant, autonomous actors, they have to make themselves into quality goods, which includes learning to speak English and acting rationally. Here, commodity forms shift from value in the extraction of surplus labor to the labor done by consumers in brand allegiance, and financialization appears in relationships like debt.[4] The goal is to remake the migrant from a mere labor unit to a self-governing, brand-bearing, and brand-making actor. In order for this transformation to occur, government officials and recruiting agents attempt to cultivate and teach potential migrants.

BRANDING LABOR

Central to the cultivation of entrepreneurial migrants is the assumption that migrants are rational economic actors. Mr. Sahil, the owner of Mancom, understood that "people primarily go overseas for earning a living, saving, and sending it back." Mr. Shah agreed, telling me that a driver in India, per month, is paid INR 6,000 to INR 7,000 (approximately US$130 to US$152 in 2010). When working in the Gulf, he said, they are paid INR 12,000 (US$260) per month and do not pay taxes. In addition to higher wages, when discussing reasons for migration, recruiting agents regularly point to the possibilities for upward mobility for workers once those workers are abroad if the migrants work hard. "Here, as drivers, there is no growth and no economic growth and when they go, they can build [careers]. Overtime is attractive to many workers, something that workers do not receive in India, but get in Saudi Arabia." In addition, Mr. Shah told me it is hard "for people to climb higher [in India] because [in India] there is such a large amount of labor. For there [the Gulf], in recognized companies, [workers] can climb up the ladder. From dishwashers to managers!"

Recruiting agents believe the economic benefits of migration extend to migrants' communities, and this approach to migration as an economic calculus allow for agents to describe the challenges migrants experience as beneficial. For example, recruiting agents are aware that Indian laborers live in isolation in the

Gulf and have limited opportunities to spend their earnings. Because of the (relatively) high pay and limited places to spend it, recruiters argue, migrant laborers are able to send their entire paycheck back to their families. Thus, when imagining Indian migration to the Gulf, remittances and development are closely associated with entrepreneurial migrants.[5] Indian migrants to the Gulf are valorized when they are seen as entrepreneurs who are contributing to the development of their communities and country.

When hiring workers, recruiting agents and their employees attempt to teach workers the need to discipline themselves in order to be good employees. To facilitate this, they select migrants they see as trying to improve themselves. With these practices, recruiting agents encourage migrants to cultivate themselves into entrepreneurs and better representatives of India's brand. In such views, migration, rationality, and entrepreneurship are closely connected. Michel Foucault wrote that migration is "an investment, the migrant is the investor. He is an entrepreneur of himself who incurs expenses by investing to obtain some kind of improvement."[6] Here, Foucault is looking at migration through a neoliberal lens in which one's subjectivity and one's work are deeply imbricated. Self and work are understood to be social and individual processes, and these processes are constantly undergoing reevaluation as new visions of the future emerge.[7]

Recruiting agents described the cultivation of entrepreneurial migrants as a key way to improve the quality associated with the brand of Indian labor and their own agencies' brands. In 2009, I attended the annual meeting of recruiting agency associations where members of the association discussed both their reputation and proposed government legislation that would affect their business, two factors that they saw as closely intertwined. At the meeting, Mr. Kumar, a board member and recruiting agent based in Mumbai, told the other agents present, "We [recruiting agents] need to upgrade ourselves." For Mr. Kumar, granting the council greater power to regulate members was the way to achieve improved status. Other members, reluctant to give the council control over their own agency's activities, argued that the improvement of recruiting agents was already underway.

During this debate over regulation, Mr. Shah stood up and argued that recruiting agents did not need improvement; rather, Indian migrants needed improvement. Outlining a shift in recruiting agents' roles in migration, Mr. Shah said, "[The] government thought of RAs as *chor* [thieves or con artists] and doing hanky-panky. But now government see us as partners in recruiting and the people on the ground." One reason for this change, he argued, was that recruiting agents were increasingly hiring Indians for more skilled positions. "We are moving away [from] ABCD requirements and toward European markets where the government needs help to better talk to HR [human resources] of European companies." The ABCD requirements, described by Mr. Shah, are shorthand for job categories that are usually filled by unskilled or semiskilled workers: A stands for *aaya*, or nanny; B for *bhaiya*, which literally means brother, but here used as slang for general laborer; C for cook; and D for driver.[8]

In Mr. Shah's assessment, Indians emigrating for work to Europe and North America are more skilled, a fact reinforced by the restrictive immigration policies of European and North American governments. He also asserted that as more Indians move to Europe to work, recruiting agents will be valued more highly because of their experience working with European companies and familiarity with work practices there. Mr. Shah's perspectives highlight the importance of the skill level of workers and the places where they are emigrating in reflecting the quality of the agency. Other agents agreed with Mr. Shah. One contributed to the conversation: "If one guy goes to Saudi [Arabia] as a laborer, his neighbors will be inspired and go. But if one guy goes to the West then slowly others will get inspired to get trained so that they can go." In this narrative, if the government offered training to potential migrants, poor Indians with the correct initiative could improve themselves. No longer confined to the Gulf, recruiting agents dream of a world where training would allow workers to go to the West for better jobs and higher salaries.

TEACHING ENTREPRENEURSHIP

Government officials and recruiting agents agree that migrants need to be entrepreneurial in order to maintain the quality of India's brand. As such, India is best embodied in the well-educated migrants who travel to the United States or western Europe. Migrants who are not properly middle class must be taught to operate in such a way. In order to improve on "India's brand," recruiting agents directly asked the government to improve migrant education. At the meeting between recruiting agents and the Ministry of Overseas Indian Affairs, agents argued that the Government of India should be attentive to their needs and learn from their hands-on experience. In its presentation, one association urged Dr. Singh, then Secretary of the Ministry of Overseas Indian Affairs, to change the current emigration policies based on the experiences of recruiting agents. One slide read:

> The [Recruiting Agent] Council has been able to create awareness to the
> Government of India (MOIA) towards flaws inherent in the implementa-
> tion of provisions of Emigration Act 1983 by giving suggestions to amend
> act and rules towards this object. In this course the Council representatives
> have been interacting with the Government authorities viz-a-viz the hon-
> ourable Minister, the Secretary and other senior Government officials. For
> example, Emigration Rules 1983 have been amended and notified on 9th
> July 2009, incorporating the suggestions given by the Council. However,
> there are many other suggestions that have not yet been accepted by the
> Government but those are most necessary to be done.

After reading this slide, the president outlined his council's achievements, including successfully petitioning the government to allow recruiting agents to
charge migrants more money for emigration, changes in the processing of paperwork by the ministry, and allowing the transfer of recruiting agent registrations.

Asserting their expertise in managing emigration processes and the applica-
bility of their insights, recruiting agents then argued that the government should
make changes in three areas. The first involved improving the skills of potential
migrants; recruiting agents wanted the government to open more trade schools
and teach English to potential migrants. The second change was reduced oversight of recruiting agents and lesser punishment for agents' procedural lapses.
In addition, agents wanted the security deposit they had to pay reduced from
twenty lakhs rupees to ten lakhs rupees (US$43,735 to US$21,867 in 2010), and
they wanted to get rid of the requirement that agents need to have graduated
from high school. Third, recruiting agents hoped the government would make it
easier for agents to attract business, and recruiting agents regularly stressed that
Indian workers were competing with men from Pakistan, Bangladesh, Nepal, and
the Philippines. In order to make Indian laborers more attractive and thus create
more business for recruiting agents, the recruiting agents hoped that the ministry
would stop implementing a minimum wage for Indian employees abroad, change
visa policies, and simplify the emigration process.

The recruiting agents present at the meeting made these suggestions in a
didactic manner. Both presidents said they wished to "inform and instruct the
government of the realities" of emigration rules and instruct the government on
how it could best fix what they saw as flaws in the emigration process. The presentations emphasized that the government ought to reduce emigration regulations

and instead focus on giving workers skills that would make them competitive for a greater number of jobs. Underlying these objectives were seemingly contradictory impulses. On the one hand, recruiting agents were arguing that the government ought to be hands-off with business, but on the other hand, they were simultaneously asking for a larger government role in the education of laborers. While this argument may seem contradictory, it reflects recruiting agents' self-understanding of themselves as rational economic actors requiring only laissez-faire regulation. In contrast, recruiting agents conceptualized potential labor migrants as not properly rational economic actors and thus needing increased government intervention and oversight.

While neoliberal governance is often thought of as a reduction of state services, here, the neoliberal position is that the government should expand to support the market position of Indian businesses. In particular, recruiting agents argued the government should teach (and pay for) the education of migrants. This education would improve migrants' skills and increase recruiting agents' business earnings. One recruiting agent told me the government should "create a school to train [school] dropouts in their understanding of cleanliness, language, and how to be office boys. . . . We need to groom them in working in the corporate sector. Grooming in all aspects and we want to give skilled people instead of rough people." Central to this notion of grooming was a disciplining of the body, which recruiting agents argued would also serve to discipline the mind. Through "uplifting" and disciplining workers, they reasoned, India and recruiting agents themselves would rise in international opinion. Agents believe such education and improvement will diffuse to other potential migrants.

Mr. Kumar also described the process of migrant improvement—a self-fashioning that Mr. Kumar saw as the moral cultivation of self that stems from individual entrepreneurship. The key, he said, to improving Indian migrants is understanding "the connection between disciplining the mind and bodies of Indian workers." Like other recruiting agents, Mr. Kumar believed the government should do this training. In particular, he argued, the government should "teach morning exercises and yoga," and he believed that a government initiative that included morning yoga would "teach discipline" to potential migrants. The underlying assumption is that unskilled and semiskilled workers are not disciplined and that only through the regimentation of (government-imposed) routine would they become proper representatives of the Indian brand. By learning yoga, migrants would develop the discipline to be entrepreneurs and as a result would present themselves as better job candidates in job interviews, be hired in greater numbers, and be better employees.

Current government training programs, according to recruiting agents, trained too few Indians, and the Indians who were trained were not learning the most in-demand skills. To illustrate their point, recruiting agents described two training schemes run by the Ministry of Labour and the Director General of Education in 2009 and 2010. One, the Craftsmen Training Scheme (CTS), was implemented through 1,896 industrial training institutes (ITIs) and run by state governments. The other, the Apprentice Training Scheme (ATS), was implemented through 3,128 industrial training centres (ITCs) and run by private companies. In total, these two schemes trained 742,000 people yearly for 107 trades. For both training programs, the education level of applicants varied based on which craft the applicant wished to learn, but many crafts require only an eighth-grade level of education. In addition, the length of programs varied from three months to two years. When I asked Mr. Sahil, the owner of Mancom, about these programs, he indicated that he appreciated the focus on training men to work in semiskilled professions, but, he argued, these programs are too limited in scope. Standing up from the table where we were drinking tea, Mr. Sahil began to pace and tick off the problems with the programs on his fingers. First, he said, these programs have limited capacity. According to the National Sample Survey data on employment (2004–2005), these programs reached only one-fiftieth of the youth who receive formal vocational training. Plans were to expand the scope of the trainings, and the Eleventh Five Year Plan of India (2007–2012) proposed to expand the capacity of vocational education and training in India from 3 million to 15 million new entrants to the labor force. But, he argued, even with this expansion, "these numbers fall far short of the demand."

While the limited number of people trained is an issue, the biggest problem, Mr. Sahil continued, is that the skills workers are trained in do not reflect job demand. After listing the problems with the numbers of workers trained, he sat down once again. Sighing, he said, there is a "mismatch between the training imparted and the skills demanded and individuals in the programs are not learning the most popular jobs and often [trainees] do not have complete knowledge of the skills [needed to do jobs]. Why," he asked, "do the programs not train students to pass international certification exams? This certification would improve a student's chances of finding a job abroad and increase the reputation of Indian workers." To address these issues, Mr. Sahil and many other recruiting agents argued there should be a national regulation of the training programs.

In addition to technical training, recruiting agents addressed changes that could be done in public education that would help Indian youth cultivate the skills necessary to emigrate to work in the Gulf. One way they suggest the government could help Indians prepare to work abroad is by offering English-language classes in public schools. During my research, I frequently saw the value of speaking English. Interviewees who could speak English were hired at higher rates than those who could not. In addition, some employers require applicants to take a test as part of their application process. This test, in my experience, is usually in English.

I first heard recruiting agents bring up language education at the meeting between the Ministry of Overseas Indian Affairs officials and recruiting agency councils in Mumbai. Such a proposal struck me as realistic; India's constitution guarantees free schooling for children up to fourteen years of age, and public schools are supported by local, state, and central government funds. Despite the fact that only a quarter of Indians list Hindi as their mother tongue, it is taught to the exclusion of English in public schools.[9] This means that English education in general remains the exclusive right of the middle- and upper-class children who attend private schools.[10] Upon hearing the suggestion for English-language instruction, Dr. Singh, the Secretary of the Ministry of Overseas Indian Affairs, responded to the recruiting agents by first acknowledging that their suggestion was a good one. "But," he said, "it conflicts with policy. The national language of India is Hindi, and people are responsible for learning English on their own. The Indian government's policy is to promote Hindi and local language." In this statement, Dr. Singh acknowledges the importance of English for Indians searching for jobs abroad but argues that prospective migrants should take it on themselves to learn English.

Articulating a neoliberal perspective on migrants, one in which migrants improve themselves for financial gain, Dr. Singh suggested that poor Indians should be properly motivated and find their own resources for language learning. Here, the failure of the prospective migrant to learn English is viewed as an individual failure of not attempting to improve oneself. This emphasis on language and the need for individuals to assess their learning needs and access the proper resources works to restrict many minorities' access to migration. Such policies both establish and reinforce religious, economic, and regional discrimination. Dr. Singh's statement regarding Hindi as India's national language also conflicts with the Indian constitution and contemporary court rulings. In section 343 of the constitution, Hindi is added as an official language of the federal government *in addition* to English. However, this emphasis on Hindi reflects popular perspectives and government policies in India on language and the relationship between upper-caste Hindu practices as properly Indian, as well as the path for national development and modernization.[11] Such policies influence pedagogy not only by dictating the language of instruction but also by influencing what characteristics of migrants are thought to best represent India.

SELECTING ENTREPRENEURIAL MIGRANTS

Frustrations concerning the lack of government training were shared by most recruiting agents. One day, Mr. Shah complained to me that men who were going abroad were not "trying to improve themselves. Even making literate people today to understand is difficult so you can understand the difficulty in making illiterate understand, of teaching them. . . . You see, I am not satisfied with this recruitment and want to improve [Indians]." In addition, he was concerned by irregular migration, which he saw as having a negative impact on India's brand image abroad. "People are saying India is being degraded by sending illegal workers and therefore losing its [India's] reputation." To address the need to cultivate entrepreneurial migrants, some agencies, including Mr. Shah's agency and Mancom, offer classes to prepare job candidates for interviews. Mancom's owner, Mr. Sahil, told me he is interested in "improving the quality" of interviewees, particularly for clients he hopes Mancom will work with more in the future. The quality of Indian labor will improve by cultivating entrepreneurial attitudes in migrants, and therefore India's brand image will improve. In exploring the work done to teach migrants, it emerges that Indian entrepreneurship is envisioned through a lens that includes Hindu nationalism and middle-class work habits.[12] Often invocations of entrepreneurial selves in India are also rooted in understandings of masculine productive labor.[13] As I watched a series of trainings at Mancom, I learned that these moral, gendered habits were as important as job skills in determining the success of potential job candidates.

While recruiters argued that the government should perform job training, such work is often privatized, as it is in other global contexts.[14] In addition, some agents extended their work to include not only prospective migrants but also their own employees. In the Mancom office, the emphasis was on teaching workers what management understood to be the most valuable skills in the workplace—those that were applicable in all oil work. Smitha Radharkrishnan describes such actions as "cultural streamlining," which she defines as "the process of sampling a dizzying diversity of cultural practices into a stable, transferable, modular set of norms and beliefs that can move quickly and easily through space."[15] In a corporate setting, the goal of cultural streamlining is adapting and producing "appropriate difference" so that Indian technologists can become "global."[16] When recruiting agents offer training, they are often explicit in the connections between skills and self-presentation, and they apply these disciplinary frames not only to pro- spective migrants but also their own employees. Because many recruiting agency employees who focus on staffing unskilled and semiskilled positions worked in the Gulf prior to working at an agency, these employees too are seen as needing instruction into how to improve themselves, so as to improve the quality of the company's and the nation's brands.

At Mancom, Mr. Sahil spent a lot of time training both his own employees and prospective migrants. One day, he complained to me, "Most [of Mancom's em- ployees] cannot plan, do not think farther than two feet." Indeed, many meetings were held in order to teach employees how to correctly speak, dress, and spend money. Mr. Sahil began one meeting by asking, "Why are we having this meeting?" The room was quiet for a moment, and then Puja, who worked at Mancom as a receptionist, responded tentatively, "To improve ourselves." Mr. Sahil nodded in approval at this answer. He then highlighted how improvement is a branded process by explicitly connecting Mancom's brand and employee improvement. At another meeting, Mr. Sahil asked Rupina, one of the few women at Mancom—she worked with clients helping to staff highly skilled positions—to give a lecture entitled "Etiquette and Grooming." The audience for the lecture was the Mancom staff who helped place unskilled and semi-skilled workers with companies, all of whom were young men who had previously worked in the Gulf. In her presen- tation, Rupina addressed four key areas that she and Mr. Sahil believed junior employees needed to learn: how to keep the washroom clean; how to talk to your boss; how to groom oneself, with a focus on brushing one's teeth and hair; and how to email correctly. In this final category, Rupina repeatedly stressed that confidential information, and particularly recruitment fees, must never be written in an email. Here, self-improvement, described as professionalization, legal savvy, and personal hygiene, are all seen as central to branding. According to Mr. Sahil, instructing his employees on these topics facilitated employees' ability to better represent the recruiting agency and also to select better-quality interviewees for clients.

Quality versus Quantity

Mr. Sahil did not limit his vision of improvement to Mancom employees, and he implemented a number of practices and procedures at Mancom to improve the quality of job candidates as well. For example, Mancom employees organized pre-interviews at the agency in the week leading up to interviews with high prestige clients. Mr. Sahil and Mancom managers believed the higher-quality candidates would impress clients and help secure additional contracts. At these interviews, Mr. Anthony and Mr. Shukla asked workers basic questions regarding the type of work for which they were applying. Both men had been managers at oil and gas projects in the Gulf for over twenty years. Although they had little experience with the work of recruiting agents, they knew more by far about the running of oil and gas projects than any other people at Mancom. For lesser-skilled positions, they conducted their interviews mostly in Hindustani or, occasionally, Malayalam. If workers only spoke Tamil, another member of the staff would translate.

During these interviews, Mr. Shukla and Mr. Anthony asked candidates about their knowledge of basic tools, evaluated candidates' ability to read technical drawings, and checked to see if candidates knew common acronyms. For more skilled positions, these pre-interviews were conducted in English, and they posed more complicated questions related specifically to the job in question. Candidates who passed these pre-interviews were supposed to be seen by the client prior to candidates who did not show up for pre-interviews at all. Candidates who did not pass these pre-interviews were ineligible to attend the client interviews. Despite the possibility of not passing, some job seekers told me they thought it was better to attend pre-interviews because it meant they would have a greater chance of being interviewed by the client. However, this was hardly guaranteed even for candidates who passed, given the large crowds and sometimes chaotic atmosphere of interviews.

Recruiting agency employees believed that workers who showed initiative in past jobs would be good job candidates. Conversely, those who did not demonstrate this initiative would sometimes be weeded out during the pre-interview process. One day, I sat with Mr. Shukla as he pre-interviewed workers for upcoming interviews for a semiskilled job at an oil and gas company. A job candidate entered and gave Mr. Shukla his CV, who looked over it and began to question the interviewee. The form of these interviews largely mimicked the style of interviews with human resources managers from oil companies. First, Mr. Shukla asked, "What kinds of things did you do in Qatar?" The candidate replied by listing the types of tools he used on the job site. Satisfied with the answer, Mr. Shukla showed the candidate a technical drawing and asked him questions about the document. The candidate faltered and said he did not know how to read it but could follow directions. Mr. Shukla frowned and then asked the candidate additional questions about the image. At the end of the interview, Mr. Shukla rejected the candidate and told him he could not attend the interviews with the oil company representative, despite the fact that the potential interviewee had the requisite job experience. After the interview, I asked Mr. Shukla about his decision not to pass the candidate. He told me, "The candidate's knowledge was not great. While [he] had the skills, he did not have knowledge. The problem was [he] showed no initiative to learn in his past experience. This means that he is not suitable for [this job]." Mr. Shukla suggested to the candidate that he try to find a job at a company with lower standards and named some upcoming interviews at Mancom.

Recruiting agents and their employees want qualified, industrious candidates to attend interviews so that companies hire many workers and continue to work with the agency in the future. Recruiting agency employees also believe that clients want large numbers of candidates to arrive at interviews. This meant that during pre-interviews, Mr. Anthony and Mr. Shukla needed to balance seemingly contradictory needs. The first time I sat with Mr. Anthony during pre-interviews, I expected him to ask challenging questions and pass along only the highest caliber of candidates. However, unlike Mr. Shukla, Mr. Anthony emphasized the need to pass as many applicants as possible in the pre-interview stage, and he gave the "green light" to the large majority of applicants he interviewed. Indeed, pre-interviews with Mr. Anthony often had a lecture-like quality in which he anticipated what questions the client would ask the job seeker. Mr. Anthony would then tell the interviewee the correct answer to these questions. One afternoon I sat with him as he conducted pre-interviews for a project in Kuwait. That day, he interviewed a man who had previous experience as a pipe fitter. As they spoke, the man immediately confused inches and centimeters. Mr. Anthony stopped him, pointed out the error, and explained the difference. He passed the interviewee and told him to study for the interviews with the oil company managers. After the interview, Mr. Anthony told me that the interviewee "didn't seem qualified," but he put him through to be interviewed by the client because he thought it best to "cast a wide net." Mr. Anthony said he would send many people to be interviewed with the oil company manager and then "see if anyone got picked up."

Regional and Religious Discrimination

Decisions made in pre-interviews are not always meritocratic. Recruiting agency employees often hold assumptions concerning how certain skills map onto Indian geography, and these perspectives on regional specialization are shared by government officials. An assumption commonly held by both recruiters and government bureaucrats working in the Ministry of Overseas Indian Affairs was that certain types of workers come from certain states of India. The mapping of skills according to state was surprisingly consistent, and I often heard, for example, that plumbers come from Orissa, carpenters from Rajasthan, laborers from Bihar and Uttar Pradesh, and engineers and doctors from Kerala. The result was that a notion of state specialization was reinforced by recruiting agent practices. For example, if a recruiting agent needed to find plumbers for a project, he would go to Orissa, thereby reinforcing the stereotype.

Some assumptions were harmful to minority community members. In many recruiting agency offices, stereotypes about Muslims create and reinforce an understanding of religious difference in which Hindu migrants are hard-working and industrious and Muslim migrants are uneducated and irrationally religious. Many told me that religion was the most important factor in defining Muslim citizens' values and that religion is the reason most Muslims want to migrate to the Gulf, whereas Hindus migrate to work abroad because they have made a rational financial calculation.

During interviews with recruiting agents and their employees, Hindu and Muslim job applicants often received differing treatment. This was the case even when the recruiting agent or employee was also a Muslim, and these interactions reflect the importance of class as well as power of Islamophobic ideologies.[17] One recruiting agent, Mr. Kumar, told me that the young generations of middle-class Hindu men want to "give India [a] try first" because they do not want to leave their homes or work in the "harsh" conditions of the Gulf. In contrast, he said, "Lower categories—Dalits and Muslims—want to go abroad and improve their category." For him, the "biggest reward is seeing people improve and helping them. For example, there was a young man who was 10 pass [he had gone through tenth grade in school] and who had taken two years of technical course in India. I was recruiting for helpers and met this enterprising young man, who had ideas of starting a business if he were alone." But, Mr. Kumar continued, the young man was not alone and had family responsibilities: "He was the eldest of three siblings and [his] father was good for nothing. So the man went as helper." Mr.

Kumar believed that after many years of working in the Gulf, the young man would eventually be able to return to India and open his own business.

This properly entrepreneurial and rational migrant may be contrasted with laborers from minority communities, who are often considered objects of development or excluded from the modernization narratives all together. Muslims, in particular, are thought to be motivated by religious beliefs, not capitalism. Some recruiting agents describe Muslims' religious motivation as a fact but are not overt in passing judgment on it. For example, Mr. Bakshi told me that "Muslims prefer to go to Saudi Arabia because hajj is free and [they] would prefer to go even at a lower salary. It is the reverse for non-Muslims who want a higher salary." This form of discourse reinforces notions of Muslims as driven by primarily religious motives. In contrast, Hindus are viewed as rational economic actors. Through such descriptions, social inequalities become naturalized.

Other recruiting agents and employees sometimes use the perception that Muslims are primary motivated by religion to reinforce Islamophobic positions. This discrimination at times has a negative impact on Muslims' ability to find jobs abroad. One day as I sat with Mr. Shukla and Mr. Anthony as they tried to find employees for commissioners' work, Mr. Anthony explained to me,

> This work is after installation, checking to make sure that everything works and showing people how to use it. It is more difficult to get people for this work because greater knowledge is required and the nature of work now is that a person in oil and gas only does one job, so they do not become experts at all tasks.

Here, Mr. Shukla interjected, reinforcing the perspectives that good migrants ought to improve themselves and act as entrepreneurs: "But if a person is willing to work hard, then they can learn." In his reply, Mr. Anthony mobilized religious stereotypes to explain the challenges they were having finding suitable candidates that day:

> But the problem is that people do not want to go abroad for work, only people with some responsibility go and they are the oldest brother and their sisters need to get married. . . . People can get good work in India. So no one wants to go. It's the few bad ones that want to go work abroad. The worst are from Jharkhand, Bihar-side, and they [are] 99.9% Muslims and they have the same problem as the Muslims in Pakistan have—they are fundamentalist crazy. Pakistan doesn't send many people to work [in the Gulf], they

have the language, like India, but they do not have the technology, India is much advanced, and Pakistan is just a terrorist training camp now.

Through deploying stereotypes such as terrorism and fundamentalism, Mr. Anthony described a Muslim ethic that was antagonistic to modernity, development, and entrepreneurship. Discrimination against individuals from certain states or from minority communities, such as Muslims, was justified, he believed, with the language of brand and failure to properly inhabit a modern, Indian entrepreneurial subjectivity.

Teaching Correct Speech

If an interviewee navigated bias and passed pre-interviews, Mancom sometimes held classes to prepare interviewees for interviews with the client, particularly if the client was one with which Mancom hoped to work more in the future. While many presentations were described as teaching best safety practices, in substance, the classes often focused on worker responsibility and interviewees' communication skills. During classes, Mr. Shukla and Mr. Anthony explained the basics of safety equipment, showing the job candidates work boots, helmets, and gloves; demonstrating the use of this equipment; and prepping candidates on what to say when interviewers asked about safety equipment. This and other classes were seen as a time to train the applicants and prepare them to respond to interviewers' questions correctly, thereby helping to normalize best business practices into a single strategy and facilitate another form of cultural streamlining. Mancom managers attempted to improve the quantity and quality of the company's applicants by hosting classes on the days leading up to the client interviews.

I attended one set of classes in 2010, just prior to an oil company manager's arrival to interview workers for jobs as scaffold riggers. Scaffold rigging is a semi-skilled occupation, and many of the people who interviewed for the jobs did not have high school diplomas and would fall into the vulnerable or Emigration Check Required (ECR) category, meaning they need permission from the government in order to migrate. The candidates in attendance had passed the pre-interviews a week earlier and sat crowded in a meeting room while Mr. Anthony and Mr. Shukla discussed "best safety practices." As his lecture on personal protective equipment began, Mr. Anthony looked to the group of men and said firmly, in a mixture of English and Hindi, "sab' se ba're baat is confidence" (the biggest thing is confidence).

After demonstrating safety equipment, Mr. Anthony and Mr. Shukla also told candidates what to do in case of an emergency. As they spoke, they underlined the importance of the equipment and the lecture itself by telling the candidates, "International law says that human safety is first." Throughout the lecture, they firmly placed the responsibility for safety with the candidates. "Make no mistakes," Mr. Anthony said, and Mr. Shukla agreed, "accidents don't just happen, they are caused." Communication, they told candidates, is the key to avoiding accidents. Mr. Shukla then concluded the lecture by stressing that interviewees needed to "speak correctly and with confidence" to the interviewers. Pausing for a moment, he added, "Communication is also key" to finding a job abroad. This means, they told candidates, that you must go and "present your knowledge" at your job interview. By attending classes in which they are taught how to "speak correctly" and with "confidence," job candidates learn to present themselves as knowledgeable laborers.

This emphasis on language and communication reflects both individual and social cultivation and strongly resembles the methods of state development projects. In 1956, the Ford Foundation awarded India a grant to strengthen local democracy, and one activity initiated with this was teaching local leaders to communicate in ways that emphasized local democratic principles in contrast to communal political identities.[18] In the contemporary moment too, communication is directly connected with development as well as morality and the fashioning of "civilized" selves and places. Unlike past efforts to cultivate moral individuals through language directed by the government, communication strategies now are cultivated in the workplace.[19] This privatization is similar to other changes that have occurred since India began liberalizing its economy in the 1990s. While the Indian state continues to focus on the development of institutions and individuals, businesses also take on this work, and recruiting agencies actively work to provide opportunities for migrants to cultivate themselves into better representations of India's brand.

HIRING MANAGER PERSPECTIVES

India's brand is imagined in terms of a global audience. In the case of migrants laborers, potential employers compose a large part of this global audience. Much like the differing perspectives of recruiting agents and government officials, employers engage with labor migration from a particularized set of perspectives. When human resources managers for oil companies describe place of Indian workers in the global labor market, they often emphasize the differing wages required by workers of differing nationalities and the comparative cheapness of Indian labor.

While the price of labor is important, managers discuss workers' pay in conjunction with their own perceptions of Indian workers' abilities. George, an American, was in Mumbai to hire Indian workers for construction projects underway at the US-based energy contracting company for which he worked. When we met, he told me that he oversaw three recruiting specialist units, based in Mumbai, Manila, and Cairo. When I asked him why one of these units is based in Mumbai, he told me the company had chosen to recruit in Mumbai because "traditionally it was an area to get high-quality engineers and craftspeople." As we spoke more, I learned that historically, his company hired only Americans and Europeans to work on projects. "But this has changed over the years. Over the last ten to fifteen years, the location of recruitment has been driven by the cost and companies had to rethink" the nationalities of workers. Blaming a "shift in the economy," George told me that Americans want five times the salary that the company pays to Indian workers. By hiring Indian or Filipino workers, the company could pay workers much less and receive the same quality work. The reason the work quality was the same was, in George's opinion, that universities in the United Kingdom and India "are almost identical." In addition, he believes that the university system in the Philippines "is comparable, and in many cases better than" the university system in the United States.

While praising the high quality of Indian skilled professionals, George was mainly hiring semiskilled workers and saw India as an ideal place to hire such workers. Overall, he estimated that his company had approximately 60,000 employees at any given time. He believed 10,000 of these employees were semiskilled or unskilled workers from India. Now the company was recruiting in India heavily "because there is cheap labor in India." On the visit when I met him, he hired approximately 250 Indians to work as laborers at just one of the oil construction projects for which he oversaw staffing. The low cost of Indian labor and the large numbers of men who compete for jobs mean that oil companies see India as having a surplus of labor, and this surplus, along with a low minimum wage established by the Indian government, means to managers like George that Indian labor is cheap.

Many companies visit the Philippines and multiple South Asian countries when hiring the large numbers of workers necessary for oil projects. Alex, a British project manager from a European-based energy contractor, visited Mumbai to hire workers for a project in the United Arab Emirates. He was accompanied by two human resources managers from Connex who would travel from Mumbai to the Philippines to hire additional workers. While discussing these plans, Alex told me, "It is better to hire Indians, if possible, for open jobs, because they are much cheaper." The low wages that companies pay Indian workers compared to workers from Pakistan, Bangladesh, and the Philippines, both human resources managers and recruiting agency employees told me, is that the Indian government sets a minimum wage for vulnerable Indian workers going abroad that is lower than any of those other countries. In conversations with Alex, George, and other corporate representatives, they do not focus singularly on India's brand. Rather, the price of Indian labor is considered an important (if not most important) feature of Indian labor.

CONCLUSION

Through lectures and demonstrations, employees at Mancom attempted to teach workers a language of communication that reflected their knowledge as well as a confident attitude toward work. These aspects of communication are strongly associated with entrepreneurship and the accompanying social and individual cultivation that goes along with it. Often practices like grooming, communication, and safety appear to be global in scope, contributing to the movability of migrant labor. While the pre-interviews and classes may seem separated from structural inequalities and individual biases, social and individualized inequalities influence the migration process. These are often based on a shared vision of India's future that focuses on upper-caste Hindu values and actions and omits other members of the Indian nation. Issues arise in how the government participates in training, the types of training recruiting agents implement, and individual biases at recruiting agencies and in the government. All are considered key elements in improving India's brand image through selecting quality migrants and teaching migrants to be entrepreneurial.

Recruiting agents and government officials are able to agree on the threat of the labor migrant to India's brand because of their socioeconomic class, as well as the ideal future of India's brand. As recruiting agents and government officials seek to cultivate entrepreneurial migrants, they reinforce select values—values that are seen as being uniquely Indian and are shaped by national histories and previous trade routes. Workers are to be representative of India's brand abroad, a brand that is unique due to these practices and an ethic that is understood to be representative of India. While the impulses of business and the government do not overlap completely, the concept of brand allows for the coordination of meanings, mediation, and translation that help overcome the threat of incommensurability between the government's and agents' understandings of migration, its history, and their roles within it. The coordination and circulation of huge numbers of papers, emigrants, and bureaucrats within and through the Arabian Sea is developed as both groups agree on the relationship between the nation's brand and migration.

Unstated in this process is the role of dispossession. In interviews, employees at recruiting agencies told me they believe that as an area benefits economically from the inflow of remittances, the education level throughout the community increases and residents of that area are no longer willing to migrate for low-wage, menial labor positions. As a result, companies recruit from agricultural areas in poor states to fill these positions. While historically many Indian migrants were from southern India, today the majority of migrants come from northern Indian states, which are the most reliant on agriculture and have higher unemployment and underemployment rates.[20] From the perspective of migrants, working in the Gulf pays six to ten times more than a job in India.

Competition for jobs is fierce, and migrants must pay large amounts of money to help them acquire their jobs and pay for emigration. This debt plays an active role in the production of labor and drives the price of labor increasingly lower. Labor migrants are the most vulnerable. Their precarity emerges as they sell their labor, often through the influence of dispossession[21] and as they take on debt to become entrepreneurial brands.

This discourse of cultivating entrepreneurship is not limited to government officials and recruiting agents. Returned migrants from the Gulf who worked for recruiting agents often repeated the importance of migrants working hard and improving themselves. Deepak, an employee at Mancom who specializes in recruiting laborers for projects, had worked in Qatar previously. There, Deepak, told me, he was hired as a laborer because it was the only position he could find. After a while, he "came up" to a job in human resources. This move, he said, was possible because he worked hard to learn English and computer skills. He shared this story with laborers preparing to travel to the Gulf and told them that they too could be promoted. He said to one group, "You will go and work in the camp.

Get up early in the morning; go early to the job site. Work on site. Be good with others, and do no politics. Be fair. Then you'll come up." In conversations like these, Deepak encouraged men about to go abroad to work hard, and this would help them be promoted. Men, eager to work abroad and dreaming of a future of financial security, listened attentively.

Chapter 3

BUILDING INFLUENTIAL NETWORKS

ON THE DAY OF THE INTERVIEWS, I ARRIVED AT THE TECHNICAL academy campus in one of Mumbai's northern suburbs before the interviews were scheduled to begin. But I was not earlier than all of the potential workers who gathered at the academy. The large campus of the academy is often quiet, but on this day, over two hundred men lined the long, paved paths that connect the academy's various buildings. The men were waiting, as many told me, for a "chance"—a chance to be hired, to work abroad, to repay loans, to help sisters marry, and to save family farms. These were some of the first interviews I attended, and I was surprised by the large number of men present—many times more than the company hoped to hire, and the interview day was relatively short. All of these men waiting seemed impossibly hopeful to me, given the long odds that any individual man would make it to an interview, let alone be hired.

In order to get a large crowd, the Mancom employee supervising these interviews, Deepak, advertised the interviews in local newspapers and called his contacts to tell them about the interviews. The interviews were for welders to work for an energy services provider based in Oman. As I continued to conduct research at Mancom, I learned that the recruiting agency often held interviews at this site because it was large enough to accommodate the many people who often showed up for interviews. In addition, the academy had many of the tools needed for interviews because interviewees are often asked to demonstrate their familiarity and adeptness with common tools used on oil projects. These interviews were for welding jobs, and men would be timed as they welded metal; those who did so quickly and with the most accuracy were usually hired.

Interview practices, like skill testing, lend the appearance that individuals with the most expertise will be hired for positions. When discussing workers in the oil industry, expertise often arises, as oil requires expertise to make it usable.[1] Expertise involves the ability to know a topic, solve problems based on this knowledge, and convey this expertise to others.[2] Within the oil industry, expertise is most often conceptualized and sought after in relation to upper-level engineers or geologists, but assumptions about expertise affect who is hired for other positions as well.[3] As this chapter examines, however, expertise, demonstrated by quickness and skill in tests, is only part of who gets hired for jobs in the Gulf. For most Indian migrants, networks and relationships structure their emigration experience and their ultimate success or failure at finding a job abroad.

Standing next to Deepak as he looked out at the crowd of waiting men, I asked him who would be hired. He responded, in English, that it was ultimately dependent on "networks and influence."[4] The importance of networks and influence was reinforced as I spoke with men waiting for an interview and throughout my research more generally. As I walked around the campus, I met Wafadar, a Muslim man from Bihar, who hoped to be hired that day. During our conversation, he explained to me how he, like Deepak, understood both networks and influence to be central to the success of his job search. Wafadar had recently returned to India after working in Bahrain for one year. Before that, he had worked in Qatar and Oman for six years. He was married and had two daughters and a son. While he worked in the Gulf, his wife and children lived with Wafadar's parents and brothers on the family's small farm. I asked Wafadar how he knew about the day's interviews, and he told me about meeting one man who introduced him to another, and this second person brought Wafadar, along with a number of other men, to these interviews. The men with whom Wafadar worked, often referred to as subagents, were both from Bihar. Later that day, I again met Wafadar, and with a large smile, he told me he had been hired. As we chatted, Wafadar told me he was successful finding a job because he had formed relationships with the right local men—men who, he told me, had "influence."

Mobilizing understandings of locality and community, individuals involved in labor recruitment and prospective migrants use relationships to shape and delineate scales through the analytic of networks, a term they themselves often use.[5] Thinking of migration as a process of making networks uses a metaphor for migration that differs conceptually from approaches to migrants as vulnerable citizens in need of protection or as brand bearers who may be taught entrepreneurial attitudes. When brand and vulnerable are invoked, the scale of the nation-state is central. Such a scale assumes that migrants move from one discrete space to another—from sending to receiving country based on push and pull factors. In contrast, the term *network* destabilizes focus on the individual and on the state in favor of examining transnational communities that are being built. Using a network view of Indian migration to the Gulf sheds light on the multiple actors who shape regional oil production.

As people—government officials; recruiting agents and their employees; subagents; oil company managers; and current, prospective, and returned migrants—interact during the process of migration, they build networks. People collaborate in these networks to navigate economic and social inequalities.[6] Migrants also use them to navigate bureaucratic processes, debts, and working conditions. In addition, they create paths for additional prospective migrants to travel.[7] In India, examinations of networks or relations (*rishta*) often arise in studies of caste identity and politics.[8] Unlike networks mobilized around caste and politics, the networks created as people migrate to work on oil projects are composed of groups thought to be quite different—different religions, castes, nationalities, and classes. These networks are formed through understandings of locality, gifts, and circulation. Hierarchies are created within networks, and they take effort to maintain. While for many workers like Wafadar these networks are the key for migration, in other cases networks do not always produce successful results, and sometimes they are disastrous for prospective migrants and their families.

AGENTS, SUBAGENTS, AND JOB CANDIDATES

> Friends of friends.
> —*Jeremy Boissevain* (1974)

Wafadar's process of moving from his village to a job in the Gulf demonstrates one way that local connections are formed and the role of community making in the migration process. In the case of Wafadar's migration, subagents were key to finding a job in the Gulf. Subagents, usually local men who have some experience working in the Gulf, are unregulated and charge fees to prospective migrants to help find them work in the Gulf. Many subagents have connections with agents who are registered with the government or recruiting agency employees. Subagents frequently describe their role as being a middleman between recruiting agents and workers.

The first subagent with whom Wafadar worked was Goopal, a Hindu man living in the same region of Bihar as Wafadar. Goopal had worked as a subagent for three years and before that in Oman as a laborer for six years. When I met him, he told me he was using the "knowledge, experience, and connections" he had gained while working in the Gulf to help others from his district to migrate. Goopal told me he had "sent three hundred to four hundred men" to the Gulf and "all [the men] are happy." He stressed that they were happy because he "sends them transparently." To Goopal, "transparency" meant that he told the workers about every stage of the recruiting process and helped them find legitimate jobs.

Subagents like Goopal often work with another subagent who has a personal relationship with employees of a recruiting agency. When Wafadar was looking for work, Goopal introduced him to another subagent from Bihar, Jagdish. Jagdish had more experience than Goopal and had lived for thirteen years in the Gulf, working in offices in Oman, Bahrain, Kuwait, and the UAE. Jagdish, who worked with many subagents, including Goopal, told me that subagents "collect" workers from Bihar and Uttar Pradesh and then send these potential migrants to him in Mumbai. As I sat with Jagdish one afternoon, he explained the importance of his work to me: "Once I get the requirement [from a recruiting agent] I call the [sub] agents and they start arranging people. I must follow up with this every day ten times." Once in Mumbai, potential migrants such as Wafadar meet with Jagdish. To help these men find jobs, Jagdish takes the prospective migrants to the recruiting agencies where he has contacts. Jagdish's role is not limited to taking people to interviews; he also helps applicants create résumés and prepare for interviews.

As he described his work to me, Jagdish emphasized his own role as a crucial link in the networks that connect subagents located in villages with recruiting agents and oil companies. Connecting migrants, according to Jagdish, is both how he helps migrants find jobs and also how he helps them navigate bureaucratic apparatuses. Once a worker is hired, Jagdish explained, he sends the worker home to wait. Jagdish also waits, and, he said, "When I get the visas [from the recruiting agent], I send copies to local agents, and local agents go to locals and tell the people to be ready and then inform them when they are coming to Mumbai. Then they come, collect papers, and fly to the Middle East."

When a subagent like Jagdish brings a worker to an interview, they usually work with recruiting agency employees. In many cases, registered recruiting agents did not personally handle the recruiting of unskilled and semiskilled workers. These agents tended to be more skilled and more educated, and they have more financial resources than their employees or subagents. Many recruiting agents spent their time building relationships with other recruiting agents, high-level government bureaucrats, and energy contracting company owners or high-level managers. As a result, many recruiting agents in medium- and large-sized agencies were removed from the day-to-day recruiting practices. For the recruitment of unskilled workers at Mancom, one manager, Pandeya, oversaw three junior employees, Deepak, Arjun, and Jimmy, who handled the bulk of the unskilled recruitment. When I met them, all three had recently returned from working in the Gulf. A few years after I first met them at Mancom, all three began working again in the Gulf, and they had used the relationships they built at Mancom with Gulf companies to find these jobs.

Employees at recruiting agencies and, in particular, the office workers who specialize in recruiting unskilled and semiskilled workers, often have close relationships with subagents. Subagents rely on their relationships with recruiting agency employees in order to help men find jobs. Similarly, recruiting agency employees rely on their personal networks when arranging interviews, often trusting subagents to bring many candidates to job interviews, thereby helping the agency employee impress the company's client. Arjun told me that he "calls subagents and they bring to him, two days before interviews, as many men as they can find for a position." Subagents also vet the quality of applicants, and, Arjun explained, "From subagents, I can get the whole history of a candidate. I want to make sure that they don't cheat and that they can get approval to work. Subagents also have networks and influence. They use networks to go find men." Like Deepak, Arjun emphasizes networks and influence as keys to migration. For Arjun, these are attributes that determine the importance of subagents, and his success in his job was determined by his own networks and influence with subagents. By working with the right subagents, Arjun was able to ensure a large number of men show up for interviews and that these men are quality applicants, with the skills or experience, or both, required to perform the job.

Recruiting agency employees typically have a few subagents with whom they prefer to work, and at interviews, they prioritize the workers brought by these preferred subagents when calling individuals into interviews. A subagent's ability to help men find jobs in the Gulf depends on the influence of the recruiting agency employees with whom the subagent develops networks. The influences of recruiting agency employees are often reflected in their relationships with subagents and with human resources managers at Gulf companies. Generally during interviews, one Mancom employee worked as a liaison with each client representative, usually a human resources manager, but sometimes a project manager or a manager who directly oversees worker activities. Each of Mancom's employees had a slightly different style for how he presented applicants to clients, but regardless of the style, it was a well-thought-out strategy that included trying to sway the client so that he would choose many candidates from Mancom.

As at the technical academy interviews, it is not uncommon for hundreds of men to show up for interviews for jobs in the Gulf. As a result, interviews are often overcrowded and so overbooked that most applicants are not able to meet with the potential employer for an interview. At interview sites like the technical academy, energy company human resources managers often quickly and efficiently quiz applicants, rapidly deciding if the applicant should be hired immediately, sent for testing, or not hired. Even given the speed with which employers interview applicants, there is no way they could see all of the applicants who arrive for interviews. In the end, most men would wait all day and still not be interviewed. In order to be interviewed by a representative of a company, interviewees hope the subagent with whom they work has influence and relationships with recruiting agency employees. In addition, subagents want to work with recruiting agency employees who are good at building relationships with energy company human resources managers.

Over lunch one day, I asked Arjun, Deepak, and Jimmy how they decided who was interviewed first, then second, and so on, particularly given the large numbers of people present at interviews. Arjun replied, "CVs are arranged in order of quality of applicant, how early they came to be short-listed, and how early they arrive today. When a requirement is told by the client as they are ready to interview, then the candidate is called," and brought into the interview room, by lower-level office workers. As Arjun continued talking, he described the strategies he used to influence hiring decisions: "I like to mix up the interviews—mix up the applicants so that the client gets confused. Also, I have the good candidates go first so that he [the client] thinks Mancom has good applicants. Then, later, the bad candidates [are interviewed], and he can reject these."

Relationships also play a key role in who is interviewed. For example, at the interviews with which this chapter began, the men, including Wafadar, who went to the interviews with Jagdish, a subagent with whom Deepak regularly works, had their résumés put on top of the pile of interviewees. This gave the men Jagdish brought a greater chance of having the employer see their qualifications. These résumés may be placed in front of those of other interviewees who had arrived early or had been short-listed in the previous days by Mancom employees. Such daily practices demonstrate the importance of relationships in determining if a prospective migrant is hired. Because of his close relationship with Jagdish, Deepak viewed the men Jagdish brought as "his [Deepak's] candidates" and explained that he would put them first even if they didn't have the qualification. "It is worth trying for them . . . sometimes, depending on the client need, I can even push the candidate into a position by talking to the client, even if the candidate isn't skilled, isn't ready." Subagents work closely with recruiting agency employees by vetting prospective job candidates before interviews, bringing qualified candidates for interviews, and managing job candidates at the interview site. In return, employees at recruiting agencies will "push" interviewees brought by subagents with whom the employee has a close relationship. This reciprocal relationship is valuable to prospective migrants because there are many more potential interviewees than time to interview them.

In addition to the strategic placement of workers in the interview queue or placing some résumés at the top of the pile, agency employees also mobilize "emotional blackmail" as a tactic to get their liaison at an energy company to comply with their requests. This emotional blackmail, as agency employees themselves call it, includes techniques such as making the client believe that the employee of the recruiting agency will lose his job if not enough of his candidates are accepted. As I sat with Jimmy during a set of interviews, he told me he will "push the candidate into a position by talking to the client, even if the candidate isn't skilled." To clients, Jimmy would say that his boss would fire him if the client did not hire enough interviewees. Jimmy would then push the candidates he wanted the client to take, including those brought by subagents with whom Jimmy has a working relationship. Through using emotional blackmail, Jimmy often could convince a client to hire additional people because the client did not want to be responsible for Jimmy losing his job.

While recruiting agency employees push subagents' job candidates, subagents also help employees at recruiting agencies get around bureaucratic apparatuses and policy issues that arise when conducting interviews. For example, one day Arjun was stressed "because there are some problems with the ad. It needs to be certified by the [Indian] embassy [in the country for which they are hiring], but this takes ten days. This is not possible," he said, because the client was coming for interviews in five days. Without the proper approval, Arjun could not advertise the interviews in the paper. As a result, he immediately began calling subagents to ensure that a "large crowd" would arrive for the interviews. Through relying on these subagents, Arjun felt he was successful at his job. In this case, he was able to place twenty qualified laborers with just one short day of interviews even though he was unable to advertise the interviews widely.

Jimmy, Deepak, and Arjun also told me that they relied on subagents to ensure that workers, once hired, actually traveled to their jobs in the Gulf. When a worker is hired, the agency processes the paperwork and buys a plane ticket before the applicant pays the agency's fees. In addition, energy companies in the Gulf pay once workers arrive on-site. Sometimes the hired worker will not return to the agency to get his papers and travel for the job. This is particularly a problem, I am told, when workers arrive without subagents because they do not pay Mancom's fee until hired workers arrive in Mancom's office to pick up their tickets and passports. However, if a man arrives with a subagent, the agency sends copies of the visas to the local subagents. These subagents tell the hired worker their papers are ready and encourage them to go to Mumbai, pick up their visas and tickets, and travel to the Gulf.

THE IMPORTANCE OF LOCAL RELATIONSHIPS

According to Wafadar, migration is a process rooted in local networks, and he described his natal village as the site from where local relations grow. Wafadar told me that relying on local networks involved less *parīshānī*, a term that could mean worry, stress, or harassment. When Wafadar began looking for work, he first met with Goopal, whom he considered to be a "local man." Recruiting agency employees also privilege understandings of locality when building networks. While some subagents who work directly with recruiting agency employees are based in Mumbai, others are based outside the city. Jimmy, Arjun, and Deepak were sometimes unable to find subagents who could bring to Mumbai the number of workers clients required. In these cases, Jimmy, Arjun, or Deepak would travel to towns in various Indian states to find potential workers, and they frequently went to the states in which they were born when travel was needed.

One week, Arjun and I went to a town in Rajasthan where a "friend" (a subagent) of Arjun lived. Because the client, an energy contractor, was "trusting"

Mancom to do the tests, Arjun called his friend, and the friend arranged for an interview site that allowed for testing—in this case, a place with enough space for men to demonstrate their ability to build scaffolding. On the days of interviews, Arjun judged the workers and selected a group of finalists from whom the client would make a decision based on the interviewee's testing score, résumé, and biodata. Recruiting agents often prefer potential migrants to come to Mumbai for job interviews because it saves the agency travel expenses and agencies can use locations familiar to them for testing. In contrast, agency employees often were excited to travel. In the case of this scaffold-builder position, Arjun explained that the pay for the job was low and people who could afford the expense of traveling to Mumbai would not want to take a job because of the pay. According to Arjun, traveling to villages for low-wage jobs is usually preferable to conducting interviews in Mumbai because, he said, when he travels to villages, he can "find one hundred qualified men in a trip." In Mumbai, for the same job, he said, he may get only twenty or thirty applicants, usually because of low wages. Thus, by traveling to villages, Arjun told me, he can give Mancom's clients "a good selection."

Deepak too often traveled for interviews, usually to Bihar and Uttar Pradesh. One week, Deepak and I went Uttar Pradesh with two Indian hiring managers who worked for an energy company based in the UAE. At each interview site, subagents brought large groups of men. When we arrived each morning, one to two hundred men would be waiting in a relatively unstructured environment, such as a field or a courtyard. On this trip, I was surprised at the orderliness of the interview site. Men were waiting in lines—a stark contrast from the interview site at the academy in Mumbai where men sometimes push forward hoping to be interviewed by the client. I asked Deepak about the difference in orderliness, and he told me, "I myself am good at managing people." But, he added, he expects subagents to "manage the people they bring." During his trips, Deepak explained that he relied on subagents not only to bring workers for interviews but also to "tell workers how to stand and present" themselves. This was particularly important, Deepak said, if he was traveling with a client, because he believed orderly lines would impress the client with the quality of the interviewees and Mancom.

Many agents tend to recruit preferentially from their home state or district. For example, Mr. Hussain, who is from Gujarat but based in Mumbai, told me he prefers to hire workers from near his natal village in Gujarat. He told me this is easier because he can call friends in his village and they send workers to him in Mumbai. High-level managers at recruiting agencies also express this. Pandeya told me that when a client needs to hire laborers, he likes to look first in Bihar. This was because Pandeya is from Bihar and he wants to "help his state people. They don't have jobs, families are dying." Pandeya went on to tell me that helping Biharis find jobs in the Gulf "is a type of social work, because they are jobs with good salaries." This preference for hiring workers from one's state or district occurred also in hiring for skilled positions.

Prospective migrants and recruiting agency employees stress that locality facilitates trust. This is particularly important as migrants may experience problems during their travels, and subagents help them navigate these problems. Deepak told me, "These people [migrants] are harassed by police in Mumbai, and I need to go and pick them up from the station. Sometimes there is a problem with ticketing, and they need to stay for four to five days. But people only trust this man [the subagent they originally worked with] [and] will not meet with or take the papers from anyone else." This indicates the trust migrants have for local agents over agents based in large cities like Mumbai. This trust continues even after a migrant arrives in the Gulf. Deepak explained to me, "When [migrants] reach [their destination country], if no one is there, they call and he [the subagent] has to say, 'Wait there!' Sometimes they wait one or two hours or all night." Subagents connect recruiting agents to workers and also provide valuable insights to workers as they look for a job and after they travel for that job.

Although these are networks with local connections, individuals are not envisioned as equals within the system, and recruiting agency employees and subagents repeatedly invoke and reinforce social hierarchies. Language is a key way these hierarchies are displayed. Early in my research at Mancom, I sat with Deepak and Arjun as they took a break from arranging interviews for a Qatari company that wanted to hire seventy-five manual laborers. During the break, they asked how "the work for my book" was going. As I began to talk, Deepak interrupted me and began a lecture that felt, at first, unrelated to what I was talking about. Deepak began, "You must not use *aap* when you are talking to these men." *Aap* is the most formal form of "you" in Hindi and Urdu and is used to show respect with elders and with strangers. It is also the plural form of "you." In general, I address most people and all strangers with *aap* because that was what I was taught when learning the languages. When I told Deepak this, he replied, "Saying *aap* is the wrong way to speak [to laborers]. You must use *tu, tere*." *Tu, tere* are the least formal form of "you" and "yours" in Hindustani. Over my years of language study, I was consistently taught that it would be both rude and offensive to use *tu*. Confused,

I asked Deepak and Arjun why *tu* wouldn't be rude for me to use. Arjun replied, "They [laborers] are lower classes. This is how you talk to them." I must change, Arjun and Deepak said, because I was confusing prospective migrants by "giving them respect."[9]

As I began to listen more carefully to the language used by recruiting agency employees and subagents, I found that *tu* is commonly used when speaking to unskilled laborers, particularly those from Jharkhand, Bihar, and Uttar Pradesh. Indeed, often Arjun and Deepak would yell "arre" (Hey!) at men looking for jobs as laborers and other forms of address used by upper-caste men when addressing people of lower castes.[10] In contrast to the hierarchy Deepak and Arjun drew with laborers, they addressed men looking for semiskilled work, such as electricians and pipe fitters, often with *tum*, the form of "you" more formal than *tu* but less formal than *aap*. *Tum* is used among friends and may also be used among colleagues working together in offices. When Deepak and Arjun used *tum*, I found their interactions with those candidates were often friendlier. By choosing to use either *tum* or *tu*, Deepak and Arjun established their relations with job candidates and signaled closeness or hierarchy.

MAINTAINING NETWORKS

Subagents and recruiting agency employees work closely together, and each group sees good relations with the other group as integral to their success at their respective jobs. For example, subagents maintain order, as Deepak described, at interview sites. They are also relied on by recruiting agencies to understand the specificities of a job and to know which of the men they are working with are qualified for positions. However, this did not always work out, as I saw at Mancom during failed interviews for a Gulf-based energy company, al-Unbub. A human resources manager and a project manager from al-Unbub were in the Mancom offices interviewing men to work as pipe fitters for the construction of an oil refinery. During the interviews, both Mancom employees and representatives from al-Unbub became increasingly frustrated, and the representatives from al-Unbub disparaged the quality of Mancom's interviewees. Despite conducting dozens of interviews on the first day, the representatives from al-Unbub hired only one person. By lunch on the second day, the representatives had hired only one additional person. I sat with the project manager and human resources manager from al-Unbub as they conducted their interviews, and I could see they were upset and becoming increasingly frustrated. This came to a head after lunch on the second day of interviews when the project manager asked the job candidate his first question. The interviewee began to respond, but after less than a minute, the project manager interrupted the interviewee. Waving his hand, the project manager said, "You don't have any basic knowledge, sorry," and the interviewee was promptly escorted out of the room. The project manager then asked the human resources manager for the advertisement Mancom had run in the newspapers prior to the interviews. As the project manager read the advertisement, he grew upset that his time was being wasted. Pointing to the advertisement, he complained to the human resources manager that "[this] has none of the technical requirements listed in it." These requirements included the ability to read blueprints, use a tape measure, and use welding equipment. In response, the human resources manager insisted he had sent the right requirements to Mancom. He then deflected blame from himself, saying, "Agents only care about crowds and think having requirements [in the job advertisement] will discourage people from coming."

As the day continued, the interviewers treated the interviewees with increasing derision and contempt, often stopping them after they had spoken only a few words. By the end of two long days of interviews, al-Unbub had hired only five candidates. The employees of Mancom, and particularly Jimmy, the employee in charge of these interviews, were upset because few interviewees were being hired and because the interviewees were being treated poorly. By the middle of the second day, Jimmy understood al-Unbub would not hire many workers, and Jimmy's attention shifted from placating the al-Unbub interviewers to encouraging prospective migrants to return to Mancom for future interviews with a different company.

The Mancom employees present at the interviews had various reasons they believed these interviews had "failed." According to Mr. Anthony, few workers were hired because the project manager sent to do the interviews was "not very high in the company and he was afraid of his own boss." Therefore, Mr. Anthony conjectured, this project manager had unreasonably high standards because he did not want to be blamed for hiring workers who performed poorly. The next day I asked Jimmy why the interviews were such a failure, particularly given that earlier that week, he had successfully run interviews in which seventy workers were hired. Jimmy shrugged his shoulders and said he did not know, but that "probably Mr. Anthony is right" and the project manager "lacked confidence." Still trying to make sense of the failed interviews, I asked Jimmy what a pipe fitter does.

Jimmy again shrugged his shoulders. "I have no idea. My job is to run the ad and tell subagents. I don't care what it is, subagents know this [job specifications]." As we continued our conversation, Jimmy indicated he was frustrated and worried that the owner of Mancom, Mr. Sahil, would be upset. But Jimmy did not complain that the subagents with whom he worked brought unqualified candidates. Rather, he found fault with the company representatives running the interviews. Once he realized that the interviews would not be a success, his main concern, he told me, was to maintain a good relationship with the subagents and job candidates.

THE ROLE OF EXCHANGE IN BUILDING NETWORKS

Gifts play an important role in forming and maintaining relationships among migrants, subagents, recruiting agency employees, government employees, and oil company managers. Through giving gifts, many hope to build networks that include individuals they see as influential.[11] In turn, these networks facilitate collaborations that produce innovative migratory processes and practices.[12] Returned migrants often brought gifts to recruiting agency employees of watches, cologne, and alcohol. In giving these gifts, subagents and returned workers built relationships with agency employees. These relationships may be called on the next time a returned migrant was looking for a job in the Gulf, and they could also have potential positive benefits for a migrants' family members and friends.

At Mancom, Deepak was trying to find men to come for interviews for positions as sandblasters and spray painters at a project in Abu Dhabi. He looked through his list of contacts, finally finding a man, Ahtesham, whom he had placed in a similar position five years earlier. Before calling the number, Deepak explained to me, "This man, Ahtesham, is a very good man." As evidence, Deepak told me that when Ahtesham returned from the Gulf, he had brought Deepak a watch that he had purchased while working abroad. After explaining this to me, Deepak called Ahtesham's number, and Ahtesham's brother answered. During the conversation, we learned that Ahtesham was currently working in Kuwait. Instead of hanging up, Deepak asked the brother if he had experience working as a sandblaster. When Ahtesham's brother replied in the affirmative, Deepak proceeded to ask the brother about his experience and the places where he had worked. Hearing that Ahtesham's brother worked in India for an international corporation, Deepak told the man about the upcoming interview and asked him to come to Mumbai for this interview. Deepak then told Ahtesham's brother to call his friends with "the correct experience" and to bring them to the interview as well. After the conversation, Deepak told me he was happy that he had talked to the brother and excited by the quality of interviewees he anticipated the brother bringing.

The following week, I met Ahtesham's brother. He too said he was happy, and he told me he had "completed" the interview and was hired. When I asked him about the phone call with Deepak, Ahtesham's brother said that at first he was unsure if he should travel all the way to Mumbai for an interview. But, he said, he called his brother in Kuwait, and his brother told him that Deepak is a good man. For this reason, the brother said he felt comfortable coming to Mumbai and meeting with Deepak. As I spent more time with Deepak, I learned that he often relied on previous people he had placed in the Gulf to help recruit workers for positions. He could call a person he had helped find a job, and they would call their friends. Deepak said, "From one reference, I get many applicants. This way I don't need to hunt."

Gifts help shape the relationships among recruiting agencies' employees, subagents, and migrants. At times, the gifts from subagents and migrants to employees of recruiting agencies are objects of much speculation and gossip in recruiting agencies. At most agencies, employees told me that they did take gifts from job candidates and returned migrants, and they assumed that their colleagues did as well. But when gifts were given or taken, workers concealed their actions from colleagues for fear these gifts would be seen as bribes, which are expressly forbidden at many recruiting agencies, including Mancom. At a staff meeting one day, Mancom's owner, Mr. Sahil, told his employees that "applicants are willing to pay money to get a job," but he repeatedly warned that "taking such money is grounds for termination." He elaborated that in the past, Mancom workers had "accepted bribes to ensure jobs, make documents, vouch for candidates to client. And Mancom has terminated on such grounds." Despite these warnings, the staff at Mancom still speculated regularly about other staff taking bribes. By describing exchanges as bribes, recruiting agents and their employees categorized these exchanges as signs of corruption. The term *corruption* morally critiques such transactions and carries a possible accusation of legal impropriety.[13]

The moral and legal force stemming from accusations of taking bribes was made clear to me in a conversation with Deepak. When I arrived at Mancom's office one day, he was upset and pulled me into a corner of the office. In a loud whisper, he said that he'd just heard from his colleagues that his manager, Pandeya, was going with him on his next set of job interviews. Deepak was upset by this and blamed his colleague Arjun. Deepak nodded to Arjun's desk and called him a *bakchod*, slang for a person who speaks nonsense or who gossips. Deepak suspected Arjun had been talking to Pandeya. In addition, Deepak said Arjun was a *chamcha*, slang for sycophant, and that Arjun had been telling "stories" that Deepak was taking gifts from subagents. Deepak also believed that Pandeya was inclined to listen to these stories because he was envious of Deepak's growing success at the agency. Deepak believed that his manager was traveling with him in order to "catch him [Deepak] taking bribes," and this would give Pandeya an excuse to fire Deepak, who was becoming a potential competitor in recruitment numbers. But, Deepak said, lowering his voice and describing Pandeya's nice car and house, Pandeya's lifestyle would be affordable only by taking bribes from subagents. Here, Deepak was responding to Pandeya's perceived accusation and threat by also invoking bribery. At Mancom, such accusations usually arose when there were tensions between individuals.

In these moments of tension between individual employees, the money or goods given from subagents and migrants to agency employees are described as bribes. However, migrants, subagents, and agency employees do not regularly use the term *bribe*, invoking it only in moments of conflict. Instead, agency employees, migrants, and subagents usually describe the goods and money exchanged as gifts. In characterizing exchange in this way, people sought to create and reinforce relationships.[14] Gifts from subagents often take the form of money but could also be jewelry, mobile phones, or other electronics.

During the time I spent conducting ethnographic observation at Mancom, the policy regarding bonuses for recruiting agency employees changed; instead of receiving INR 500 (roughly US$11 at the time) for every worker who was chosen, employees no longer received any bonus. The express reason for this change was the poor economy following the 2008–2009 recession and its effects on Mancom's business. This policy shift, however, also may have reinforced the bonds between subagents and the recruiting agents at Mancom, as employees may have been inclined to pad their incomes without management knowledge by working with the subagents. By working with subagents with whom they already had relations, employees of recruiting agencies might receive a cut of the money that the subagent charged the worker.

Usually subagents charge prospective migrants a substantial fee—between INR 70,000 and INR 120,000 (approximately US$1,531 to US$2,624 in 2010)—to help them find a job in the Gulf. Money and gifts are often used as ways to cultivate influential relations. Building influential networks was needed, according to recruiting agency employees and subagents, because of the complexity of emigration regulations and their irregular enforcement.[15] The fees paid in excess of allowed amounts and gifts from migrants to those who have influence on their migration prospects are often framed as bribes and are the subject of gossip. In such discussions, *bribes* and *corruption* are terms that are at times mobilized to morally critique others.[16] In addition, when government functionaries are the recipients of items, these interactions may be moments in which the boundaries between government and companies are blurred and, in these cases, where people develop their own perspective of the state.[17] Often activities that would be labeled as corrupt become "collectively legitimated in everyday practice."[18] However, many migrants, recruiting agency employees, and subagents differentiate between gifts and bribes—"bribes" usually used to critique others' practices and "gifts" when discussing relationships.

Wafadar paid Goopal, the first subagent with whom he worked, INR 70,000 (US$1,531). Goopal, and Goopal's experiences "catching" job applicants, demonstrates a way relationships are formed through gifts. When I met Goopal, he told me the reason he charges men looking for jobs in the Gulf fees is because he must build networks with other people in order to be effective at his job. He particularly stressed how much money he needed to build relationships with government functionaries, including police officers. In part, his relationships with government functionaries were necessary because he was not registered with the Indian government, so his work as an agent was illegal. This illegality caused problems and drove up the fees he charged migrants. Goopal told me, "There is trouble, lots of pressure from police, and they ask, 'Where is your license?' and so I have to give them money and they go—usually rupees 5,000 to 10,000 [approximately US$109 to US$218 in 2010] is given. And I drink, eat with the [policeman], and he is happy." As Goopal explained how he engaged with police officers, he did not frame these interactions as moments of bribery or symbolic of the police's corruption. Instead, Goopal described his encounter as one in which social relations were built through consuming food and drinks with the police officers. When considering gifts from the perspective of those who give them and the role that food sharing has in connecting people, Goopal's story highlights that this is an interaction in which relationships are formed, often with an emphasis on local communities.

Here, Goopal stresses sharing food, an act that many Indians consider to be one that connects individuals.[19] Through such actions, people are able to create

networks with influential individuals. These encounters between low-level government employees and subagents are key moments in the migration process,
during which workers, subagents, and low-ranking government employees in-
terpret, translate, and work around policies that were, and continue to be, also
negotiated by recruiting agents and higher-ranking government officials.

Obtaining passports and emigration permission situates migrants within the
state,[20] but migrants often narrated their relationships with others as the most
important feature of their migration. Although the government may describe
vulnerable migrants as unable to act on their own as political actors, these migrants are in fact navigating complex bureaucratic apparatuses through forming
relationships. As subagents, migrants, and government employees interact, their
differing agendas may spur unequal results.[21] Inequalities, in these contexts,
are not the result of participants enacting a radical program of inclusion and
exclusion. Rather, they emerge and are reified as participants shape differing
contractual engagements with the state.[22]

For Wafadar, local networks not only helped him access interviews; he also
told me he was able to rely on friends of friends to host him in Mumbai while he
looked for work. Such a perspective regarding the bureaucratic structures and
the importance of local agents was echoed in Wafadar's expectations concerning
the documents needed to travel. Now that he has found a job, Wafadar told me,
he would "rest in Bihar" until it was time to leave for the job. While he was there,
he would get the requisite forms filled out, such as a "No Objection Certificate,"
from the police in his village. The rest of the paperwork he trusted would be
completed by the recruiting agency. Wafadar could then simply arrive, pick up
his passport with visa and plane ticket, and travel to the Gulf. In this narrative,
Wafadar emphasized the need for relationships with the right people in order to
navigate the bureaucratic paperwork required for emigration clearance.

ROLE OF CIRCULATION IN BUILDING NETWORKS

Locality and exchange are important parts of building influential networks. Another aspect of these networks is their formation through circulation. Subagents
and recruiting agency employees had experience working in the Gulf, and they
use the relationships they developed while working there to facilitate their jobs
in India. In addition, men who had migrated previously sometimes build relationships with recruiting agency employees as they moved from their villages
to Mumbai to the Gulf. Through building relationships directly with agency em-

ployees, prospective migrants could often avoid working with a subagent the next time they went abroad, often saving quite a bit of money in terms of the fees normally paid to subagents.[23]

Returned migrants mobilize relationships they built while working in the Gulf to find jobs, and they built relationships with subagents and recruiting agency employees, as well as with European and American oil company employees, who usually work as site managers at oil projects. Because most Indian migrants traveling for unskilled or semiskilled positions go to the Gulf on two- to three-year contracts, the relationships they form with oil company managers may be beneficial when they search for their next jobs. Workers drew on the relationship created by working for someone to navigate a competitive job market rooted in socioeconomic inequities.[24]

In Mumbai, I attended interviews held by Connex, a European energy services provider that was hiring pipe fitters and electricians, semiskilled labor, for a construction project in Abu Dhabi. As I observed interviews, I found that for oil company managers too, relationships and networks are central in hiring workers, and localized networks also structured the actions of and evaluations by managers working in the oil industry. When I arrived at the Connex interviews, I met Alex, a project head originally from the United Kingdom. He had worked previously in Norway and in most of the countries of the Arabic-speaking Gulf. This was his first visit to India, and he was there to hire hundreds of workers for the construction of an offshore oil rig in Musaffah, Abu Dhabi. With Alex were the head of Connex's human resources in the Gulf, the head of human resources' assistant, and one of Alex's site managers, all of them Indian nationals.[25] When the interviews began, Alex's colleagues warned him that he should not depend on an interviewee's CV to establish if the person had experience. The men who showed up that day, like men at most other interviews, had CVs that the subagent with whom they were working had helped them write. In fact, it is not uncommon for groups of men to arrive with the same résumé. Alex's colleagues therefore encouraged him to be skeptical of the credentials and degrees that applicants listed.

Alex read résumés carefully, but he did not ask workers about their skills or what work they had performed at certain job sites. Rather, he read résumés to see if migrants had previously worked in the Gulf and, if so, to see with whom they had worked.[26] Alex was particularly interested in workers who had been previously "sold," or subcontracted, to other companies, and he immediately approved them for employment with his company. He told me these workers "were probably okay, or else the company wouldn't keep paying for them." Alex also hired people who had worked for Connex or for his friends at other companies. If candidates claimed that they had worked for Connex or another American- or European-based company in the past, Alex tested this assertion by asking what project they had worked at, who the boss was, and if the worker could describe any of the managers on the site. Alex told me he was familiar with many of American and European project managers currently working in the Gulf. The reason for this was both that Alex had been "sold" to other companies in the past and because Connex was always one of dozens, if not hundreds, of companies working at any given oil project site.[27]

The most important factor for many project managers like Alex when hiring was with whom the interviewee had previously worked. For example, when interviewing an applicant who had previously worked for an American-owned energy contractor operating in Qatar, Alex asked if the interviewee knew Henry, a European manager who had worked on that project. A Mancom employee translated the question, and both the Mancom employee and the interviewee seemed confused. Usually human resources managers ask about skills and then send interviewees to be tested on these skills. Instead, Alex asked about networks. Finally, the interviewee admitted that he could not remember the names of his White managers. But, he said, there was this large guy with red hair. Alex, recognizing this description to be a former colleague of his, hired the interviewee immediately without testing the worker's skills. Throughout the week of interviews, Alex repeated this line of questioning, focusing not on the work men had previously performed but with whom they had worked. The men he hired were the ones who could reference European or American managers, often by describing the manager's appearance or mannerisms.

When candidates could demonstrate knowledge of the right people and networks, Alex viewed this as more important than the length of time they claimed to have previously worked in the Gulf or any certificates they might include with their CV. Workers who had previously worked for a project manager personally known to Alex did not even have to go to the testing center; he immediately hired them. Workers who did not know a manager Alex knew but could read technical drawings and answer Alex's questions were taken to a technical testing area where Mr. Anthony showed the candidates a task and asked them to perform it. For example, people applying to work as electricians were asked to pull and connect wires. The candidates were then evaluated based on their ability to complete the task correctly, as well as the speed with which they did so. Roughly one-quarter of the candidates who were asked to take the technical test passed. Thus, workers build networks not only with subagents but also employers, and these networks may help them navigate the job market.

Sometimes a worker was unable to answer Alex's questions about the people he had worked for or answer human resources managers' questions concerning job technicalities. In these cases, interviewees sometimes tried what they called "emotional techniques" to be hired. For example, interviewees would plead with Alex to give them a job and ask Alex to "take a chance" on them. Alex was moved by these pleas and told me he would like to hire everyone, and he gave many chances to those who were pleading to answer questions not only about previous managers but also regarding job skills. These emotional requests were less effective with Indian human resources managers who worked in the Gulf. For example, the assistant to the human resources manager, Akbar, was from India, and he was much harsher in his tone and demeanor, usually judging candidates with a standard rubric regardless of what the employees at Mancom said about the candidate. The differences in how Akbar and Alex hired, however, should not be reduced due to personality differences. Rather, Akbar's position at Connex was significantly lower than Alex's position, and Akbar feared losing his own job if he made poor hiring choices.

WHEN NETWORKS FAIL

The success or failure of migrants is often determined by the luck of connecting with an honest subagent, but the amount of money a subagent takes is not determinative of the quality of the network. This was made apparent to me when I met Ibrahim in a village outside Hyderabad, where Ibrahim lived with his mother and paternal uncle's family. He worked on the family farm, but the small plot of land did not produce enough to support his family. When I met him, he was looking for work in the Gulf. He had traveled "irregularly" to the Gulf before—that is, his migration had not followed the proper processes and he lacked valid work documents. In Ibrahim's case, he had gone to Dubai on a visit visa that was valid for only two months. In order to get this visa, he had paid one lakh rupees (INR 100,000 or around US$2,000 in 2009) to a man who had an office in a nearby town. In return, this man was supposed to provide a work visa and get the necessary clearance from the government that would allow Ibrahim to travel. When he received the visa, Ibrahim was told it was a work visa, and he went to

Dubai, where he stayed with friends from his village, and he expected to find work immediately. But Dubai was suffering from the 2008 financial crisis and no one was hiring; in fact, most companies were sending workers home. In this economic climate, Ibrahim was unable to find work or a more permanent living situation. After three months, he was arrested for overstaying his visa. Through some timely intervention by the Indian government, Ibrahim spent only a short period of time in jail and was then sent back to India.

The man to whom Ibrahim paid money for the visa was from a district near his home. Although he did not know the man personally, Ibrahim felt that the man's nice office and the fact that the man said he was from a nearby village made him trustworthy. When Ibrahim returned from Dubai and tried to find the man he had paid, he was told that the man had "run away in the night with crores of rupees." I asked Ibrahim if he would now go to Mumbai or Hyderabad in order to meet with a recruiting agent approved by the government, and he told me, "No. I only trust the ones I know." For Ibrahim, the people he knows did not mean the people that he had already met; it meant people from near his home and with whom he could relate based on language, place of origin, religion, or the spatial proximity of daily lives. Ibrahim had a deep engagement with what he considered local, and local connections were central to his attempts to migrate. This emphasis on local relationships had a profound impact on his experience and mediated the ways in which the bureaucratic apparatuses used to regulate migration were mobilized.

When I met him, Ibrahim was again trying to travel to the Gulf, and not only for repayment of the loan. He told me that he felt pressure to earn money to increase his "chances" and support his family. As he looked for a job in the Gulf, Ibrahim told me he did not care if he had to travel irregularly; he only wanted to go. He hoped that once he was in the Gulf, he would find work as a driver or a cook and begin to repay his rising debts. For Ibrahim, the regulations of the government—such as procuring a visa or getting permission to travel—were restrictions on his movement and produced barriers that he needed to negotiate. These restrictions, however, did not curtail his aspirations or plans, in part because he knew many other workers who had migrated without formal documentation and without clearance from the Indian government. The key to his travel, he believed, was finding the right man to facilitate it. Ideally, he wanted a work contract before traveling to the Gulf, but he was willing to "take risks" again in order to travel.

One result of the uneven application of power and the burdensome nature of document verification was that many workers chose to migrate "irregularly," thereby bypassing official channels. The irregular path could be equally problematic, however, as lower-level government officials helping to develop an alternative network for migration kept driving up the costs workers must pay. Charging migrants fees in excess of the legal limit for help finding a job abroad certainly reinforces the structural violence caused by normal bureaucratic structures and debt.[28] In order to pay the fees, workers frequently borrow from moneylenders, who often charge high interest rates, and migrants often put family farms and other property up for collateral. This debt is key in forming social relations, structuring obligations, and creating wage labor; and it is part of how migrants build and maintain networks.[29]

CONCLUSION

Negative experiences such as Ibrahim's are well known by those who hire workers for oil projects. For their part, some multinational oil companies do not hire workers who come with a subagent and hire only through registered recruiting agents. These companies specifically ask the registered recruiting agents with whom they work not to work with subagents. In enforcing this preference, some companies are even known to have stopped working with an agency once it is discovered that the agency works with subagents. In practice, such policies usually lead to either workers arriving on their own or subagents being more furtive in their role. However, only a small number of companies adopt such a policy; not coincidentally, those that do have higher standards than other companies in their employment criteria. Veteran workers in the Gulf who meet these criteria are able to get these better jobs and, by avoiding subagents, pay less money to do so. Some recruiting agencies, particularly smaller ones with few employees that rely on localized networks in their home states, capitalize on this. For example, Mr. Hussain's office mostly hired workers from near his natal village in Gujarat. Prominently placed on the door to his offices was a sign: "No subagents by order of the management." Such signs, he told me, add legitimacy to his work, particularly to international companies that are concerned about their own companies' reputations.

The companies that do not allow subagents also make it harder for the employees of recruiting agencies to arrange for large numbers of workers to arrive at interviews. One day Jimmy, an employee of Mancom, was trying to find qualified job candidates for a company that did not want Mancom to use subagents to help fill the position; the company believed this policy would increase the quality of candidates and reduce the amount candidates paid to get jobs. Jagdish, a sub-agent, sat with us. Jimmy was having trouble finding enough candidates for the interviews and was calling people he had helped place in jobs in the past. Jimmy hoped Jagdish would put Jimmy in touch with some of the candidates he works with, but this would, of course, hurt Jagdish's profits because the candidates, if hired, would not pay Jagdish for his services. When Jimmy left the room briefly, Jagdish said to me, "This company doesn't want to use subagents. Maybe I should let them fail and then [the company] can see what happens without subagents." In this observation, Jagdish pointed to his frustration that his work is characterized negatively despite its centrality to the emigration of workers to the Gulf.

The process of migration and circulation in the Arabian Sea are shaped by local social connections and hierarchies. As Wafadar's and Ibrahim's experiences show, migration exists within overlapping networks of connections between South Asia and the Gulf. These connections inform how workers move. In addition, the deployment of structures used to move goods, such as mangoes, also shapes how workers move. The success or failure of a worker to migrate and how workers move are part of a much larger network that includes oil companies, government, agents, migrants, and local communities. Workers used these networks in order to secure jobs. They often privileged local contacts in forming and maintaining these networks, but these contacts often took greater advantage of workers than did professional contacts. Managers, including human resources staff and technical experts, also relied on networks in order to evaluate workers. This evaluation was important because of common inconsistencies between workers' stated knowledge and their actual skill levels. In the process of developing and negotiating networks, workers and employers created hierarchies, navigated bureaucratic hurdles, and increased their incomes. The logic of the networks shaping oil production were not (solely) dependent on the requirements of the industry or of the participating states but also dependent on localized affiliations, past relationships, and the shape of worksites.

Part II

CONNECTIVE SUBSTANCES

IN 2009, I SAT IN THE LARGE FOYER OF A BUILDING LEASED BY MANCOM, A RE-
cruiting agency in Mumbai, India. At a table, Mr. Shukla and Mr. Anthony, two
men who had worked as managers in the Gulf for many years and now worked
at Mancom, were interviewing workers on behalf of a large energy services
contractor. Human resources managers at the company had hired Mancom to
recruit and then facilitate the emigration process for roughly one hundred general laborers who were needed immediately to complete a refinery construction
project in the Gulf. As Mancom employees collected résumés, a group of young
men who had recently returned from working in the Gulf arrived. They wore
large golden watches, button-up shirts made of shiny, iridescent material, and
trendy sports shoes. Their fashion choices set them apart from the dozens of men
already standing in the office building's hallways and courtyard, all of whom
were dressed simply and without accessories. When this group of men entered,
the recruiting agency employees with whom I sat began to talk about them.

Mr. Shukla glanced at these young men and said that they had clearly not
spent their Gulf money wisely and had "forgotten" their families. As the employees of Mancom gossiped, they quickly reached consensus that these young
men had been "seduced by Dubai *ki chamak*," or the glitter of Dubai.[1] *Chamak*,
a Hindi term meaning "shiny," may describe the shininess of modern and new
things, such as Dubai's high-rises or shopping malls. Indian laborers in the UAE

often use it to refer, derogatorily, to men who wear name-brand clothes or dress stylishly. It may also be used to describe Indians trying to present themselves as Arabs. As all of the employees with whom I sat had previously worked in the Gulf, their choice of chamak gestured toward the allure of Dubai's modernity, a recognition of the Gulf's racialized hierarchies, and a criticism of these young men's consumption choices.

As the group of Mancom employees continued to discuss the young men who were "seduced by Dubai ki chamak," Mr. Shukla and Mr. Anthony decided it was time for lunch. I ate with them and a number of other Mancom employees as the group ate food prepared by their wives at home, packed by their wives into *tiffins* (lunch boxes), and delivered, hot, to the office by *dabbawalas* (lunch box delivery persons). My lunch companions regularly shared their lunches with me, often lamenting that I was a single woman, living alone in Mumbai, and suggesting that I learn to cook so that my parents could find me a "good match," meaning a husband. If I were married, they argued, I would no longer "have to" do research abroad. During our lunches, Mancom employees would keep track of what food I ate, and if I ate more of one dish than another, the employee would boast at the office and call his wife to tell her that she had cooked the best food that day.

Despite a growing crowd in the waiting area—one that was rapidly spilling over into the hallways and courtyard of the building—Mr. Shukla and Mr. Anthony ate their lunch at a leisurely pace. As we ate, Mr. Anthony decided to explain to me more how Dubai ki chamak is seductive and dangerous. While both Mr. Shukla and Mr. Anthony wore expensive watches and finely made clothes, they did not see themselves as falling into this trap. Rather, migrants who work as laborers—those who come from poor communities and are often from low castes or minority communities—are the most susceptible to this seduction. The young men who wear such clothes, they pointed out, must have spent the money earned in the Gulf on unnecessary material goods and had forgotten their obligations while working abroad.

As we ate, Mr. Anthony told a story to illustrate this point:

A number of years back there was this boy and girl living in Mumbai and they wanted to get married, but they didn't have any money so the boy decided to go to work in the Gulf for two years, and then he would come back, and they would get married. The boy was a Christian. . . . He went to the Gulf, but he didn't come back after two years; he stayed on and met someone else and fell in love and married her. Then, after some years, the boy and his wife—who was pregnant—returned to Mumbai from Dubai just for the Christmas/New Year holiday. The boy decided to go with some friends to a dance place for the Christmas or New Year dance, and the wife did not go because she was pregnant. The boy saw his friends and danced with some girls there, and then, who should come but the old girlfriend, the one he did not marry. She came up to him but did not say, "Why did you leave me?" or accuse him for not coming back. They danced to a song and before the beginning of the next song, the girl said she was cold, so he gave her his jacket. She then went to the loo—this is a toilet—and the boy waited but she did not come back, and finally they were closing up the dancing place and he decided to leave. The next day, he went to the girl's house and her mother was there. She also did not ask why the boy never came back to her daughter. Finally, the boy said, "Auntie, where is Anita?"—Anita was the girl's name—"She took my jacket!" Anita's mother replied, "That is not possible! You don't know? She died last year! But if you don't believe me, come. I'll show you the grave and the marble in which her name is carved." They went to the grave, and there she was buried, but also there was the boy's jacket. Anita, the girl, had killed herself the year before.

As he finished this story, Mr. Anthony, paused, stared at me gravely, and then continued:

And you may not believe that ghosts are in Mumbai, but this is true and it happened. And would you know that not fifteen days after this, the boy died from fever and chills. This is why people have to be careful when they are running around with girls, because girls take it too serious and too many boys go to the Gulf and forget about their girlfriends here in India. A jilted girl in India will kill herself, but in the Western Europe and America, they are not like that; they are too easy-going.

Other Mancom employees crowded into the cramped office space where we ate lunch in order to listen. Mr. Anthony is an excellent storyteller, and his theatrical pauses, fluctuating voice, and enthusiasm held everyone's interest. When he concluded, another Mancom employee, Latif, broke in: "The boy was not a Christian. He was a Muslim. I know where this graveyard is!" A second

Mancom employee, Iravan, a Hindu, disagreed, arguing that the story was about a Hindu migrant. Despite this disagreement on the religion of the young man, I heard versions of this story throughout my research, often by older, returned migrants who were illustrating the dangers posed for communities and families when a young man moves to the Gulf.

While I've heard this story in multiple contexts, it nevertheless retains certain salient features: the motivation of going to the Gulf for a few years in order to fund a marriage or support one's family; the gendered and class aspects of this migration; and the potential danger that when young men go abroad, they will forget their obligations. In addition, there are multiple spectral presences in Mr. Anthony story: the ghostly woman, one's past relationships, the seducing "modern" future, and the missing young man in his community. Anthropologists find ghosts appear in moments of rupture and change.[2] When ghosts do appear, they often remind individuals and communities of their histories and social obligations.[3] Moreover, one cannot ignore a ghost, because ghosts are often powerful, with the power to protect or harm individuals,[4] as the death of the young man at the end of Mr. Anthony's story demonstrates.

Ghost stories are one way people situate migration. People also make migration and labor meaningful in ways additional to labor's economic value through such practices as giving gifts to reenforce kinship ties or using money earned abroad to help "develop" one's community. Anna Lowenhaupt Tsing argues that commodities become gifts through a process of translation—a process in which mediators confer on certain commodities "relation-making powers."[5] This process of translation becomes necessary because of alienation, which Tsing defines as how things (including labor) are made commodities by being "torn from life worlds."[6] Labor alienates people from the product of their labor, their work, themselves, and their community. As Indian migrants and their families participate in kinship practices, development of their communities, and imagine the future, they complicate understandings of alienation as rupture, as migrant labor works simultaneously in multiple value systems.

Migrants often navigate tensions between labor and home, glitter and obligation, ghosts and dreams through poetic engagements. It is with gold and oil that migrants build and maintain their relationships with their families, communities, and country. The semiotic materiality of these substances allows for an extension of relationships and arguments for new futures. In exploring migrants' discussions of migration, we find that they and their families are not, and do not see themselves as, passive victims of larger forces. Examining both the kinship practices of migrant laborers and migrants' imaginations about the future makes clear that capitalism creates "value from non-capitalist value regimes" and that local practices and value systems shape global capitalism.[7]

Chapter 4

MAKING KIN WITH GOLD

WHEN I MET YOGESH IN THE UAE, HE WAS WORKING AT A FACTORY that built parts for oil rigs. He came from a rural, economically depressed part of India, where his father and two brothers farmed a small plot of land. When he finished high school, his parents insisted that he take a job through a cousin who also worked in the UAE to pay for his sister's marriage and contribute to household expenses. Yogesh had been working in the Gulf for about three years when I met him, and he had no plans for moving permanently back to India, although that was what he eventually wished to do.

During the week of Eid al-Adha, Yogesh and his friends allowed me to accompany them as they ran errands and made the most of their vacation time. As we traveled through Dubai, our group visited outlet stores, and everyone, with the exception of Yogesh, took advantage of the sales and bought clothing, shoes, trinkets, and snacks. Yogesh did not shop with us because he was saving his money for the gold souk. He told me repeatedly that his "primary obligation" was his sister's marriage, and to help his sister marry, he needed to buy gold, which would be a gift from his family to his sister's fiancé's family at the time of marriage. While Yogesh did not use the word *dowry*, anthropologists use it to describe gifts given by the bride's family to the groom's family at the time of marriage.

It was November when Yogesh and I visited the gold souk, and the weather was hot and humid. Despite the heat, Yogesh did not want to shop for gold in the air-conditioned mall. The stores in the mall were largely empty due to the global financial downturn in 2008, and they were advertising sales on the television. But the mall felt uncomfortable for Yogesh because the workforce of the Arabic-speaking Gulf is defined by a racialized labor hierarchy in which South Asian laborers fall near the bottom.[1] As a result, Indian workers face social discrimination and feel under scrutiny in many public spaces. Yogesh, similar to other Indian working-class men, told me that he perceived patrons and mall employees as unwelcoming. Instead, he and I ventured into the gold souk in Deira, the historic commercial center of Dubai that houses more than three hundred gold retailers. As we walked, Yogesh looked for a shop with the lowest gold prices. Finally, he decided on a little stall with some design pieces, but mostly ropes of gold. Yogesh was reluctant to spend money on jewelry design as he felt unsure as to what styles his sister preferred, and he did not want to waste money. In the little stall we entered, we heard Tamil, Malayalam, Urdu, and Hindi being spoken by South Asian workers buying gold to take home to their wives, sisters, and mothers. After much deliberation, Yogesh chose a plain chain, its price determined by weight.

Yogesh expressed worry about the amount of gold that his family asked him to bring home. On his annual trips to India, he spent more than three-quarters of his salary buying gold to accumulate for his sister's dowry. He had wanted to buy his mother some gold, but she instructed him to focus only on getting gold for his sister's wedding. He disliked speaking to his sister on the phone, because his sister was "mera dimaag ko kha rahi hai"[2] (eating my brain) by making demands about the quantity of gold she wanted him to buy that seemed impossible for him to meet. Yogesh attempted to satisfy his family's requests by living frugally, which, he told me, included sharing a one-bedroom apartment with eight men and refraining from buying unneeded items. He said he felt *phans gaya*, stuck or trapped, in the UAE and forced to spend all his money buying gold. An especially large amount of gold was needed because his sister wanted to marry a man who worked in information technology and lived in Australia. This marriage would allow upward mobility for his family that would be impossible without his income.

Yogesh felt obliged to provide gold for his sister's dowry, and he also felt he needed to provide money to support his family. After buying gold and paying for his daily needs, Yogesh sent the remainder of his paycheck to his father to use for household expenses. The family Yogesh helped support included not only his sister and his parents but also his brothers, his brothers' wives, and his brothers' children. This type of family organization, referred to as a joint family, is based on the practice of patrilocal social organization and involves a group of adult male joint heirs and these males' dependents living together. Joint families, considered by many Indians to be the ideal family structure, are found among Christians, Muslims, and Hindus throughout India.[3]

With remittances, Indian migrants and their families make sense of labor migration and frame it as a way to fulfill familial obligations and be good sons and brothers. Focusing on kinship obligations and gendered roles within families demonstrates that kinship motivates migration, and migration in turn influences kinship practices by providing opportunities to reshape kinship ties and express gendered roles within families. In particular, this chapter focuses on the purchase of gold for their sisters' and daughters' marriages. The gold that Indian migrants working in the Gulf buy becomes a kinship substance that maintains family relations and informs gendered labor. To understand the transmogrification of gold from commodity to kinship substance, this chapter explores contemporary perceptions of dowry in India, fears that families will be forgotten by family members abroad, and the role of substances in Indian kinship. It then historically situates dowries and gendered labor practices and examines the role that colonial capitalism and state policies play in shaping kinship practices, illuminating how kinship and economics were, and continue to be, mutually constituting.

In the contemporary moment, the gift of gold is used to improve a family's status, maintain and shape natal family relations, and fulfill gendered kinship obligations. Often migrants find that accumulating gold for marriages offers a way to demonstrate they are good sons and brothers; migrants who do not buy gold for marriages are often viewed negatively by their peers. As sons contribute to their patrilineal joint families, their work abroad is enabled by their wives, who help their husbands fulfill kinship obligations by caring for their husbands' aging parents. As women cook for their in-laws, the food they prepare, like the gold their husbands buy, operates as a kinship substance, but wives often receive little recognition for their kin work. In this context of transnational labor migration, gold provides a way for migrants and their families to shape and maintain kinship relations and fulfill gendered roles within their families.

GENDER AND KINSHIP

Gender and kinship are inextricably imbricated: "Kinship is a system of categories" given form by sex and gender relations, and gender is dynamic, relational, and given context through kinship.[4] Often kinship is studied through a focus on procreation and birth, reinforcing the assumption of a natural dichotomy between men and women, males and females. Instead, anthropologists argue, the focus should be on the process by which this dichotomy appears.[5] The gift of gold and gold's position as a kinship substance demonstrate how kinship and gender are defined, understood, and enacted within Indian migrant families in the Gulf. Rather than emphasizing moments of procreation and birth and the accompanying substances of semen or breast milk, an analysis of gold as a kinship substance demonstrates how familial relations and gendered roles in contexts other than procreation and birth shape kinship practices.

The pressure that Yogesh felt to buy gold for his sister's wedding was not unique to Gulf migrants, despite the fact that dowry is a contested practice. In India, dowry is technically illegal and described regularly in the Indian news as a "social evil." As a result, many families deny giving or asking for dowry, but nevertheless engage in large expenditures of gifts from the bride's family to the groom's family, including the gold focused on here. To acquire these gifts, families go to great lengths, including, in extreme cases, selling a kidney.[6] Some middle- and upper-class Indians see dowry as a traditional practice that continues despite the 1961 Dowry Prohibition Act, which made it illegal, and many assume the practice will change with modernization.[7] Indians who see dowry as a social evil most often cite its negative impacts on women. These negative impacts are made clear in an amendment to the act in 1984 that endeavored to offer greater protection to women by explicitly making dowry demands and dowry harassment illegal. Anthropologists have found that dowry contributes to and reinforces Indian preferences for sons, skewed gender demographics, and the higher value placed on male children.[8] In addition, it is strongly associated with violence against women, and dowry demands may escalate to domestic violence and even murder.[9]

Despite the negative impacts of giving dowries, in my conversations with Yogesh and other migrants, I was never told that giving a dowry is illegal in India, and dowry was never discussed as a reason for the poor treatment of women. Nonetheless, negative depictions of dowry by Indian newspapers or politicians may have influenced how migrants describe the practice. Notably, migrants did not regularly use the word *dowry* (or *jahez/dahej*, in Urdu/Hindi). Rather, men told me they worked in the Gulf to "buy gold for their sisters' [or daughters'] marriages" or to "help their sisters marry." In framing their reason for working in the Gulf as "buying gold," they describe buying gold for their sisters and daughters as a practice that connects the natal family and extends those relations as women marry.

When Pandeya, a Hindu from the state of Bihar, narrated his life story to me, he stressed the importance of kinship practices and gendered obligations in his choice to migrate. Pandeya moved to the Gulf in his mid-twenties. He was hired as a manual laborer and, after decades, earned a promotion to a position as a low-level supervisor on an oil project. When I met him, his parents had passed away, and he, with his wife, Padma, lived in Mumbai, India. In Mumbai, Pandeya had used the connections and skills he had developed in the Gulf to find work at a recruiting agency. He told me that when he was a young man, his father had farmed a small plot of land, but this land did not produce enough money to support his large family, which included Pandeya, his parents, and his seven sisters. During the first decade that Pandeya worked in the Gulf, he focused on helping provide dowries for his seven sisters. Like many of the other men I interviewed, Pandeya felt it was his obligation to help his sisters marry before he did; as a result, Pandeya did not marry until his mid-thirties.

When I asked Pandeya what he provided for his sisters' dowries, he stressed the importance of gold. "In North Indian style of marriage, of course, THE GOLD is an important item for the marriage." As I took notes, Pandeya, who had learned English while working in the Gulf, looked over my shoulder and offered corrections, insisting that I capitalize "the gold" to indicate its importance. After he was satisfied with my transcription, he continued: "But it is not as important as it's emphasized in South India. Say if it is 50 grams in North, then it would be 500 grams in South Indian marriage. South Indians are more fascinated towards gold. However, one thing is true in all Indians' marriage—i.e., DOWRY—which a girl has to carry to [her] in-laws place." This conversation exemplifies that dowry, also capitalized at Pandeya's direction, is given from a bride's family to the groom's family at marriage. Many Indians consider these gifts to be unidirectional: the bride's family gives a dowry, and the groom's family gives no return gifts.[10] Often a woman's ties and obligations to her natal family are thought to be severed when she, with her dowry, moves to her husband's home.[11] However, as migrants acquire gold in the Gulf for their daughters' or sisters' marriages, the gift of gold maintains natal family relationships and informs ongoing kinship practices. It is in this sense that I view gold as a kinship substance.

When anthropologists discuss kinship substances, they often focus on bodily substances, such as blood, semen, and breast milk, and on how these substances are mobilized in the "symbolic constitution of social relations."[12] In David Schneider's analysis of American folk theories of kinship, kinship is organized by a dichotomy between substance and code of conduct, in which "substance" refers to a naturalized, biologized bond of relatedness represented as blood, or a biogenetic contribution of each parent, whereas relatedness by "code of conduct" is "only" a matter of cultural convention.[13] Subsequent anthropologists have shown how the "seemingly unproblematic distinction" between (fixed) nature and (malleable) culture that underlies the substance/code distinction in American culture obfuscates the interconnectedness of people, socioeconomic practices, and the environment.[14] Kathryn A. Mariner's recent work on adoption in the United States, for example, demonstrates how materials such as paperwork merge substance and code in American understandings of kinship.[15]

In folk theories of Indian kinship, by contrast, substance and code are more explicitly imbricated in one another since kinship substances are understood as malleable, not biologically determined or fixed. People develop relatedness through intimate interactions, including breast feeding, sex, and eating, during which organic substances, like breast milk, semen, and food, are shared.[16] Anthropologists approach these organic substances as cultural phenomena that people use to define both the closeness of individual relations and larger social hierarchies.[17] Inorganic matter may also be used as a kinship substance, and Indian migrant laborers working in the Gulf draw on gold to reinforce, modify, and extend kinship relations. As men like Pandeya work in the Gulf and use their incomes to purchase gold for their daughters' and/or sisters' marriages, they strengthen natal family ties and fulfill gendered family obligations.

COLONIAL CAPITALISM AND GENDERED LABOR

Although many Indians tend to regard dowry as traditional, a historic examination of gold and migration reveals how colonial capitalism and state laws have significantly influenced Indian dowry practices, including the central role of gold in dowries. During the British colonial period, the enactment of laws, the commodification of labor, and the formation of the market society contributed to shifting social and familial landscapes.[18] Dowry is one practice that was affected as the British colonial government in India altered property rights to more effectively collect taxes. Before the implementation of colonial tax laws, dowry often took the form of immovable assets such as land, and this property was considered women's own (*stridhan*). As concepts around property changed, dowry increasingly took the form of movable assets, such as gold. The conversion of property to movable capital allowed for the control of capital to move easily from a woman's father to her husband or parents-in-law, and women no longer held control of this property.[19] The taxation of dowry and the process of state building influenced how gold as part of the dowry over time became a central aspect of contemporary Indian kinship while appearing to be a fixed and time-less tradition.

Gold's importance relates not only to colonial taxation but also to historic circulations in the Arabian Sea. As Yogesh bought gold and we wandered through the gold souk, he was participating in these circulations. Prior to independence in 1947, India was one of the main exporters of gold in the world. After independence, gold smuggling constituted a lucrative endeavor for merchants in the Gulf, as the Indian government charged duties on its import and placed restrictions on its export.[20] Gold smuggling continued until the early 1990s, when the liberalization of India's economy included the lifting of trade restrictions and custom duties.[21] Today Indian gold merchants in Dubai characterize the city as a "golden frontier" of India.[22]

RESTRICTIONS ON WOMEN'S MIGRATION

As gold, colonial officials, and traders circulated through the Arabian Sea, Indian workers also traversed the area, but how individuals traveled and for what jobs was, and continues to be, gendered. When Mancom held in-terviews for jobs in the Gulf with hundreds of Indian men, I never ran into a woman looking for work in the Gulf at a recruiting agency. This absence of women surprised me, given that approximately 20 percent of the Indian workers in the UAE are estimated to be women.[23] Having spent time in the Gulf, I knew that a common job for an Indian woman was working as an *aaya* (nanny) or domestic worker.[24] Domestic work does not pay as well as jobs in the oil industry, and domestic workers in the Gulf (as in much of the rest of the world) work unregulated hours and are at higher risk of experi-encing physical and verbal abuse.[25] One reason uneducated Indian women are unable to find work in the oil industry derives from current emigra-tion restrictions, which build on colonial laws and nationalist discourses, as well as the perceptions of recruiting agents who facilitate migration to oil projects.

During my first meetings with recruiting agents, I asked if they helped place women in jobs as domestic workers, food servers, or salespersons in the Gulf. My questions provoked offended responses from recruiting agents, and they would express moral indignation that I would ask such questions of them. As I spent longer periods of time in recruiting agencies, I learned that one of the reasons for this moral offense was the assumption that working-class Indian women in the Gulf must be trafficked persons. Recruiting agents explained to me that women who migrate in search of unskilled labor, in particular, are frequently exploited and forced to work in the sex industry.

I had one such awkward conversation with Mr. Zakir, an owner of a recruiting agency in Mumbai. As we drank tea, he explained his company's operations to me. During this conversation, we were repeatedly interrupted by men who wanted to drop off their résumés, receive updates on recent interviews, or learn if there were any upcoming job interviews. I asked Mr. Zakir why there were never any women looking for work at the recruiting agencies I visited. He responded, speaking in both Hindi and English, by explaining that only "unscrupulous" agents work with women. The reason, he continued, was "ve faydain utha raha hain" (they [unscrupulous agents] take advantage [of women]). In particular, he said, it was commonly known that women are sexually exploited while in the Gulf. Given the predominance of this knowledge, he assumed that a woman who wanted to work in the Gulf could best be characterized as *achchhee larki ki tara nahin* (not the good type of girl). Other recruiting agents with whom I spoke also used this euphemistic expression. The phrase is meant to convey that women, and particularly uneducated women, who want to travel abroad must be sexually promiscuous.

Newspapers also repeated this view that sexually promiscuous women migrate to work in the Gulf, and Indian women working in the Gulf as entertainers face particular scrutiny. While I was conducting my research, newspapers frequently ran articles concerning Indian "dancing girls" working in the Gulf.[26] In these articles, reporters interviewed "concerned patrons" who claimed that "girls ply the trade"—meaning that women dancers were also selling sex. Patrons supported this claim by stating that performers were not allowed to take tips, so the only reason to dance well would be to entice clients. In these articles, the Gulf is portrayed as a place where unskilled women could make large amounts of money, but only by participating in the sex industry.

In both newspaper accounts and the stories that recruiting agents have told me, working as a sex worker is considered inherently exploitative, and working-class women are particularly vulnerable to this type of exploitation once they travel outside India.[27] This understanding of sex work and coercion is strikingly similar to the Immoral Traffic (Prevention) Act, which the Indian government passed in 1956 and amended in 1986. One of the original reasons for writing and implementing the legislation was efforts by the United Nations to stop trafficking. In the Immoral Traffic (Prevention) Act, prostitution, defined as "the sexual exploitation or abuse of persons for commercial purposes or for consideration in money or in any other kind," is conflated with trafficking.[28] This association of trafficking, sex work, gender, and class means that today, recruiting agents are reluctant to help facilitate women's migration because they do not want to be seen as profiting from women's sexual exploitation.

In the stories about women migrants to the Gulf relayed by newspapers, government bureaucrats, and agents, the emigration of uneducated women is linked to their potential sexual activity and the commercialization of sex. Although women working in the Gulf report a wide variety of experiences, the intersection of sex work, class, and migratory status meant that women are left rapidly vacillating between an excess and an absence of sexuality.[29] This is seen in the two most common characterizations of working-class women migrants. The first is that these women are of "loose morals," and they participate in sex work for financial gain. The other is that Indian women who are of a morally high character, and therefore sexually unavailable, are forced to participate in the sex trade when they travel to the Gulf. This tension between promiscuity and purity restricts the possibilities for female emigration. Because working-class women are thought to have limited options outside sex work, all emigration by poor women becomes suspect. As working-class women are envisioned and treated as potential victims of sexual predation, their vulnerability means that the state needs to protect them by regulating the emigration process.

During the colonial period, nationalist and anticolonial writers positioned women's work as ideally located in the home, with an emphasis on the (re)production of future citizens.[30] Motherhood was women's primary role, and beginning in the late eighteenth century, the idea of *Bharat Mata* (Mother India) became increasingly popular. As Bharat Mata grew in popularity, India became representable pictorially and verbally as a woman.[31] Through this repeated association, women came not only to represent, but also to embody, the Indian nation. In nationalist texts, Indian women were discursively situated in the private sphere and valorized for "remain[ing] essentially unwesternized," thereby becoming emblematic of tradition and metonymically representative of the Indian nation.[32] Laws enacted by the postcolonial Indian state reinforced the association between women and the home. After independence, citizenship provisions drew on colonial law and the legal doctrine of coverture to establish citizenship by domicile and birth. A woman's citizenship became legally dependent on her father's or husband's domicile and birthplace.[33] The close association of women, the home, and India continues, and Indian women working in the information technology industry abroad cultivate a "respectable femininity" that they consider emblematically Indian through their balance of work and home life.[34]

Today men and women must meet different criteria to emigrate for work. For example, the Emigration Act of 1983 makes it illegal for a woman under 30 years of age to emigrate to work in the Gulf if she has not passed tenth grade in school. Government officials responsible for overseeing the implementation of the Emigration Act argue that these restrictions protect the "most vulnerable" Indians from trafficking and safeguard India's reputation abroad. Poor women have unequal access to migration and employment abroad, and this reinforces the inequalities they face in India due to their gender and their economic position, as well as their reliance on their brothers to help supply gold for their weddings. This inequality is in marked contrast to the relative freedom that upper-class women have to move abroad. For example, upper-class young women, such as daughters of recruiting agents, frequently go abroad to England or the United States to study. Recruiting agents tell me proudly that their daughters studied at American or British universities, and no one has ever suggested that this was an immoral activity.

In contrast to the ability of wealthier women to travel and work abroad, many poorer women continue to face challenges to migration. One such woman is Mary, the sister of the Mancom employee Jimmy. Jimmy and Mary's family is from Goa, but they both grew up in Mumbai. After spending years working in Abu Dhabi as an office boy, Jimmy returned to work at Mancom. At that time, he used the money had he earned in the Gulf to marry a Hindu woman who lived in the neighborhood in which he grew up. Although both families opposed this interfaith marriage, the income Jimmy earned in the Gulf was enough to support his parents and rent a separate apartment for him and his wife. This financial independence had also allowed Jimmy to marry a woman whom his parents did not choose. After living for a few years in Mumbai, Jimmy once again returned to the Gulf, this time finding work in Kuwait.

Jimmy's sister, Mary, told me she benefited from Jimmy's work in the Gulf; she particularly appreciated that he paid for her to attend postsecondary school to learn computer skills. When I met Mary, she worked for a company in Mumbai but did not make enough to live apart from her parents. During one of our conversations, she told me that she wished she could work abroad, see the places her brother spoke about in the Gulf, and live independently from her parents. But, because she was neither wealthy nor educated enough to move to America, Mary told me, she would not be able to migrate because it would bring "shame" to her family—a shame that is based on gender and dominant community beliefs that "good girls" do not migrate alone to work in the Gulf.

Laws restricting women's emigration more than men's emigration, and the discursive location of women's labor within the home, mean that women often rely on their male relatives for their dowries. The gendered exclusion of socially reproductive work from wage labor occurs globally, and scholars have demonstrated the need to attend to "points of gendered contradiction and conflict" as we approach work.[35] By considering how gender, kinship, and labor are historically situated within the expansion of capital as it seeks out new revenues in the form of taxes, commodifies labor, and creates market societies, we are able to see that dowry, something considered traditional in an Indian setting, is actually shaped by liberalization, contemporary statecraft, and transnational migration. Attention to the meaning of gold for dowries and gendered labor highlights these interconnections.

THE GIFT OF DOWRY

As I began my fieldwork, my understanding of dowry was influenced by my conversations with women's rights advocates in India. I had assumed that in cases like Yogesh's family, because his sister wanted to marry a well-educated young man who lived in Australia, the fiancé's family would not ask for a dowry. Yet, contrary to my expectations, migration and increased participation in transnational, neoliberal economies do not decrease the practice of giving a dowry, but, rather, have the reverse effect. Although most men do not explicitly use the term *dowry* and instead use phrases such "buying gold to help their sisters marry," all migrants stress that sisters and daughters need to take gold with them when they move to their in-laws' homes. Ramchandra, a lower-caste farmer's son from Uttar Pradesh, began working in the Gulf when he was twenty years old after "dropping out of school" and spending years unable to find work in India. In the Gulf, he said, he could "find" more money—money needed because he had "two sisters and no money in India." As he explained, "helping his sisters marry" was his "first responsibility." When I asked Ramchandra what was needed for his sisters to marry, he was shocked that I would not know. After staring for a moment, Ramchandra said, simply, "Gold." Like other migrants with whom I spoke, Ramchandra was involved in neither negotiating his sisters' marriages nor deciding what other gifts his sisters would bring to their in-laws' houses. These arrangements, Ramchandra and others told me, are done by family members in India; the duty of family members in the Gulf is to buy gold for these marriages.

Ramchandra's sisters are now married, and he sends money for his father to build a *pucca* house, made of concrete and bricks, an expense often taken on by a family before a son's marriage to ensure a "good match." While Ramchandra married before he began building his family's pucca house, other migrants told me they were building such houses in preparation for their own marriages. Building a pucca house, they said, would help their parents find them "good" wives. When I asked what makes a woman a good wife, migrants often described a woman's ability to look after or care for the home, children, and parents; a woman's religious piety; and a wife's family's economic status. Men never discussed with me the amount of dowry they anticipated their wives would bring, and when I asked, they told me that their parents arrange such matters.

Nonetheless, anthropological studies of Indian transnational migration suggest that this type of migration drives increasingly large dowries. Men working in information technology, in particular, have seen the largest increase in the amount of dowry that they are able to obtain from a bride's family, in part due to their potential to migrate to Australia, the United Kingdom, or the United States for work.[36] In many anthropological studies, the importance of dowry is considered within the context of marriage and building relationships between families. In contrast, examining how men acquire gold for their daughters' and sisters' marriages demonstrates how gold operates within the natal family as both gift and kinship substance. The value of this gift exceeds its financial value, and migrants and their families represent dowry as a gift that maintains and recreates kinship ties and gendered roles.

The Value of Gold

Shabana, an Indian Muslim woman from Tamil Nadu, described to me the multiple values dowry holds for a family. Her husband, brother, and father work in the Gulf, and she lives with her two sons and her husband's parents. While much of her day revolves around caring for her children and in-laws and overseeing the household's daily tasks, Shabana also maintains close ties to her natal family and regularly visits her sisters and mother. In summer 2011, Shabana and I chatted frequently, and most of our conversations included a discussion of the price of gold. At that time, the US and European stock markets were volatile, and the price of gold was consistently increasing. While I had known Shabana since 2009, we had never before discussed the price of gold. Her new interest, Shabana explained, came from her younger sister Asma's marriage preparations. One day, in a conversation with her friends, Shabana asked, "Why is gold increasing at a skyrocketing pace? What has gold rates to do with the US dollar or oil? Or is there no gold in the gold mines?" Sighing, she said that the increased prices "make people's life more miserable than it already is." Shabana's friends commiserated with her and offered their perspectives on the gold market. One friend explained that gold is expensive because "people don't trust any commodity but gold; shares on the stock market are rubbish." Another friend made the case that Indians played a direct role in gold's price, saying, "Maybe if Mallus [Malayalam speakers from the state of Kerala] and Gujjus [people from the state of Gujarat] stop buying so much, it will probably drop." Another friend also commented on this link between Indian wedding practices and gold's price, with the conjecture that gold was so expensive because "more and more Mallus are getting married." Both Kerala and Gujarat are Indian states known for their trading and have a visible presence in the Gulf, often by middle- and upper-class workers. The (joking) assumption in the conversation was that the wealthy from these Indian states were getting married in higher numbers and therefore driving up the price of gold.

In Shabana's conversation with her friends, gold was explicitly discussed as a commodity, with its market price a concern. As many anthropologists have demonstrated, the value of a commodity is not rooted in what an individual will pay for it. Rather, the value is a "momentary instantiation of coagulation out of an open, dynamic, and interactive process" involving alienation, wage labor, and historical context.[37] While the price of gold certainly held importance to Shabana, as we continued to discuss Asma's dowry, it became clear that giving gold for a dowry was valued for its expression of kinship ties as well as its economic value. Colonial capitalism played a key role in gold's emergence as a central component of dowry. In addition, Indian migrants and their families often note that gold bought in the Gulf is purer than that bought in India (even if this does not empirically hold true) and that they see gold as an item that retains its value over time. Shabana believes Indians trust gold more than money because money fluctuates in value according to the global markets, but gold's value remains stable. It is this stability and purity that contributes to gold's importance in Indian kinship.

When discussing the importance of gold for Asma's dowry, Shabana described it as a gift that situates one's family within a community, maintains relationships, and expresses care. She told me that her family felt "compelled" to supply a large amount of gold for Asma's dowry because her family worked in the Gulf. Through providing a large dowry, the family was attempting to assert its relatively new class position. This position was further improved by Asma's marriage, like Yogesh's sister's, to an Indian information technology worker who lived in Australia. For both Shabana and Yogesh, gold's value went beyond demonstrating family wealth. Rather, they saw gold bought in the Gulf and given for dowries as a way to uplift women's natal families. This uplift becomes possible because gold operates as a kinship substance that maintains ties with female kin, as seen in changing gift practices.

In a later conversation with Shabana and Asma, Shabana told me her husband was contributing "a handful" of gold for Asma's wedding. Because this movement of goods from a husband to his wife's family differed from descriptions of gifts moving only from the wife's family to the husband's family, I asked if this contribution was related to Shabana's *mahr*, or the gift given from the groom to the bride in Muslim marriage (*nikah*). Asma dismissed my question and explained, "Dowries are very important in India. For Muslims, the rich are expected to give a house, gold, and a car. The poor are only expected to give a car and gold." In contrast, Asma told me, mahr, the groom's gift to the bride, is a "menial amount. Poor Indian Muslim grooms only give INR 100 [US$2 in 2011] and the rich give AED 100 [approximately INR 1,400 or US$27 in 2011]." As our conversation continued, Asma clarified that mahr constitutes a religious obligation and that, as a self-described devout Muslim, she expected only a small gift from her husband. In contrast, there is no religious obligation for a dowry, and the gold her fiancé's family expected from her natal family at the wedding was substantial and openly negotiated. To clarify why gold for Asma's marriage was so important and why her husband was contributing to help Asma marry, Shabana explained that her husband's actions were both "practical" and a way to ensure Asma's happiness. Asma's marriage to an information technology worker living in Australia, Shabana told me, would mean that both Shabana's natal family and her husband's family would "rise in status." Simultaneously, the family would be caring for Asma by ensuring her husband was a "good match."

Masculinity, Labor, and Making Kin

To understand how gold transmogrifies into a kinship substance, we must think about the value of dowry not in economic terms but as a gift.[38] Here, I consider the gift's value as it emerges in action, specifically how migrants and their families understand buying gold for dowries as representative of masculinity and familial obligation.[39] As men migrate to work in the Gulf, they extend not only the reach but also the geographic scope of their kinship networks. Indian migrants maintain and restructure kinship relations by sending remittances and purchasing gold for their sisters' dowries. Migrants navigate tensions between commodities and gifts through representing the gift of gold as indicative of gendered labor and gendered obligations. For Indian migrants, bestowing gifts of gold to their sisters and remittances to their fathers demonstrates that they are men within their families and communities. Established by fulfilling roles as good brothers and sons, this masculinity provides an alternative to hegemonic representations of adult masculinity in India that are predicated on marriage. In many poor farming communities in India, young men cannot get married because of increasing unemployment and lack of opportunities.[40] In the face of high unemployment, northern Indian families may allocate resources to prioritize a son's employment or marriage at the expense of a daughter's marriage.[41] Transnational migration, on the other hand, provides routes through which men may express adult masculinity by being dutiful brothers and sons.

In 2010, I met often with Ramchandra and his colleagues during their lunch breaks as they worked to build an oil rig in Abu Dhabi. One day, I ate lunch with a dozen men, and as we talked, they described how they regularly sent money home, as well as purchased gold for their female relatives' weddings. During lunch, Ramchandra introduced me to Mohammed, a young Muslim man from northern India who was new to this crew. When he introduced us, Ramchandra said, "Voh achchha beta hai" (He [Mohammed] is a good son). Mohammed responded in English, telling me, "I [am] supporting fully to family" by sending all of his paycheck home, because "[I am] fully devoted to family." While some workers send money monthly, others told me they send money "every five months because it is a more substantial amount and avoids fees." Workers generally send money using UAE Exchange, a popular wire-transfer service. Migrants buy gold in the souk and then wear it home as chains around their necks to avoid import duties. While they differed in how often they sent money home, my lunch companions agreed that sending this money and taking home gold was their *farz* or *karm*, the

Urdu and Hindi words, respectively, for "duty." By fulfilling this duty, they told me, a man demonstrates he is a good son and dutiful brother.

During lunch, one man told me that doing one's duty and working in the Gulf may also lead to a migrant's family "giving [the migrant] more respect." This respect manifested in their opinions being sought on topics ranging from family conflicts to household purchases to children's education. Ramchandra, worried that I would not understand, turned to me and told me that working in the Gulf "elevated him" in the eyes of his family. This, he said, was due not only to his financial contributions but also because no one else in his family had flown on a plane or traveled far from home. To demonstrate his "elevated" status, Ramchandra described how his family had called him the week before to ask his advice before buying a piece of farm equipment. As we talked, my lunch companions described their work as integral to their families, as the household's relationships and interactions extended from rural villages in India to construction sites in the Gulf.

Despite agreeing on the importance of sending money and buying gold for dowries, my lunch companions did not agree on what percentage of their paycheck they needed to give to their families. As lunch continued, Ramchandra and Sunil, a Hindu also from northern India, became embroiled in a heated debate over this question. Ramchandra had been working in the Gulf intermittently for more than a decade, and he had recently started listening to a radio show in which the host (an Indian living in the UAE) encouraged listeners to save their money instead of sending it home. The show resonated with Ramchandra, and he had recently opened a personal savings account that no one in his family could access. The reason, he said, was that "whatever you send, they [your family] upgrade the needs"—meaning that families would spend all the money migrants earned on both necessary and unnecessary items and would ask for increasingly larger amounts of money. This meant, Ramchandra told us, that if a migrant did not build his own savings, "when you go back, [you] will have nothing." He continued by telling us that of course personal saving needed to be weighed against family needs. While the show's host recommended that migrants save for themselves at least 50 percent of their income, Ramchandra said he sent home 60 percent, keeping the remaining 40 percent. Ramchandra's discussion of personal savings upset Sunil, and Sunil dismissed the radio show. Loudly, Sunil argued for sending the entirety of one's paycheck to one's family, except the money used to buy gold for weddings or minutes for a mobile phone. He felt that sending money was a son's duty. To enforce his point, Sunil quoted the *Bhagavad Gita*, a Hindu religious text:

"*karm karo fal ki chinta na karo*," a phrase that could mean either "do your duty and don't expect a reward" or "do your duty and don't worry about the outcome." Sunil used this phrase to stress the importance of actions in fulfilling one's familial duties. For Sunil, the issue resided in the question of how he could be a good son or brother, not how his family might spend the money. Refusing to speculate as to what may happen in the future, Sunil stressed that the importance of the gift (either money or dowry) lay in the act of giving.

The families of migrants often express concern that they will be forgotten after a man moves abroad. As in many other contexts, transnational migration has the potential to destabilize families and disrupt gendered roles within them.[42] This holds particularly true when migrants' access to cash provides an opportunity for them to express masculinity outside their families.[43] The possibility that men might spend money on unneeded luxury goods came up regularly in conversations at the recruiting agency Mancom. One agency employee, Jimmy, told me he lectured "noobies," or first-time emigrants, on the best way to spend money.[44] He explained, "Noobies [have] totally funny ideas, and they don't know that they are making tax-free money and they should be doing things like buying gold. They are going to earn and save—not to spend." When I asked how common this was, Jimmy replied, "People think they are in the Gulf and they can spend, but then the workers return to India with nothing." According to Jimmy, the Gulf's place in popular imagination contributed to young men's choices to consume luxury goods and not support their families. "People have certain habits that they need to support. They also want to buy good clothes because they think 'I am in the Gulf, so I can spend money, and I need nice clothes and to get fat to show that [I was] in the Gulf.'" Jimmy and his colleagues believed that when young migrants returned from the Gulf wearing flashy new clothes and other ostentatious displays of wealth, what they were exhibiting was their failure to fulfill kinship obligations and care for their families.

Women's Work and Migration

Workers who did not forget their families often discussed their families' importance in facilitating migration. Amit, an older man who had worked as a manual laborer in the Gulf for more than twenty years, focused primarily on his family when I asked him why he was once again moving to the Gulf for work. He said,

> I am going only for work. My family needs the money. You can find jobs in India, but they don't pay as well. I will compromise to whatever . . . I have to,

because I am sacrificing to go to make money for my family. So, I will adjust, just like my family will need to adjust, because I am not at home.

During our conversation, Amit told me about his family, which included his wife and children, as well as his mother, brothers, brothers' wives, and brothers' children. Amit understood that both he and his family were sacrificing in order to send him to the Gulf. His family sacrificed by missing his presence in the household, but also by initially borrowing large amounts of money from a moneylender to facilitate Amit's migration. Amit's story demonstrates a common one in which joint families and shared responsibilities both motivate and facilitate migration.

As Amit described, living in joint families provides support for migration, and men like Ramchandra often say they receive greater respect from their families after going abroad. Gendered obligations influence this choice to migrate as well. Women's work, meanwhile, often supports men's migration to the Gulf. Yet this work often remains unrecognized, and many wives do not feel they receive the same respect that their husbands do.[45] Migrants repeatedly told me that their wives care for their parents while they are in the Gulf, and migrants see this care—conducted on their behalf—as one of their duties as sons. Many women, however, find it hard to live in their in-laws' homes without their husbands. Pandeya's wife, Padma, told me she found it challenging to live with her in-laws when her husband was away because, she said, her mother-in-law treated her as a servant and demanded that she do all the household chores. She also told me that Pandeya's sisters regularly visited their parents and then berated her for not properly caring for their parents. According to Padma, without Pandeya present, she was "alone" living with his parents, without anyone to care for her. Her description of being "alone" points to the importance of a husband in building a relationship between a wife and her in-laws.

When Pandeya worked in the Gulf, Padma said she wanted to live abroad with him rather than live "only" with her in-laws. Despite her wishes, Padma never traveled to the Gulf, in part because Gulf governments place restrictions that make it challenging for lower-wage employees to bring dependents. Yet even if it had been legally possible, Padma told me, Pandeya would never have agreed for her to leave his family. At a later date, this topic came up when I spoke to Pandeya, and he told me it was hard to live apart from his wife, but that it was his duty (*karm*) as a son to care for or look after (*dekhbāl karna*) his parents. Padma fulfilled this duty on his behalf by living with his parents. In this context of patrilocal social organization, neither Padma nor Pandeya argued that Padma had a responsibility to look after her own family. Rather, after marriage, Padma's duty became to care for Pandeya and to help her husband fulfill his obligations to his family. During the time Padma lived with Pandeya's parents, she cared for them by cooking food, and this food shaped and informed Padma's relationship with both her husband and her in-laws. As wives cook for their parents-in-law, they enable the generation of additional kinship substances, including gold and money. It is a wife's care of her husband's aging parents that facilitates migration, a migration on which the Gulf's oil industry depends.

CONCLUSION

Although we often understand money and love to form connections between people in different, noncomplementary, ways, this distinction does not resonate globally. In many contexts, money is used to express intimacy and care. As Cati Coe's work in Ghana demonstrates, children of migrants see the money from their parents as expressions of intimacy.[46] In the case of Nepalese migrants, Ina Zharkevich shows that remittances constitute a substance of relatedness that helps span the distance created by transnational migration.[47] For Indian migrants to the Gulf, gold too has an economic value within families, and the gift of gold is seen as an expression of care. Unlike monetary remittances, however, the semiotic materiality of gold means that within the context of kinship, it not only economically uplifts a family but also constitutes a gift that operates as a kinship substance.[48] While food and other kinship substances inform relatedness through proximity and daily interactions, gold bought in the Gulf transcends geographic distance. It manages to do so because of its role as a gift that connects people, a gift perceived as pure because it is bought in the Gulf. As a kinship substance, gold also calls into question distinctions made between substance and code, fixity and malleability. Like blood, gold is seen as durable, in contrast to cash, which fluctuates with the markets. Gold is also seen as malleable, as the plain ropes of gold bought by migrants such as Yogesh are often reshaped by their recipients. Here, gold's qualities as pure, stable, and malleable are mutually constituted with its role as a gift that builds and maintains kinship relations and indexes one's gender.

As they buy gold for their sisters' and daughters' dowries, migrants view it as a gift and a fulfillment of gendered kinship obligations. Men often feel their status within their households improve as a result. Their gift of gold reinforces relations by maintaining connections within natal families; simultaneously, it informs a malleability of relations by extending broader kinship networks. Women, meanwhile, actively support the migration of their husbands and brothers through their own labor, although this work often goes unacknowledged. The femininity of migrants' wives becomes reinforced by their role in helping fulfill their husbands' duties of care. These dynamic interactions of kinship and gender shape and are shaped by migratory movements and economic practices.

In the case of Indian migrant labor to the Gulf, kinship practices and economic necessity are deeply intertwined. The Gulf's oil industry depends on Indian kinship relations in order to have access to the large numbers of temporary workers required by oil projects. In turn, migrants use money earned in the oil industry to provide financial support to their families, to purchase gold for their sisters' or daughters' marriages, and for possible further migration. Gold, a key component of dowry, becomes a kinship substance that continues natal family ties after men's transnational migration and their sisters' subsequent marriages. Migrants represent giving gold as the fulfillment of their gendered kinship obligations as sons and brothers. Exploring this gift of gold as historically and culturally situated illuminates how it forms part of contemporary kin making, how gold is imbricated in economic transformations and class relations, and how it becomes a gendered kinship substance as salient as semen, blood, or breast milk. As the first three chapters demonstrated, in order to obtain gold, migrants must move through a series of steps and work with recruiting agents and their employees, government officials, oil company managers, and other migrants. The following chapter considers how migrants use the money they earn in the Gulf in order to engage with modernity and position themselves as members of the Indian nation-state.

Chapter 5

THE RIG AND THE TEMPLE

IN 2010, I MADE MY FIRST OF WHAT WOULD BECOME REGULAR VISITS to a site in Musaffah, UAE, where an offshore, semi-submergible oil rig was being built. I was invited to visit the rig by Alex, a project manager working at Connex, an energy contracting firm. I had first met Alex a year earlier in Mumbai, when he was hiring workers for this project and others. As I drove through the industrial area of Musaffah, I had trouble finding the street names that were on the map he had emailed me prior to my visit. When I finally realized I was hopelessly lost, I called Alex for directions. Explaining that he had never driven himself to the construction site, Alex handed the phone to one of the company's drivers, Kewat, and asked Kewat to give me directions. Kewat asked me where I was. As I tried to describe the area in which I had parked to make my call, I could find no distinct landmarks. With this little information, he encouraged me to continue driving forward and told me, "Mandir ke lie dekho!" (Look for the temple!). When I heard this, I was worried that I had misunderstood Kewat, and I asked for clarification. Kewat replied that I understood correctly—I should drive straight and look for the *mandir*, or Hindu temple. "It is so large," he added, "you cannot miss it." I was confused as to how a Hindu temple could be in Musaffah near this construction project. In 2010, there were no Hindu temples in Abu Dhabi, and the only Hindu temple in the UAE was located in an old department store in Dubai.[1] Lost, as I often was during my research, I continued driving and began looking for a mandir.

FIGURE 3. Offshore Oil Rig.
Source: Mustang Joe (https://www.flickr.com/photos/mustangjoe/43258021631).

Eventually an oil rig's derrick appeared to my left, peeking over the buildings lining the road. I turned and, as I drove toward the construction site, I saw how the features of the oil rig (Figure 3) mirrored the architecture of a Hindu mandir (Figure 4). The derrick was reminiscent of a *vimaana*, or tower, and the crown, which is at the top of the derrick, resembles a *shikhara*, a peak or domelike cap that sits on the vimaana.[2] Meeting me at a security checkpoint, Kewat waited as I gave my passport to the guards, and the guards called a manager at Connex to check the legitimacy of my visit. After this process, Kewat ushered me to a group of trailers where Connex managers worked. As we walked past the partially constructed rig, Kewat gestured to it and asked, "Ye mandir jaisa dekhata hai, hai na?" (It looks just like a temple, don't you agree?). Pointing to the Indian men working throughout the structure, he added, that because of hundreds of Indians moving around the area, Kewat believed it looked like a temple on a festival day.

Kewat was not the only person who referred to the rig as a temple. During the time I spent conducting research at this site, many men working in unskilled or semiskilled positions would refer their worksite as *hamaara mandir* (our temple). As Kewat's directions indicate, describing the rig as a temple served to locate and differentiate this worksite in the industrial area of Musaffah. Musaffah is a large area, and there are always multiple construction projects underway, but during

FIGURE 4. Vimaana at Tajore Temple, Tamil Nadu.
Source: Pixabay (https://pixabay.com/photos/brihadishvara-temple-thanjavur-2358280/).

this first visit, none of the other construction projects in the area had the tall, imposing outlines of a semi-submergible, offshore oil rig.

Describing the rig as their mandir not only referenced the rig's place in Musaffah but also the importance workers gave their migration and labor. This poetic reference to the rig as mandir highlights the aesthetic features of both the rig and the mandir. The description also reflects the pride workers experienced by working on such a large infrastructure project, particularly one that was related to oil. As I spent time with men working at the site, they regularly described oil, as well as oil infrastructure, as symbols of modernity, development, and the future. This chapter explores the importance of describing a rig as a temple through considering how workers also use the poetics of rigs and mandirs to define modernity, make claims for their inclusion in the Indian nation, and envision the future.

Mohammed, a Muslim from northern India, worked at this project for Connex. As he described the importance of his work building oil infrastructure, he told me it helped him be a good son by allowing him to send money to his father. But the meaning he gave his work at this project extended past fulfilling his familial obligations to also reflecting a way he contributed to the future of India. Explicitly, Mohammed connected his work to the process of "making India modern" and described his migration as a way to help both his country and his community progress economically and ideologically. Mohammed was not the only person who situated work on Gulf oil projects as part of India's modernization. Both prospective migrants and current migrants tell me, with sincerity and excitement, that they work, or want to work, in the Gulf to "make India modern." When men like Mohammed tell me this, I usually inquire as to what "modern" means, as the word seems, to me, to be amorphous and fleeting. In their answers, Indian migrants describe modernity and development as improvements to infrastructure, which includes airplanes, electricity, and clean running water. They also describe it as the increased consumption of commodities. In addition, workers from groups that face structural inequalities, such as Muslims, Adivasis (indigenous Indians), and Dalits, tell me their work in the Gulf contributes to modernity because it helps their community "stop being backward" or improves their community's socioeconomic status. However, "making India modern" is not limited to material consumption and infrastructure; it implies more difficult-to-articulate dreams, including freedom; living in the city; doing what you want; and love matches as opposed to arranged marriages.

Discussions around modernity, participation in the Indian nation, and what the future will look like were of particular importance for many of the Indian men Connex employed at this rig construction site. Indian migrant laborers to the Gulf are often members of minority communities, and they face discrimination and exclusion in India. While the Indian government does not collect data on the religion of migrants, I have found in my research that a disproportionately high percentage of laborers migrating to the Gulf are Muslims. Roughly 13 percent of India's population is Muslim. Yet over 40 percent of my interviews with Indians abroad have been with Muslims, even though I make no selection for religion. In particular, at Connex's rig construction site, over 50 percent of the workers from India were Muslims.[3] For many young Indian men facing limited opportunities in their home villages, migration to the Gulf offers opportunities to fulfill their dreams and "move forward" or "move up" in what they saw as a graduated hierarchy of modernity. As I spoke with workers, and particularly those who are members of minority communities, many said they had more opportunities available to them while working in the Gulf than in India. This is because, they told me, multinational corporations did not discriminate against individuals due to their religion or caste, a practice they felt was common in India.

In exploring the poetics of the oil rig and the mandir, I draw attention to the work that migrants are doing in the space between the state, or the sovereign government of an area, and the nation, or the "imagined community" inhabiting the territory of the state. Through such poetics as the rig and the mandir, migrants draw attention to and reframe the meanings of state and nation. In particular, they position themselves as part of India's development, and they critically insert themselves as part of the national body. Migrants also use poetics to engage with the inequalities inherent in the state and capitalism. By taking seriously the poetics of rig as mandir, we see how differing narratives of modernity and progress are developed and implemented.

The association migrants made between their work and modernity is reinforced by the ideological significance that oil and oil infrastructure play in Indian development plans. In the mid-twentieth century, oil facilitated dreams of expansive capitalist frontiers, and the state governed via reference to the future.[4] Today oil is often overshadowed by the specter of disaster.[5] As migrants drew parallels between oil rigs and temples, they articulated their role in India's future. In this case, at the construction site in Abu Dhabi, the architectural style allowed for reference to Hindu temples, and the representation had meaning in the context of the Indian state and engagements with development.

MODERNITY, INFRASTRUCTURE, AND THE STATE

Migrants are not unique in associating oil and infrastructure with development and modernity. After independence, Indian engineers and politicians, including India's first prime minister, Jawaharlal Nehru, and the author of India's constitution, B. R. Ambedkar, argued that electrification and other state infrastructure projects were vital and necessary components for India's development.[6] Infrastructure projects, along with research laboratories and factories, were so central to the state's development that Nehru, at the inauguration of a large dam, described the dam and similar infrastructure projects as "the temples of modern India." With such projects, politicians argued, Indian farmers would be lifted out of poverty.[7] This perspective merged infrastructure and the economy, and as a result, the state economy and its future become sites where politics and development programs converge.[8]

Anthropological studies of infrastructure highlight the importance of considering how infrastructure is embedded in social contexts, drawn into social relations, and made symbolic of state development.[9] Fernando Coronil's ethnography of the Venezuelan state describes how oil and modernization projects are used to legitimate state power. Untangling the multiple meanings of the state, Coronil describes how the state itself was produced as an ensemble of practices, institutions, and ideologies of rule as contestations arose over the state's regulation of oil production and its control over oil-derived money.[10] Through this process, the state becomes "magical" as it is "constituted as a unifying force by producing fantasies of collective integration into centralized political institutions." This collective integration occurs around development projects that by engendering "collective fantasies of progress, it casts its spell over audience and performers alike." Through these development projects, the state situates itself "as a magnanimous sorcerer," meaning the state seizes its subjects by inducing a condition of being receptive to its illusions. This is what Coronil refers to as the "magical state."[11] Oil is a particularly strong signifier of state power and modernity.[12] The interplay of politics and oil affects state policies and oil companies.[13] Rigs, seen from a poetics of oil infrastructure, may be viewed as avenues to energy production that are often tied to nationalist projects.

In contemporary Indian politics, energy is seen as a way the state can build infrastructure and thereby lift citizens' living conditions. Political parties mobilize these developmentalist claims as a way to legitimate their projects. Emphasis on modernity and development within a Hindu nationalist framework is common in Indian politics, both historically and in the present. As I got to know Kewat, I learned that he was a supporter of the Bharatiya Janata Party (BJP). I was surprised because the BJP often emphasizes upper-caste practices, and Kewat is a member of what the Indian government labels a "scheduled caste."[14] I mentioned my surprise, and he laughed and explained that it should be obvious he supports the BJP because it "is bringing development [to India]."

The BJP is the political arm of the Sangh Parivar, an umbrella term that refers to a group of affiliated Hindu nationalist organizations. While Congress, not the BJP, was the majority in government in 2010, when I first met Kewat and his colleagues, the BJP was the main opposition party in Indian Parliament at that time. In 2014, the BJP became India's ruling party in Parliament, despite receiving only 31 percent of the popular vote. In 2019, the party won reelection. A popular slogan by Prime Minister Narendra Modi, the head of the BJP, is *acche din anewalle hain* (good days are coming). A shortened version of this slogan, *#acchedin* (good days), became, and continues to be, a popular hashtag on social media sites, including Facebook and Twitter. The hashtag is closely associated with Modi, who has become a brand unto himself, referred to popularly as *vikas purush* (development man). "Brand Modi" is developed as Modi is represented as the physical ideal of masculine development, as well as a leader who will improve the life of the common man through capitalist policies.[15] As #acchedin continues to be used on social media, it is a site for the celebration of Modi's and the BJP's accomplishments, as well as critiques of their implementation of policies.

Acche din, according to Modi and the BJP, will arrive through the modernization of India, and pro-business policies are key to this modernization. In the BJP's vision of India's future, capitalism is the vehicle of development, and access to energy is one pathway for this capitalist development to occur. Interest in energy, often conflated with the production of electricity, has led to the BJP's active development of both large solar projects as well as expanded oil and gas exploration in India. In 2016, the Cabinet Committee on Energy Affairs, chaired by Prime Minister Modi, approved thirty-one contract areas in India for oil and gas exploration and production. This approval was part of the Discovered Small Field plan, which aims to maximize oil and gas production through the exploration of large and small oil fields.[16] In 2019, the BJP's interest in securing oil intensified, and Modi traveled to the United States and Russia in order to secure oil and gas partnerships. Modi's BJP government has also spent billions backing Indian exploratory drilling in eastern Russia.

Development and Ethnonationalism

Energy infrastructure is seen as central to the growth of Indian businesses, but Indian development, according to the BJP, is also closely associated with an understanding of India built on Hindutva, or Hindu nationalist, principles. The BJP campaigns on an ethnonationalist platform that argues for "Hindus first," a policy that equates India with Hindi, Hindus, and Hinduism. The modernity envisioned by the BJP is deeply steeped in Hinduism—specifically, upper-caste, Brahmanical Hinduism. For example, educational programs put forward by the BJP government teach students from politically excluded groups that modernity is closely tied to Brahmanical Hindu culture and lifestyle.[17] In addition, the BJP includes groups such as Adivasis as part of the Hindu nation. But, the BJP argues, the lack of development in Adivasi communities is because "they failed to advance" through taking on upper-caste practices.[18] Such rhetoric brings Hindutva perspectives into conversations with neoliberal reasoning because it obfuscates inequities and naturalizes socioeconomic differences.[19]

Indians who are members of minority communities often saw discrimination within India as a barrier to finding jobs. Mohammed, for example, wanted to "make India modern" but also critiqued state actors whom he believed treated Muslims with discrimination. Mohammed's narration of his departure from India highlights how he experienced discrimination firsthand when he was traveling to Abu Dhabi for work. Here, Mohammed describes passing through customs at the airport in Mumbai:

> When I was coming here [Abu Dhabi], I was asked ten types of questions [by Indian emigration officials] and when non-Muslims went through immigration, they [the emigration officials] just stamped [the passports] and let them go. This is the reason that Muslims tend to go abroad. We don't get opportunity there [in India]. And this is the same in most every state.... The good thing about [Connex] is that they don't care about religion, caste, sect. They just see skilled workers.

This account of discrimination is far from unique, and Muslim and Dalit migrants, in particular, often share similar experiences of discrimination they face at job sites and by state actors in India. At the oil rig construction project in Abu Dhabi, migrants like Mohammed told me that they had more opportunities for advancement because they worked for a European company.

Despite the importance of the economy and infrastructure in defining and directing state-driven modernization projects, the state economy in India is subordinate to membership in the national imagination.[20] Temples, like dams and rigs, are symbolic of state power and modernity.[21] Historically, temples represented a king's power. Today temples are sites where individual disciplinary practices, particularly those related to citizenship and modernity, are expressed. Through emphasizing the heritage and ritual bodily practices that occur at temples, temples are seen as a place where citizens may learn to become modern,[22] and they are places where lower-caste groups are taught upper-caste Hindu culture. This entails a "civilizing process," the exclusion of certain groups, and efforts to sanitize the area around a temple to appeal to an upper-caste aesthetic.[23] This process, however, is far from hegemonic, and temples are also sites where the past and the future are contested.[24] Within this context, signs of modernity, visions of the future, and narratives around the nation's past become intertwined, and temples, like energy infrastructure, become places to exert political power and are, at times, sites of violent conflict.

Temples and rigs, through their connection with the past and future, serve as monuments. As such, they become places where national belonging is defined and political agendas are mobilized. The BJP was elected to power in 2014 on a promise of development, but it was criticized because, some argued, it failed to implement their promised changes. In order to secure reelection in 2019, the BJP implemented a "divisive strategy that pits minority groups and their concerns in adversarial relation to one another" and "represent[s] minorities and their allies as collectively oppositional and menacing to majority lives."[25] As in many other places throughout the world over the past forty years, members of privileged communities have increasingly positioned themselves as persecuted minorities through, in part, a conflation of politics and morality.[26] In India, this builds on a longer history of exclusion from political power. As groups battle over membership and representation in the nation, understandings of the nation's past and dreams for its future become symbolized in places like temples or rigs. These sites often become the battleground of contemporary politics.[27]

In India, Muslims are considered a marginal community and ambiguous members of the nation, and in the context of a nation-state, the idea of the minority is particularly ambiguous when combined with religion, ethnicity, or culture.[28] As Muslims face discriminatory policies, they feel the need to prove loyalty to India. Immediately following the Partition (a violent period following the end of British colonialism in 1947 when colonial India became the independent countries of India and Pakistan), the nationalist imperative was that Muslims must "decide where they stand" and state allegiance to either India or Pakistan.[29] In India in 1949, Muslims were thought to participate in disruptive and antinational activities because of their connection with Pakistan. This trope continues to reoccur and is told and retold in newspapers, films, magazines, and novels into the present. In response, Muslims feel the need to take a stand against terrorism and restate their loyalty to the Indian nation. For example, immediately after the terrorist attacks in Mumbai from November 26 to 29, 2008, Indian Muslims gathered and held signs at vigils to express their membership in and solidarity with the nation. In addition, they made statements to journalists expressing disapproval of terrorism and a general feeling of patriotism for India. Nevertheless, exclusion continues. Today this narrative of Muslims as outsiders is prominently featured on the BJP's official website, which describes Muslims as "invaders." In addition, stories about historic Muslim "invaders" destroying temples are falsely framed and perpetuated.[30] The consequence of depicting Muslims in such a way is that they are not included in the nation's future.

Monuments and the Nation

The impact of discrimination against Muslims was referenced by the challenges Mohammad had in finding a job in India and navigating interactions with government officials. Moments of violence against the Muslim community are also referenced in connection to reasons for Indian migration to the Gulf. In particular, many Muslim migrants describe the violence in the wake of the destruction of a mosque, called the Babri Masjid, in Ayodhya, India, in 1992. Twenty years after the destruction of the mosque, Ayman, a Bihari subagent based in Mumbai who had previously spent over a decade working in the Gulf, continued to narrate how the events around it affected him as well as the men from Uttar Pradesh and Bihar whom he helped migrate. As we spoke, Ayman told me that Indian Muslims migrate to the Gulf because in India, there is "increased Hindutva, violence against Muslims, and a lethargic approach by the [Indian] judiciary." He continued, "Some Muslims are not getting justice [and they are stuck because] the judiciary plays a role in promoting Hindutva." Because of this, Ayman said, there is a "decline of [India's] secular image." To support his point, Ayman pointed specifically to the communal violence that occurred in Bombay (today Mumbai) after the destruction of the Babri Masjid. The destruction of the Babri Masjid and following violence continues to serve not only as a reference for Indian Muslims, but also plays a role in contemporary politics.

In 1989, the BJP publicly included in its political manifesto a call to build a temple at the god Ram's birthplace (*janmabhoomi*) in Ayodhya, Uttar Pradesh. This began a serious of incidents concerning monuments and national belonging that reverberated to (at least) 2020. Ram, often referred to as Lord Ram, is an incarnation of the Hindu god Vishnu. His life was the subject of a still popular television show made in 1987 and 1988 that brought much attention to a proposal to build a temple for Ram at his birthplace. At issue was that Ram's birthplace was already occupied by a Muslim *masjid* (mosque), known as the Babri Masjid, built in 1528 by the Mughal emperor Babur, the founder of the Mughal dynasty in India. This dynasty controlled much of India, particularly in the north, from 1526 to 1857. Many Hindus believed that Babur destroyed a temple that marked Ram's birthplace in order to build the Babri Masjid. While independent archaeologists and scholars find no evidence to support this claim, it continues to persist and works within popular discourse to reinforce Hindu nationalist claims that Muslims are outsiders in India.

In 1992, a group of *kar sevaks* (religious volunteers) attending a rally organized by the BJP and the religious arm of the Sangh Parivar, the Vishwa Hindu Parishad (VHP), destroyed the Babri Masjid. Following the destruction, there were riots in the state of Uttar Pradesh and the city of Bombay (Mumbai). The government at the time was a right-wing, religiously conservative party that is also part of the Sangh Parivar umbrella (as are the VHP and the BJP). An Indian government commission, the Srikrishna Commission, filed a report on these riots in 1998. It found a "deliberate and systematic effort to incite violence against Muslims," and said that state actors, including police, were actively involved in killing Muslims and destroying homes and businesses.

Issues around the Babri Masjid continued to be the catalyst for communal violence. In Gujarat in 2002, Hindu activists returning from Ayodhya on a religious pilgrimage were killed on a train. While the assailants are still unknown, rumors circulated that Muslims killed these pilgrims, and the chief minister of Gujarat, Narendra Modi (India's current prime minister), facilitated the photography of the victims and called it a "preplanned attack."[31] In response, Hindus organized attacks on Muslims in Ahmadabad, Gujarat. During this period of communal violence, the Gujarati government, under Modi's leadership, facilitated the selective attacks on Muslims and their homes and businesses. State services, including the police, participated in the violence rather than protecting Muslims. In response to accusations that Modi, at best, did not do enough to stop the violence (including the extrajudicial killing of Muslims by the police), Modi argued the violence was legitimate because the state was fighting against "terrorism."[32] Conflicts also continued in courtrooms. After the destruction of the mosque, a twenty-seven-year legal battle ensued over who had rights to the site. The case, known as Ram Janmabhoomi–Babri Masjid land dispute, was decided by the Indian Supreme Court in November 2019, which granted the entirety of the land to the deity Ram.[33]

As the contestation over space in Ayodhya demonstrates, monuments and history, within an ethnic nationalist context, are key sites for shaping national identity and catalyzing citizenry. The impact of ethnonationalism continues. When former American president Donald Trump visited India in February 2020, his visit coincided with public protests over legal measures taken by the Indian government to politically exclude Muslims as well as police violence against Muslims. During Trump's visit, the Citizenship Amendment Act was highly contested by many Indians. This act, passed in 2019, fast-tracks citizenship for South Asians of all religions who are entering India, with the exception of Muslims. Following the passage of the act, protests over the exclusion of Muslims erupted throughout India. During Trump's visit, protests in the capital of New Delhi led to violent clashes between Hindus (including members of the police force) and Muslims in riots that left at least fifty-three dead, two-thirds of them Muslims. During these riots, a group shouting "India for Hindus" and other Hindu nationalist slogans paraded around a burning mosque and set a Hindu god's flag on top of the mosque's minaret. During his visit, Trump argued that India and the United States have a shared ideology that involved both development and morality and was based on economic growth, strong borders, and fighting radical Islam.[34] In Trump's visit to India, as well as Modi's visit to the United States earlier in 2019, both leaders argued for similarities between the two countries as they described future economic growth within an ethnonationalist framework.

Temples and infrastructure become symbols of the nation, modernity, and development. They are also sites where national identity is imagined. Increasingly, under ethnonationalist politics, the majority identity is framed as under threat from minorities. Protecting national symbols is depicted as the key to protecting the nation's morals, particularly from "radical Islam." Within this rhetoric of security and protection, violence is legitimated and perpetuated as minorities are excluded from India's development and its envisioned future.

MIGRATION AND INCLUSIVE GROWTH

For many former and current migrants, the solution to exclusion from the nation is the improvement of their communities' economic standing. For example, Ayman argued that the "lack of justice [following violence in Mumbai] is bad." But, he said, it is not "the biggest problem for Muslims." Rather, "the most important issue is our [Indian Muslims'] financial exclusion and exclusion is the most important problem for the community." Through facilitating migration to the Gulf, Ayman told me, he saw himself as "working for inclusive growth" of Indian Muslims through the financial stability and the opportunities for upward mobility that the Gulf provides.

Migrants working for Connex also understood upward economic mobility to be important for improving their community. In addition, they argued that they needed to work abroad because of discrimination in India. Firhad, a Muslim man from the city of Kolkata, reinforced the differences between how Muslims are treated by employers in India and how Connex treats workers. Connex hired Firhad to work as an unskilled laborer. Before that, he had gone to school part time and also worked at his father's store in Kolkata. When he began at Connex, Firhad worked under one of the Arabic-speaking managers. Firhad told me, that he "worked hard for a year" and then his manager and Alex, a British construction manager, saw Firhad's hard work and "upgraded" his position. Regarding this promotion, Firhad said, "The company has recognized my hard work—promoted me to charge hand [worker in charge of a small group of workers], then to store-keeper." Firhad was proud of his upward mobility at Connex and said it was all due to "education and hard work." Migrants described employers as meritocratic, and they saw Connex and other European energy contractors as largely free from discriminatory practices. According to migrants, these corporations' emphasis on meritocracy is symbolic of modernity. In contrast, laborers from minority communities respond to stereotypes and the discrimination they experience in India by reframing discrimination practices as a sign of India's lack of modernity and approaching migration as a process closely related to modernization.

Class, Modernity, and Movement

Associations between migration and modernity are not new. In the first half of the twentieth century, British magazines equated good citizens with those who traveled by plane and argued that the technological "backwardness" of not traveling by plane made the "nation sick."[35] During that time, modernity and the future were connected to the idea of speed, and people needed to speed up in order to modernize.[36] Today, communities around the world associate mobility with development and modernity.[37] Class, however, plays a large role in who is considered to be an actor driving development, and modernity and development are most often associated with Indian middle-class information technology workers who migrate for work to Europe or North America. Anthropologists have found that these middle-class Indians see their work abroad and the skills they learn as personal development, and they understand their personal development to be closely connected to state development.[38]

As skilled, middle-class Indians migrate to Europe and North America and continue to be active in their home communities, they are seen as the main contributors to India's development. According to Amy Bhatt, these middle-class development practices occur as Indians are exposed to Western workplaces and society and as migrants living abroad envision their own return to India.[39] The Indian information technology worker who returns home from the United State becomes a "model of neoliberal success—measured in disposable income, leisure time, and global sensibility."[40] The role of middle-class workers in the tech industry to introduce development projects reflects neoliberal attitudes related to self-disciplining and self-improvement is not unique to India, of course. Aihwa Ong describes a similar process throughout South and East Asia: "Ordinary citizens are expected to develop new mindsets and build digital capabilities, while professionals are urged to achieve norms of 'techno-preneurial citizenship' or lose out to more skilled and entrepreneurial foreigners and be reduced to second-class citizenry."[41] As skilled workers refine themselves as entrepreneurial figures, they simultaneously participate in development projects in their home communities. These projects do not necessarily disrupt the power of modernity as a hierarchical process that generates difference.[42] Instead, skilled migrants are often mobilizing models that reinforce general tenets of neoliberal development projects, projects that are marked by the fact that their driving force is not the state but individuals. In India, the result is that middle-class workers abroad are seen as introducing development projects, and labor migrants to the Gulf are seen as the object of these projects.

Upper- and Middle-Class Indians in the Gulf

Indians in the Gulf work in multiple class levels and in a great diversity of occupations, and the meaning of "Indian" is not coherent among Indians living there.[43] Often the Gulf is viewed as an extension of India, and it is not surprising to read articles that describe Dubai or the UAE as "India's gateway to the world." This is reinforced by the demographics of Gulf cities. For example, in 2017, Indians were the largest set of tourists to Dubai, and it is estimated that Indians living in the city outnumber Emiratis in Dubai three to one.[44] Large numbers of Indians move through and reside in the Gulf, and the Gulf is often drawn into the geographic imagination of India. According to Caroline Osella and Filippo Osella, the connections and remittances that connect migrants from the southern Indian state of Kerala with the Gulf mean that many residents of Kerala are more "familiar with Dubai" than India's capital, New Delhi. "The Gulf could be considered part of the place that is Kerala."[45] As Indians travel to the Gulf and the Gulf is represented increasingly in popular media, more Indians imagine the Gulf as a space that is part of India.

In the 2010s, the Gulf was seen as part of a cosmopolitan extension of India. Dubai, a city that is often used to metonymically signify the Gulf, "has come to signify, for upwardly-mobile Indians, what Hong Kong represents for affluent mainland Chinese: A place to trade, invest, shop and connect."[46] Advertising for tourism actively promotes this image of the Gulf as a place where wealthy Indians congregate. A series of advertisements in 2019 by the UAE government was branded with #BeMyGuest. In these commercials, Bollywood actor Shah Rukh Khan invites Indians to Dubai for activities such as shopping, fine dining, and skydiving.[47] Through the use of "guest," Shah Rukh Khan flags the city as a home for him or a place where he, as an Indian citizen, is able to invite other Indians. Online communities in the Gulf also create a space for cultural production, as well as commercial and political messages.[48]

Middle- and upper-class Indians, particularly young adults who have grown up in the Gulf, participate actively in this process of cultural production. For example, middle-class Indian Muslims often use social media in ways that demonstrate both their Indian identity and their sense of being at home in the Gulf. YouTube videos regularly show young, wealthy Indians comfortably moving through public spaces in the Gulf. Ahmad Al Kaashekh and Muhammad Akief are two YouTube personalities who post comedy video parodies of their lives as young Muslim Malayalam men living in the UAE. In these videos, they represent Indians as upper-middle-class office managers who drive luxury vehicles, are multilingual, and have an international array of friends.[49] Like in Shah Rukh Khan's advertisements that welcome wealthy Indians to the UAE, cosmopolitan Indians see the social fabric of India as extending to the Gulf as a place where cosmopolitan Indians of many religions belong and are at home.

During my research, I frequently met middle- and upper-class Indians who have lived in the UAE all their lives but retained their Indian citizenship. In part this was due to the restrictive nature of citizenship in the UAE and the Gulf more generally. Only children born to an Emirati father automatically qualify for citizenship. When I began my research, children who were born to Emirati women married to non-Emiratis may apply for citizenship at the age of 18, but this law was amended in 2017, when Emirati women were allowed to confer citizenship on their children when they turn 6 years old. The process for people not from the Gulf to become citizens is difficult, and it is rare for noncitizens to be granted citizenship even if all requirements are met.[50] Within this context, voluntary associations serve a key role for middle- and upper-class Indians living in the Gulf.

These associations often host holiday celebrations, support projects run by the Indian embassy, and provide social services to Indian laborers working in the Gulf.

Indian voluntary associations' performances celebrate the diversity of India. In 2010, Eid al-Fitr, a Muslim holiday celebrated in South Asia and the Middle East, fell close to the dates for Onam, an autumn religious festival celebrated by Hindus in the Indian state of Kerala. As a result, one of the Indian voluntary associations based in the UAE held a joint Eid and Onam celebration that involved a feast of southern Indian cuisine, performances by children and adults, and a competition in *pookalam*, floor art using colors and flower petals. As I watched children perform a dance they had learned at a nearby Indian dance school, an outgoing woman named Rania came and introduced herself to me. Soon many of her friends joined us. Rania, an Indian Muslim from Kerala, lives in Dubai and oversees the day-to-day operations of her father's factory, which manufactures parts used in machines commonly used for oil production. Aside from her attendance at an Ivy League university in the United States, Rania had lived her entire life in Dubai and is now raising, in Dubai, her own children, with her husband, who works in banking.

Despite her busy schedule, Rania felt it important to be connected to her community of fellow Indians and had helped organize the joint Onam and Eid event. She thought this event was particularly important because it demonstrated the closeness of the community of Indians living in the UAE. As the children's performances on the stage moved from what Rania characterized as a "Hindu dance" to one she described as a "Muslim dance," Rania explained to me that the content of the celebration, as well as the agreement to celebrate a Hindu holiday and a Muslim holiday simultaneously, indicated the "harmony" among differing religious groups within the Indian community in the UAE: "India is a combination of different cultures, religions, caste and system. These are Hindus, Muslims, Christians, and many religions. But all comes under one unity, with one strength . . . ekata mein bal hai [There is strength in unity]." For Rania, this strength and unity were also reflected by the fact that diverse Indians had gathered together outside the actual boundaries of the state to celebrate. Many of the women who sat with us, all of them Muslims, smiled at Rania's description of Indian unity.

Throughout the evening, the size of the group of women sitting near me swelled and then dwindled as women went to care for children, eat, and chat with other friends. Close to the end of the evening, only a couple of women remained sitting near me. It was late, and I was having trouble staying awake. However, I kept anticipating the celebration would end soon and promised myself I would leave in just a minute. As I tried to plan my exit, Fahmida, an Indian Muslim from southern India, turned to me and abruptly told me that she likes living in the UAE more than in India. The reason, she explained, is that in the UAE, she is able to openly practice her Islamic faith. Her friend joined the conversation, and they explicitly discussed the benefits of living in the Gulf because of the discrimination she experiences in India. To emphasize their point, Fahmida pointed to her headscarf. "If I wear hijab [a head covering] in India, I am harassed. But here, in the Gulf, I wear hijab without fear." Not wearing a head covering was not an option, Fahmida explained, because "I must wear hijab because this is required [by Islam]." As a result, when she lives in India, every time she prepares to go outside her house, she must wrap her head with her headscarf and also wrap her head with *jur'at* (boldness).[51]

Fahmida and her friend recognized that discrimination against Muslims in India made living in the UAE easier for them, but this did not mean that they understood themselves as outside of or apart from the Indian nation. The importance to their identity of being Indian was reinforced as the conversation continued and shifted to their plans for the future. As Fahmida's friend flipped through the program, she pointed to an advertisement for a construction company that was building luxury housing in Kerala. The advertisement encouraged Indians living in the UAE to begin their retirement homes now and explained the process of building a home at this housing development. Both women looked at the construction information and discussed the retirement homes they and their husbands had already built in India. As they chatted, they also shared the charities they supported. Some of these charities were in the UAE, such as an organization that gifted toiletries to Indian laborers. Other charities, based in India, included a school for girls. In addition, they expressed hope that the money they sent to their families in India would improve their communities. Throughout this conversation, despite the discrimination they experienced in India, they stressed their role as Indian citizens to help improve and develop their country.

Middle- and upper-class Indian Muslims articulate their participation in building India's future through their remittances and donations. However, poor Indian Muslims and others from minority communities are excluded from these development narratives as well as the events held by voluntary associations. This exclusion occurs even as they work for middle-class Indians and as working-class migrants also build homes in India and send remittances to their families. Instead,

Indian laborers in the Gulf, much like those in India who do not follow upper-caste practices, are often thought to be the objects, not agents, of development. This assessment, however, is not shared by working-class Indians living in the Gulf.

REIMAGINING THE NATION AND ITS FUTURE

Despite working in the lowest-level positions at job sites, many Indian laborers describe their work as a direct contribution to their community's and their country's modernization and development. But these engagements did not always reconcile with middle- and upper-class Indians' engagements with modernity and development. As workers such as Mohammad and Firhad referred to the rig as a mandir, they were not uncritically repeating Hindutva development narratives or middle- and upper-class views of development. Rather, the poetics of rig as mandir highlights the importance of infrastructure and their job experiences to India's future, one that is not exclusively defined by upper-caste Hindu or upper-class practices. The poetics of mandirs and rigs is an echo of Nehru's descriptions of dams as the temples of modern India. Through these poetics, migrant laborers, and particularly migrants from minority communities, describe themselves as active participants in shaping India's future. In these descriptions, their approach to modernity and development diverged at times from state and national models.

Over the course of my research, Indian laborers frequently described modernity as a hierarchical process with several steps. These conversations usually focus on development and India's position in a global hierarchy of development. It is common for people to tell me, "America is ahead of India" or "India is behind America." This is often temporally specific, and my interlocutors assert that the United States is a certain number of years "ahead of India," usually twenty-five years or fifty years.[52] The Gulf, too, is situated within this temporal ladder of modernity. Many migrants will tell me that Dubai is still not as modern as the United States because, they say, Dubai lacks the international centrality of the United States, and, more important, Dubai is not as "free" as the United States.

Such temporal framings of modernity may seem to echo colonial civilizational hierarchies and mid-twentieth-century development projects. Like the "waiting room of history" that Dipesh Chakrabarty argues the British used to temporally and culturally situate colonial India,[53] in the aftermath of decolonization, the epistemological tropes that informed the colonial world continued with only some alteration. In post–World War II academic approaches to postcolonial states, modernization theory was used to explain the "third world" as lagging behind (and unable to catch up to) the "modern, free West." In the United States, area studies and modernization theory informed academic categorizations of countries and underpinned conceptual binaries, such as developed and developing countries. The division of first, second, and third worlds was "based on a pair of very abstract and hardly precise binary distinctions" in which there were the traditional and the modern countries and the modern was subdivided into communist versus free.[54] Similar to the spatial and temporal assumptions that informed colonialism, modernization theory continued the temporal and spatial distancing seen in earlier colonial approaches, and the assumption, in the 1950s, was that all countries would eventually become modern.[55] These colonial logics of modernity have continue to inform people's daily lives and engagements with development.[56]

When migrants describe the multiple features of modernity, freedom is always a central aspect of it. For example, one of my neighbors in Mumbai, Manu, had worked in Saudi Arabia for a few years in the mid-1990s, and today, two of his brothers live in Dubai and work for oil companies. When Manu lived in Saudi Arabia, he worked for Aramco as an air-conditioner repair person. "I did not like living in Saudi [Arabia]. It is too hot and it is like living in jail. Dubai is better. It is still hot, but like Bombay [Mumbai], a person is free." For many migrants, Manu's comparison highlights the ways in which freedom and modernity are deeply connected.

Other migrants told me how they knew America was "modern" because of how their American managers interacted with them. Kewat, a driver at Connex (and the first person I heard refer to the rig as a mandir), told me that at his last job, he drove for an American company. One day, he said, "Seven American guys [managers of the company] needed to travel to an oil refinery by car, but there were no other cars available. . . . Seven of them—and they were big, like Americans are big—all drove ... one hundred kilometers from their site to the refinery—in one car!" Here, this adaptability was a sign of Americans' modern perspectives. Later, Kewat contrasted this with Indian managers, who, he argued, were "not flexible" because, he said, Indian managers wanted to "show they are important." In such conversations, migrants talked about American and European managers as "free" because migrants saw them as less concerned with hierarchy and status than Indian managers were.

Migrants also saw Americans as free because they felt Americans had fewer restrictions in their daily lives. As I spoke one day with Ramchandra, an employee at the rig construction project in Abu Dhabi, our conversation began with a discussion about the role of company managers in shaping workers' experiences in the Gulf. After listing the many companies he had worked for, Ramchandra told me that "the best managers are Americans." When I asked why, he explicitly connected the quality of American managers with their "modern attitudes." To explain what he meant, Ramchandra said,

> Working for Americans is the best. While I worked with Americans in [the Gulf], I thought "they understand the things necessary to live life well and never go without the basic necessities at least." I like also that Americans do not have as much paperwork as the English. With Americans, they believed me if I said I would do something and they [Americans] did what they said they would do. When I worked [with an American company] it was in the middle of nowhere. . . . The Americans built a landing strip and got a plane so that you could fly directly to Dubai. The Americans also gave [workers] an alcohol stipend and on Fridays [the day off work in the Gulf], they would play cricket and bet alcohol. But since the Americans don't know how to play cricket—they throw the ball like this [mimics how one throws a baseball], then [the Indians] always won. Me and my friends would drink too much.

For Ramchandra, some of this freedom came from the access to capital and the ability to build infrastructure, as was evidenced by the landing strip for airplanes, "living a good life," and general emphasis on having fun during one's free time. Ramchandra also references here the ease of mobility that building an airstrip allowed for his American managers, a mobility that may be contrasted with the emigration permissions he needed to get from the Indian government before emigrating to work in the Gulf. This mobility also may be contrasted to the challenges Mohammed faced when departing India for the UAE.

As our conversation continued, Ramchandra repeatedly stressed that his perspective on American freedom was based on the fact that American managers drank and played sports *with* their Indian employees. His description pointed to a connection between freedom and the disruption of strict social hierarchies. Drinking alcohol without shame seemed somewhat surprising and a sign of freedom. Of course, some of this emphasis on the freedom of Americans related to my position as a White American woman, living far from family, unmarried, and living alone. To many Indian migrant laborers, this struck them as a sign of my freedom, a sign of my questionable American virtue, or a combination of the two.

What laborers saw as less ambiguous, however, was that their managers shared drinks with people who were in lower economic standing than they were. In addition, as Ramchandra drank with his managers, he too was setting aside the practice some Hindus follow of not sharing food with people of lower castes, a practice he follows while in India but not while working abroad. By setting aside this practice, Ramchandra further destabilized social hierarchies. Here, the rig is embedded in a sociality of development that is on migrants' own terms—one that may share a Hindutva discourse of technological improvement. But it also allows for migrants to reimagine social hierarchies that expand who is a participant in the nation and its modernization.

Migrant workers in the Gulf engage with development, modernity, and freedom as three deeply interwoven concepts. Their work in the oil industry and building infrastructure gains importance due to the associations between oil and development. Migrants used the practices of the corporations for which they worked to critique the Indian government's discriminatory practices as well as their active exclusion from middle- and upper-class Indian social activities. However, migrants also critically engage with American and European discourses around modernity. Often migrants would articulate a future that was not based on individuals improving themselves. Rather, they described a future based on interconnection and mutual obligation. This perspective came to the fore in conversations about oil and its role in climate change. Indeed, it is around visions of the future that migrants often reject European and American development models and the futures implied within those models.

In December 2009, I was hanging out in Mumbai with a group of returned migrants. At that time, the United Nations Climate Change Summit was meeting in Copenhagen (also referred to as the Copenhagen Summit). This meeting was covered in newspapers, and the group of returned migrants I knew discussed this summit, often with great criticism. Deepak, a Mancom employee who had recently returned from an oil project in the Gulf, was upset by the prospect that India would have to curtail its emissions, which, he argued, would impede the country's development. As a group of us sat together and drank tea, Deepak angrily told me, "You [Americans and Europeans] made yourselves modern by burning oil and killing the planet. Now you say we must stay behind?" The other men present agreed, and Ayman, who spent many years working in the Gulf and now works as a subagent, interjected that "India is being held back" from achieving its developmental goals due to carbon emission restrictions. This group of men had all worked on an oil and gas project in the past, and none of them disputed the harm fossil fuels caused to the environment. I was surprised that they recognized this harm but still advocated for the unrestricted burning of fossil fuels. Burning these fuels, they believed would be only a temporary step in India's development.

As we continued to discuss climate change, I argued for greater carbon restrictions for all countries, and the group of men with whom I sat debated me vigorously. Finally, Jagdish turned to me and explained that they too were concerned about climate change and its dangers, but that I was not understanding their position. When he said this, I felt chagrin that I wasn't listening but instead was arguing for my own perspective.[57] Having successfully quieted me, Jagdish began by telling me he was concerned about "the future of the world and how sea levels are rising and glaciers are melting and its getting hotter and something must be done. But India can't hurt its development for this." As he finished speaking, Arjun began to speak, telling me that India's development would not be as destructive as European or American development had been historically. The reason, Arjun argued, is that the common ground in all of India's various religions is a respect for the interconnection of humans and humans with the environment.

> Indians have a belief that nature is alive. That tree [gestures towards a near-by mango tree] is alive, the sea, nature, all is alive. You know those fishermen who live in Bombay? [They] believe in the god of the sea and that it's alive. And they know that if the sea is angry, then they cannot fish that day. And they will also put flowers on the shore at high tide and pray, like the sea is a god. Westerns—Europeans and you, Americans—don't believe this and just use it up.

As Arjun finished speaking, his colleagues agreed with him and reinforced this perspective. Deepak turned to me and told me that the fishermen Arjun was referring to are members of the Koli community, an Adivasi, or indigenous, community that also faces discrimination in India. Arjun's description of their activities suggests that Adivasi engagements with the environment will serve as a model for how India will care for the environment in the future. Such perspectives include Adivasis within the nation and does not coincide neatly with BJP political presentations of India's future that closely associate upper-caste Hindu practices with the country's development.

As the group continued to speak, it became apparent that they felt this perspective was not limited to a single religious community in India but a way all Indians, regardless of religion, oriented themselves to the world. In this conversation, they described an approach to development and modernity that emphasizes the interconnections between humans and the environment. Because of these interconnections, they argued, development requires a perspective that is based on interconnection and mutual obligation.

CONCLUSION

Rigs and temples are symbols of a nation—its past and its future. Both are monuments, and they serve as sites of remembrance and places where contestations over the nation's past and future are negotiated. Hindutva, an ethnonationalist policy, equates Hindus with Indians and positions people of other religious groups as outsiders. This politically situated development of difference also defines who is a Hindu. Within this context, groups use symbols to claim and define national identity. Part of this is how monuments act as focal points where contestations arise between memory, or the affective experience of the past, and history, or the story we tell about the past. They also define who will be part of the nation's future.

As they engage with the state and the nation, migrants make claims of membership in the nation and as participants in the state's development. At times, migrants make claims that push against contemporary Hindutva politics and Indian social practices through praising the practices of European and American companies and individuals and equating these practices with development, modernity, and freedom. Workers, however, do not accept all European and American practices. One area in which workers frequently invoke criticisms of Europeans and Americans is around climate change, and in these discussions, it is apparent that freedom for migrants does not mean freedom from social obligations or social relations.

By describing the rig as a mandir, migrant laborers reckoned with the Indian state's development policies and modernization projects, and workers positioned themselves as agents of India's modernization. In exploring migrant engagements with modernity, we find migrants may situate their migration in ways similar to Hindutva developmental projects. Here, much like middle-class Indians working abroad, migrants make claims to shaping India's future by learning new skills and bringing new wealth to their communities. This is particularly clear in migrants' engagement with modernity's relationship to transferable skills that will help India, in their words, "develop."

Migrant laborers come from rural areas, are disproportionately from minority communities, and are usually from lower economic groups, and as a result, they are often excluded in development narratives of the nation. In order to understand how migrants see their role in development and their understanding of modernity, this chapter examined how workers discussed modernity and explored what models of modernity and development migrants drew upon and critiqued. Using the poetics of the rig and the mandir, laborers gestured toward the similarities in aesthetics between temples and rigs and also made a claim for the role of their labor in a context of energy production, statecraft, and changing values. In this examination, we see a critique not only of politics but of the political exclusion of members of minority communities in the Gulf and in India. As workers critiqued a Hindutva vision of India, they put forward a modernity in which minorities are active members of that state. Describing their work site at the rig as a mandir lets Indians from lower socioeconomic communities occupy the contested monuments of the nation. As migrant workers described their visions of India's future, modernity and freedom repeatedly arose as two concepts that are closely connected. Migrants' emphasis on freedom often drew on their interactions with American and European managers. Despite this engagement, American and European practices were not uniformly accepted. In the example of climate change, workers argue for modernity and development through recognition of one's interconnection with the environment.

Part III

THE WEIGHT OF TRADITION

CONNEX'S TRAILERS AT THE RIG CONSTRUCTION SITE IN ABU DHABI were small, but they felt even smaller with almost all of the highest-level managers crowded into one of them. In the trailer, a few tables served as desks that were covered in stacks of paperwork, hard hats, tools, and computers. Alex, my contact at Connex, had dropped me off at this trailer and then quickly left to oversee a pressing issue. I entered the trailer and was met by a group of Connex's highest-level managers, all White men from the United Kingdom and western Europe. The managers had converged on this trailer in order to meet with me. There was an awkward silence as we sat staring at each other while drinking instant coffee. I hoped they would allow me to conduct research at this Connex construction site, and I smiled at them, unsure of what to say. Finally, Alex's supervisor, Scott, broke the silence and asked me about my research. I began to talk about Indian migration to the Gulf, and he interrupted me. "But why are *you here*?"

Part of this question, I believe, was in jest, as Scott, Alex, and other European managers were later quite vocal about their preferences to work in Europe, Australia, and the United States. Another part of this question relayed a bit of suspicion or concern that I was a journalist writing an exposé about labor in the Gulf (a concern shared by recruiting agents when I began my research in Mumbai). Awkwardly, I began again, linking my first visit to Dubai with my current research. As I explained my project in greater detail, the managers began to nod. After asking several questions regarding my research and how I will anonymize my data, Scott approved my work. This research, he told me, is "important" because South Asian laborers in the Gulf are "like slaves." All the managers agreed, and one suggested that I watch a recently aired BBC documentary, *Slumdogs and Millionaires*, which depicts the "appalling" living and working conditions migrant workers in Dubai experience.[1]

A popular explanation for contemporary working conditions centers on the belief that traditional *khalījī*, or Gulf Arab, culture was reified through the state building that occurred in the mid-twentieth century and formalized undemocratic political institutions and restrictive definitions of citizenship. Today, labor migrants' ability to access state resources and participate in governance is limited.[2] An increasing number of scholars have focused on the experiences of migrant workers and how these experiences are connected to citizenship practices in the Gulf. Often these arguments focus on citizenship and the administration of the Gulf's *kafala*, or sponsorship, system to argue that the Gulf is different from other areas of the world. According to popular discourse and some scholars, the result is that immigrants, particularly those who work as laborers, are, as Scott articulated, treated "like slaves." The consequence of such a discourse is that it implies that Gulf labor relations are "precapitalist" and therefore exceptional in the contemporary world.[3]

Such discourses are not limited to oil company managers and scholars. The director of International Labour Organization, in response to Qatar's changing laws, called the kafala system *lliebudiat aleisriata* (modern slavery), and similar language has been used by human rights organizations, including Amnesty International and Human Rights Watch.[4] Often the poor treatment of South Asian laborers in the Gulf, by employers and in general social interactions, is attributed to perceived homogeneity of Gulf culture and that oil rents allow for the continuation of *khalījī*, or Gulf Arab, tradition.

Here and in the following two chapters, I push against this characterization of the Gulf through considering the histories of colonialism in conjunction with the historic and contemporary practices at oil corporations. This builds on work that examines how oil companies were, and continue to be, the invisible participants in the restructuring of governments in the wake of oil discovery.[5] While contemporary labor practices are often explained as traditional, or rooted in an unchanging past, examining historic and contemporary corporate practices situates contemporary labor practices squarely in line with neoliberalism, modern resource extraction, and the global management of carbon production. In the contemporary moment, managerial practices at worksites, the isolation of labor camps, and unequal access to the legal system all shape the experiences of migrant laborers. In this analysis, it becomes apparent that governance and oil company practices depoliticized the oil fields and that these practices continue to reinforce labor hierarchies in the Gulf.

A focus on colonial and corporate practices does not mean that the historic practices of Gulf cultures did not influence contemporary social relations[6] or imply that laborers do not experience precarious working and living conditions. Differences in expectations, experiences, and processes of migration, combined with the huge numbers of migrant workers, lead to the separation of workers from host societies. This separation is most strongly felt among the least skilled workers, and their positions are often extremely precarious. Such precarity is un-evenly distributed among groups and arises out of modern state efforts to manage populations.[7] This precarity is also constructed through the use of contracts and safety standards that increasingly limit workers' rights and mitigate corporate risk by displacing this risk onto individual workers.

In scholarly, popular, and government examinations of labor in the Gulf, the kafala, or sponsorship, system is often discussed as underpinning and enabling worker abuse.[8] In this system, all employees in the Gulf are under the oversight of a *kafīl*, or sponsor. In other words, all noncitizens working in the Gulf must have a citizen act as a sponsor for their visas. One's sponsor is most often one's employer. Not only are workers dependent on employers to enter the country, but they must also receive permission from their employer in order to change jobs, and employers often physically keep employees' passports.[9] Needing a sponsor for a visa does not differentiate the Gulf States from other countries like India, the United States, and Great Britain—all of which require valid visas with a work sponsor. What is often argued to differentiate the Gulf is the extent to which this process seems to affect the lives of migrants. The conflation of sponsors and employers, combined with labor laws that favors employers, means workers are particularly vulnerable to abuse from their employer. Such approaches understand the kafala system to be a formalization of pre-Gulf oil relations and citizenship that is tied to a pre–World War II model defining tribal membership.[10] Migrant laborers, in these approaches, are mistreated because they are situated within an employer-employee relationship that is based on older models of slave–slave owner relations.[11] This formalization, scholars argue, was particularly important

due to the increasing wealth that accompanied the intensification of oil production in the region.[12] As a result, in the contemporary moment, migrants find there
are no strong labor laws to protect them, they are unable to appeal to the state for
protection, and legal structures formalize their exclusion.

Scholars have also described the kafala system's importance for the production
of the state and legitimation of state power.[13] Because the Gulf countries are small,
they delegate certain authorities to their citizens through the kafala system, and in
turn, the system creates a way for citizens to acquire wealth.[14] This fulfills the social
contract in which citizens are required by law to receive a share of the economic
benefits from oil and gas endeavors and the subsidiary industries built around
them. While wealth from oil rents is unevenly distributed among citizens, almost
all citizens receive financial payments from oil profits, as well as free or highly
subsidized energy and water services. In addition, citizens are able to benefit from
the oil industry by, for example, charging fees to sponsor visas. Closely associated
with the kafala system are three policies that govern the ownership of businesses
and property in the Gulf. Laws of commercial companies require that all businesses
be majority owned by Gulf nations. Alien residence laws require immigrants to
receive permission to reside in the country and limit the length a foreign residents
may stay. Finally, property ownership laws limit the ownership of land or property
to citizens or to those who have received permission from the government.

Overemphasis on pre-oil traditions or on change as representative of modernity often has the consequence of representing khalījī culture as not as modern as
Europe or North America and reinforces international development hierarchies.
They are built on the colonial dream of the colonized and repeat British colonial
tropes about the Gulf.[15] These colonial tropes include a perspective that the Gulf
was an isolated area before the discovery of oil and an assumption that Gulf Arabs
are "backward" and resistant to modernization.

As oil exploration grew in the Arabic-speaking Gulf, narratives concerning
the Gulf's "backwardness" were repeatedly mobilized by colonial administrators
and oil company managers. Oil companies had difficulty exploring and then
accessing oil in the Arabic-speaking Gulf, and the colonial administration believed
that distrust by local sheikhs and people created barriers for oil exploration. For
example, British officials observed that people living in the area viewed many
"modern" items, such as cars, with distrust. As late as 1938, the British administration claimed, "Some people thought cars were animals and drank water from
troughs, while [another tribe] believed that we had some 'medicine' which, if

poured on to the hills, would turn them into silver." The "ignorance" of the people was compounded by the "ignorance" of the sheikhs, many of whom the British felt did not even understand Arabic properly. The result was that the sheikhs were "obstructive in spirit" during oil exploration. Imposing what the British perceived as arbitrary demands, the sheikhs of the Trucial States put restrictions on where oil exploration parties could visit and the length of time groups could stay in areas. One sheikh also asked that the exploration parties not use "motors" when looking for oil.[16] This last point was particularly difficult for the surveyors, who were not willing to travel by camel and thus greatly hampered by the request.

Today, international hierarchies of modernity are bolstered with economic models in which the wealth garnered from oil rents allows governments to selectively modernize while maintaining illiberal traditions, including practices like the kafala system.[17] In particular, the "resource curse," a theory in which oil and the wealth produced from oil rents hinder democracy and democratic institutions and forms,[18] has been applied to the Gulf to demonstrate how the Gulf States are able to maintain undemocratic processes through the redistribution of oil rents to citizens.[19] For the Gulf, paradoxically, oil wealth is associated with ushering in material modernity, but oil is also perceived as delaying or staving off social and political modernity.[20]

Recently, the proposed solution to laborer precarity is to modernize the Gulf's policies. The importance of modernization and its role in changing labor conditions is clearly articulated by international organizations and government leaders of the Gulf States. This perspective comes to the fore as laws in the Gulf States have been recently amended. In 2019, Qatar shifted its labor law to allow workers to freely change jobs without receiving permission from their current employer. In response to this change, Sharan Burrow, general secretary of the International Trade Union Confederation, commented, "Qatar is changing. The new tranche of laws will bring an end to kafala and put in place a modern industrial relations system."[21] Here, Burrow situates the kafala as a nonmodern practice. Similarly, in 2019, changes to real estate laws in Abu Dhabi were described by Sheikh Mohammed bin Zayed Al Nahyan, the crown prince of Abu Dhabi, as "modern." At the announcement, Sheikh Zayed stated in Arabic, "Modernizing the real estate laws reflects the rational/wise leadership's support of the government visions aimed at developing the economic sector in the emirate."[22] These descriptions of changing laws in the Gulf present a perspective in which changing laws move the countries toward modernization, rationality, and development.

These modernization efforts, however, are not successful in exorcising the ghosts of the past because cultural tradition is used to obfuscate historic colonial and corporate practices. Analysis of past and contemporary policies and worker experiences demonstrates that the Gulf is not an exceptional, unmodern space; rather, it is a place deeply imbricated with and shaped by colonialism and contemporary neoliberalism. Historically, the British administration in the Gulf worked in conjunction with oil companies to formalize labor practices, including the kafala system and laws of commercial companies. Today these policies are maintained through the housing of workers in camps, contracting and subcontracting, and, perhaps ironically, safety standards.

Chapter 6

BLOWING SAND

RANIA STOOD OUTSIDE ONE OF HER FAMILY'S FACTORIES, LOCATED in an industrial area in Sharjah, and waved at me happily as I arrived. Rania's factories make specialized parts for oil projects, and the family had been making parts used in oil production since the late 1970s, when her father moved to the United Arab Emirates from India. These factories are 49 percent owned by Rania's family and 51 percent owned by an Emirati sponsor. Rania was born in the United Arab Emirates and had spent her entire life living in the country, with the exception of the four years she attended an elite university in the United States. Now, Rania's father was aging, and she was gradually taking over more and more responsibilities for running these factories. With Rania's and her father's permission, I had visited the factories a number of times and spoke to workers on their breaks. Rania was always busy on my previous visits, but on the day of this visit, she had some open time in her schedule, and she was eager to give me a tour of the factory.

As we walked through the factory, Rania pointed to machines and raised her voice above the din of the factory to describe the machines' roles in the manufacturing process. Men worked purposefully, and the machines thumped and hummed with regularity. Finishing the tour, we entered Rania's quiet office. As we chatted, I asked her about worker relations at her factory. Did workers ever complain? How did they settle workplace disputes? From conversations and observations of their daily lives, I knew that some workers felt their job conditions were far from ideal, but also that most workers in the Gulf felt they could not negotiate for better conditions. In response to my questions, Rania indicated that there were no problems with workers. She praised the "strong laws" in the UAE. If men "disrupt work," she said, "the police come and [they] go right back [to work]."

Rania was not alone in her positive appraisal of the police's swift response to labor unrest. For example, Navin, an Indian human resources manager at an oil company in the UAE, told me, "The greatest thing about the UAE is the strong laws. Here workers cannot strike and cause problems. If there is any problem at a worksite, you just call the police and they come and take care of it. It saves so much stress." When I asked whether there were more strikes at sites in the desert given their isolation from the city and thus far from police stations, Navin replied, "No! There are none. The police will even come to the desert."

In the twenty-first century, strikes by workers are extremely rare—so rare that in the more than a decade I've worked in the Gulf, I've witnessed only one. This small strike looked quite different from strikes I have seen in the United States, where workers may hold signs and chant slogans. At the strike I saw, workers stood, in relatively straight rows, quietly, and fully dressed for work. As they stood, they refused to pick up their tools. After about an hour, a manager emerged from an office and said he would meet with a representative for the workers. Hearing this, the workers picked up their tools and resumed their work.[1] Infrequently, there are also news reports about strikes, such as when, in 2015, hundreds of South Asians took to the streets to protest unpaid wages and the Dubai government mobilized riot police in response.[2]

Worker actions are illegal in the Gulf. Workers are forbidden from collectively organizing to improve their working conditions, and they face grave consequences when they try to do so. From the perspective of Indian migrants, the inability to strike is often discussed in connection with the surveillance and other security measures in place at oil projects, as well as the isolation of their labor camps and the general precarity workers feel while living in the Gulf. From having to clock in and out of project sites to worrying that they will be reported to government authorities or company officials if they "step out of line," migrants tell me they feel constrained. This chapter considers labor conditions that emerged from colonialism, imperialism, and oil production in the Gulf. The focus is on how management practices, including worker accommodations and labor contracts, increase worker precarity. Of course, management practices do not exist in a vacuum, and social inequalities are also structured through exclusion of workers from many spaces and the racialized labor hierarchies that inform interactions. In extreme cases, the consequences of these practices include the abandonment of workers.

HISTORIC RESTRICTIONS ON STRIKES

In order to understand the inability of workers to collectively organize, one must attend to the historic practices of oil companies and how these practices continue into the present. From the early 1940s through the 1960s, oil companies and the British colonial government implemented segregation of worksites based on nationality and regularly intervened in worker agitations with militarized responses. These two processes began in the mid-twentieth century and continue to be relevant for understanding today's labor hierarchies. Oil company managerial practices relied on racial classifications to increasingly segment workers based on nationality and sought to undermine worker solidarities that cut across linguistic or national borders. In addition, oil companies and the British colonial government became increasingly focused on national and corporate security, and security became closely associated with control over oil production. This emphasis on security spurred governance and management practices that were better suited to working with immigrants whose recourse to government support was tenuous. It is this merging of managerial practices and the securitization of oil, I argue, that provided the foundation for the current labor laws in place in the Gulf.[3]

As the oil industry grew in the Gulf, the British administration and oil companies (many of them majority owned by the British government) created governable spaces and ushered in a time of oil capitalism that involves a monopoly over mineral exploitation, the security apparatuses of the state, and institutional mechanisms by which oil revenue is distributed.[4] In the Gulf, oil company management practices reinforced national identities in efforts to depoliticize labor in the oil fields. An analysis of strikes at oil projects in the mid-1940s to the mid-1960s demonstrates the various and shifting ways in which people form solidarities in order to influence politics and improve their working conditions. These solidarities were not neatly bound by colonial or national boundaries, but during this period, worker action became increasingly fragmented along national lines.[5] Below, I briefly explain a case where oil companies changed worker living accommodations in order to mitigate against possibilities for large-scale strikes.

In 1952, British Petroleum (BP) hired over six hundred Indians to help build a new refinery in Aden.[6] These workers included a couple of Indian doctors hired exclusively to attend to workers from Asia, as well as a few clerks; the rest of the Indian employees were hired as cooks.[7] At the Aden refinery construction project, workers were employed for a contract of eighteen months.[8] They worked most Sundays, and workers reported putting in at least ten hours a day.[9] Indian workers at this project were unhappy with their working conditions. While the company claimed ten-hour workdays were stipulated in the contract, workers reported that these hours were too long and that they had not been informed of these hours before arriving in Aden.[10] Furthermore, workers were confused by the payment system for overtime hours. The company claimed that workers would be paid overtime upon completion of their contracts, but workers were unaware of this condition.[11]

Indian workers also complained that their camp was twenty miles from the site of the refinery. As a result, they commuted a long distance every day for work and were not paid for this time. The isolation of the camp also affected how workers could advocate for changing conditions. First, the distance of the camp from the city meant that it was hard for workers to contact the Indian government and ask the government to negotiate with the company on their behalf.[12] A second way the camp's isolation affected workers was that it was challenging for them to form solidarities with Arabic-speaking and Farsi-speaking workers through regular interactions and shared experiences. In addition to isolating groups, oil company managers allocated different privileges to different nationalities, which helped foster discord between groups.[13] Separate work camps were not new at this time, but with isolation, camps becoming increasingly strict in their segregation practices.

The isolation of these camps differed from the location of earlier labor camps at British oil projects. For example, in the late 1940s at the oil refinery in Abadan, Iran, Indians lived closely with Iranians as well as Arabic-speaking workers. These Indian camps were understood by the British to operate as a buffer zone between Iranians and the British.[14] Such spatial separations, particularly in cities, exist far more strongly in colonizer imaginaries than in practice. In addition, these separations are largely discursively constructed within an Orientalist framework and are frequently transgressed as workers move through colonial spaces.[15] Proximity and practice facilitated affiliations across national lines, and in the 1940s, Indians were active in strikes alongside Iranian laborers and other Arab migrant laborers. In contrast, the isolated camps in Aden in the 1950s helped to minimize such coalitions and were used by managers to reduce strikes.

From the perspective of oil companies and the British government, labor unrest was fraught: oil was used in the military, and the price of oil meant that workplace strikes were costly for oil companies. Concerns over strikes came to the fore in 1951 when Iran nationalized the Anglo-Iranian Oil Company (later British Petroleum), including the world's largest oil refinery in Abadan, Iran. This nationalization was spurred in no small part by multinational worker strikes at the oil refinery at Abadan. After Iran's brief nationalization of the oil industry from 1951 to 1953, British oil companies and government officials showed an interest in maintaining a workforce that could be controlled or replaced. For example, when Indians participated in collective action at Abadan, those who went on strike or organized politically were easily deported and new workers hired. Because from the late 1940s through the early 1970s oil company managers could replace Indian and Pakistani employees who disrupted worksites, workers from these countries came to be increasingly hired for unskilled or semiskilled positions.[16]

During the 1960s, a series of strikes by khalījī workers in Qatar, Abu Dhabi, and Bahrain were characterized as threats to national security and, as a result, Gulf governments, British administrators, and oil companies worked together to reduce the impact of future strikes.[17] Frustrated by lost revenue and fearful of nationalization, oil companies increasingly focused on the stability of the workforce—in both the oil fields and the industries providing support for oil production. Workforce stability, as oil company managers and British administrators argued, was the central feature of political stability. The result was an evacuation of politics from the oil fields through the replacement of khalījī workers with precarious South Asian workers who today compose the majority of laborers at oil projects and who have limited success in calling on the government to protect their rights. Following worker strikes in the 1960s, the British protectorate and oil companies responded by writing labor laws friendly to oil companies and replacing local khalījī workers with workers from South Asia because managers thought they were less political and easier to fire.[18]

LABOR CAMPS

Oil infrastructure is a key site where the idea of national security was and continues to be invoked. Historically, this resulted in the depoliticization of the oil fields. In the UAE, security uses state-of-the-art technology to survey expatriate populations.[19] In addition, many of the managerial practices developed in the mid-twentieth century continue to be implemented at oil and gas projects in the Gulf. One such practice is providing living accommodations for workers in isolated camps.

Anthropologists engage with camps as spaces built by states to contain or control populations.[20] In the Gulf, many laborers live in camps that are segregated based on nationality, gender, and race.[21] These camps are grouped together in the Emirates, and every morning company buses arrive to take workers to their various worksites. Two companies that I worked closely with, Connex and Rania's factory, contract with companies that own dorm-like buildings to house their employees. The fee that companies pay per individual includes electricity, water, cable television bills, and meals. The fees for electricity and water are standard, but many companies do not pay for cable television and meals. In the camps I have visited, men live in bunk beds, with eight to twelve to a room; a small kitchen is included in the rooms of some workers, based on their job in the company's hierarchy; and there are communal bathrooms.

Within camps, workers are organized by company and often by nationality. Sometimes within nationalities, people are further grouped by their religion. As George, an American contractor explained to me, his company tries to "split people based on religion. This avoids conflicts, suits religious beliefs, and canteens are there to suit dietary needs. Of course, people can go and eat in other areas, but this is very unusual." At Connex's camp where the rig was being built, language, more than religion, seemed to dictate how men lived in the camp, and many workers who identified as Hindus and Muslims told me they shared living spaces with those who were from the same state in India but of other religions. Most important to the workers at Connex was speaking the same language and being from a similar location. Sociality at camps is not limited to eating and sleeping; workers also spend leisure time with their roommates. For example, many sites I found have weekly cricket games. Teams were often interreligious but nationally homogeneous. Despite the homogeneity of the teams, workers banter and talk with members of opposing teams during games, at times opening spaces for conversations and friendships.

Locality, which often affects how migrants move, also informs how workers experience their migration. A couple of years after I first met a group of men with Ayman, subagent, while he was helping a group of men from Uttar Pradesh find jobs in the Gulf, I met those same workers in the UAE. As we sat and drank tea at a restaurant near their camp, the men told me that they were happy with their experience migrating and were particularly pleased they had worked with Ayman.

One man said that he liked working with Ayman because he felt that Ayman often helped many people from the same area find jobs. As a result, the man told me, there "are many people from my village, all at this work site. It makes it easier" to work in the Gulf, away from one's family. Despite these connections, the segregation of worker camps does create challenges to forming workplace solidarities or collectively requesting changes to their working conditions.

As laborers create social lives in their working and living spaces, particularly the camps in which they reside, they are excluded from other social spaces in Gulf cities. Camps most often are outside city centers and separate from the restaurants, beaches, and shopping malls frequented by middle- and upper-class residents. While workers may travel to the city, they are usually aware of discrimination. This means that while buses may run between camps and the city, they are often underused by workers. In part, this is because small shops around the camps provide many of workers' daily necessities, but it is also because of the discrimination workers experience.

On the rare occasions when migrant laborers do visit public spaces in the Gulf, they frequently experience discrimination. On a Saturday in 2011, I sat on the beach in Dubai and watched as a group of young South Asian men arrived and stood at the edge of the beach. They did not fit in with the well-dressed Europeans, South Asians, and Arabs who were using the beach, sitting under umbrellas to shade themselves from the sun, and wearing both expensive watches and designer swim or leisure wear. These young men were dressed in the clothes worn by laborers on oil projects on their days off—polyester pants, faded T-shirts, and worn shoes. As they stared out at the crowded beach, a group of young White men walked up to the group and, to my horror and shock, they chased the Indian men off the beach, acting as informal state actors to socially police the beach to keep out lower-class workers.[22] I was so surprised by the interaction that I barely registered what had happened before both groups had disappeared in opposite directions. On the day following this beach encounter, I described my distress about the situation to a Lebanese friend who works as a human resources manager at an oil project. He explained to me that the men who had been chased off were "dangerous" and would have made "women uncomfortable" with their presence. This perception of South Asian men as dangerous and lecherous is informed by migrants' socioeconomic position as migrant laborers.

Generally an individual's nationality, race, gender, and class influence many of their daily interactions as well as their structural support or lack thereof.[23] In the Gulf, racialized labor hierarchies often collapse one's nationality and class, and they shape one's perceptions of social space and their access to such spaces. In 2019, I was in Abu Dhabi and spending a few evenings catching up with Arjun, an Indian man I first met in 2009 while he was working at the recruiting agency Mancom in Mumbai. Arjun had been working in Abu Dhabi for about five years at that time, and we arranged to have a meeting near one of the malls in the area. He wanted to walk outside the mall, but I was exhausted from jet lag and insisted that we go into the mall to find a cup of strong coffee. I made a beeline for Starbucks, ordered the largest coffee on the menu for myself and a frappuccino for Arjun, and sat down in the comfort of the air-conditioned mall café. Arjun, who the day before in an Indian food stall was confident and gregarious, was quiet and fidgeted in his seat in the Starbucks. As I tried to make small talk, telling a story about my daughter, he simply nodded and looked around. Suddenly I realized that the café was full of Whites, Arabs, and South Asians who were clearly dressed in designer clothes, wearing expensive jewelry, and using cutting-edge technology. In contrast, Arjun worked as an office boy and was dressed in what I knew to be his best clothes, but these clothes were ill fitting and worn. I asked Arjun if he wanted to leave. In response, he nodded and quickly walked out of Starbucks. I caught up to him as he waited for me at the mall exit. As we left the mall, Arjun told me he had never been to Starbucks before, and he did not think it was a "good" place to be. "I could see those [White and Arab] men watching me, wondering why [I am in Starbucks]." He then told me that he began to worry that someone would call the police on him for harassing a *gori*, a White woman. In contrast, I felt comfortable in Starbucks, even though I was dressed casually, wearing nondesigner jeans, a T-shirt, and no jewelry. After we left the mall, Arjun and I began walking toward an area where South Asian men, as well as workers from the Philippines and Ethiopia, gathered to eat and watch football (soccer) matches on television.

As we ate and watched the matches, Arjun quickly returned to his gregarious self and began to tease me for being "single" (unmarried) and telling me, in partial jest, that I was now "too old" to find a "good match." As he talked, I reflected on the differences in Arjun's experiences and mine in Starbucks and how these are directly related to the Gulf's racialized labor hierarchies. In this case specifically, white privilege allowed me to sit in Starbucks and simultaneously excluded Arjun from that space; white privilege is also one reason I did not initially think of Arjun's discomfort when I insisted on Starbucks.[24] At the time, I was tired and had not been to the Gulf in about six months, but also, I generally do not have to worry about or fear discrimination or harassment based on my race, class, or nationality when in the Gulf.

These moments on the beach and in Starbucks are reflections on the social isolation in which labor migrants live their daily lives and the racialized labor hierarchies that dominate social interactions in the Gulf. In these hierarchies, South Asian laborers fall near the bottom.[25] Racialized hierarchies are reinforced through daily interactions, wage discrepancies, legal practices that favor employers, and social separation. Migrant laborers from South Asia and Africa are not alone in this system.[26] Race, nationality, and class inform one's experiences, and workers from many nationalities experience discrimination,[27] often reinforced by the strict regulation of space with groups of laborers walking in the city often seen as "gangs."[28] As I saw at the beach in Dubai, these racialized hierarchies are reinforced by middle- and upper-class residents of multiple nationalities. In addition, workers like Arjun internalize these hierarchies and avoid disrupting them for fear of the consequences, which could include arrest, physical harm, and deportation.

These security practices, according to Noora Lori, are how the state attempts to mitigate the risks of large expatriate populations, thought to be rooted in the criminal threat of migrant laborers and also the threat immigrants pose to Emirati values.[29] Public fears map directly onto laborers and other poor migrants, who come most often from sub-Saharan Africa or South Asia.[30] Such security measures work in conjunction with contracts and have the impact of further precaritizing migrant laborers. These measures build on and reinforce the isolation of laborers into camps.

FINANCIAL PRECARITY

Workers who were unhappy with their work were unable to form workplace coalitions *and* they could not easily leave their jobs and return to India. A point of contention Connex workers discussed was that they were required to pay fines if they wanted to leave their job before the end of their contract. Connex implemented this policy by withholding a portion of workers' salaries for the first year of their employment. According to their contracts, if a worker broke his employment contract or was unable to perform the duties outlined in his contract, then he was sent home and Connex kept this fee. The fee differed depending on a worker's nationality. Workers from India were charged US$250, and Nepalese and Filipino workers, in contrast, were charged US$175 and US$200, respectively. Government regulations in Bangladesh did not allow the company to collect this fee from employees. Workers who had been at the company longer than a year largely were unfazed by this Connex policy. Connex's human resources managers argued that they "had" to charge these fees because they feared high turnover rates and because they were required to pay fees to both the UAE government for workers' visas and to manpower supply companies in India to help them recruit workers and navigate India's restrictive emigration policies. Whenever this topic arose, senior workers would dismissively tell junior employees that Connex was a trustworthy company and that the men would be happy to have "their bonuses" after their year had passed.

These fees were not unique to Connex: all of the companies that I have talked to charge them.[31] Ganak, an Indian working as a human resources manager at a different energy services company, explained to me, "If we don't charge [employees] for a visa, then we lose money. They also come and don't want to work hard. They have the idea that Dubai is the easy life and don't want to work. Also [the employees'] homesickness increases and [employees] miss babies, mom, wife." This, he told me, was why they needed to charge fees. Sometimes this fee was not charged up front; instead, the worker has to pay to leave a contract early. One oil company contractor included in its employee contract that workers needed to pay approximately US$900 if they wanted to go home before their contract ended. Because most unskilled workers at the company were paid approximately US$245 per month, this termination fee equaled almost four months' wages. At yet another company, a manager told me these fees encouraged employees to work hard. Indian workers at Rania's factory paid the fee before they began their work: the newly hired workers gave the fee to their recruiting agency, which then gave it to factory management. Many workers at all companies told me that they had borrowed large sums at high interest rates to pay these fees if they needed to pay them when they were hired.

The fact that companies require workers to pay a deposit did not usually deter unskilled and semiskilled workers from applying for jobs, but the deposit is a large sum and may keep them from leaving their jobs early once they are in the Gulf. At times, workers do not want to continue working in the Gulf, but, they tell me, their families are in precarious financial circumstances. Fear of losing money prevents workers from leaving their jobs early and also safeguards the money the company paid for visas, plane tickets, and training. Managers will sometimes "hide" or ignore a worker who is not as productive as others, but keeping this fee ensures that employees who are unhappy working in the Gulf will not leave the company before the end of their first year. In this way, the costs of visas and airfare are a risk that the company places firmly on the worker—the person least able to negotiate the contract or afford the lost money.

MANAGERIAL PERSPECTIVES

While workers often live in isolated camps and are charged fees to deter them from breaking their contracts, not all migrants experience similar conditions. In contrast to the workers depicted in the BBC documentary that characterized migrant laborers as slaves (*Slumdogs and Millionaires*), Alex and his colleagues told me that workers at Connex were treated better than most other workers in the Gulf. For example, Alex said, workers are given leave to return home annually, as opposed to the norm throughout the Gulf of receiving leave every two years. The reason, Alex said, is that "the owner [of Connex] can't sleep if they go home once every two years." Alex also told me that the camps where workers live were much better than the general living conditions and that Connex's safety record guaranteed better working conditions for employees.

Managers often express concern for the welfare of their workers and a desire to improve workers' daily lives. In fact, Alex told me that one of the reasons he initially approved my visit to his worksite was that he thought it would convey care to his employees. After I had been visiting the site for a few months, Alex and I were chatting one day and he told me that his Indian employees "couldn't get over a White woman [is] here, speaking their language, and listening." Alex's concerns for his employees were repeated by most managers I met in the Gulf, and I understand this to be sincere. However, this does not mean that their workers experienced optimal working conditions. While Connex employees' circumstances are significantly better than most others employed as unskilled or semiskilled laborers, many of the critiques of working conditions in the Gulf apply to employees of all companies operating there.

Today managers often acknowledge that even their own workers, as Alex described it, live "hard lives." The reasons include the hot climate. Working to construct a rig with so much steel, Alex told me, is extremely hot—so hot that only South Asians are able to handle the heat—an assertion that assumed a racialized difference in bodies while simultaneously acknowledging the difficulties of the work laborers perform.[32] In addition, managers at Connex told me workers have hard lives because workers live away from their families and are excluded from social spaces in the Gulf.

Workers in my presence never suggest striking over labor issues or petitioning the Indian government to intervene on their behalf. In part this is because of the restrictive labor laws and strikes are illegal. Rumors circulate in both India and the Gulf concerning the severe repercussions for labor agitation, and these rumors are strengthened by recruiting agency employees. As workers arrive at an agency to get their visas for a new job, employees will tell workers to "be sure not to cause problems" at their jobs because they may be "thrown in jail" and possibly "never return to India." Recruiting agency employees told these stories because they wanted to be sure that the workers they sent to clients "behaved" and that the agency would not get a reputation of sending workers who are "troublemakers." Additionally, these agency employees had also previously worked in the Gulf, and they also heard stories there of unsuccessful labor agitations.

Despite restrictive working conditions, workers still agitate against labor practices that they feel are unjust. Often managers do not view these labor actions as rational. Rather, in addition to viewing the cause of poor labor conditions to be rooted in traditional Gulf Arab culture, managers often view the reasons for worker unhappiness as rooted in emotions. For example, when I was visiting a Connex project in Kuwait in 2019, a British manager described a recent work agitation among workers constructing oil infrastructure for a British energy contractor. As we chatted, the manager told me that during the past week, his workers had gone "wild" and "their heads were [makes head-exploding gesture and the sound of an explosion]." He attributed this to high emotions that workers were unable to control when watching a soccer match. As a result, he told me, he called security, who came to the job site. Security, he continued, are like police, and the presence of the "police" stopped the worker "riots." The workers returned to work when they saw security officers. In this manager's experience, security forces responded quickly to any reporting of labor unrest. His description of unruly workers in response to a sporting event depoliticized the actions of workers.

Assumptions concerning worker actions as "wild" are reinforced by racialized labor hierarchies—a hierarchy that many managers have naturalized. At worksites throughout the Gulf, racialized labor hierarchies are prevalent, and the oil rig construction project in Musaffah was no exception. Upper-level managers are usually from Europe and North America; lower-level supervisors are from the Arabic-speaking countries outside the Gulf, the Philippines, or South Asia; and laborers are primarily from South Asia and the Philippines. As Robert Vitalis illustrates in his history of US involvement with oil production in Saudi Arabia, key methods developed by American oil companies to curtail labor strikes included the racial segregation of workers and discrepancies in pay based on race.[33] Importantly, the institutionalization of racism as a management technique was not unique to the oil industry in the Middle East; racial labor hierarchies were also mobilized in, for example, the oil industry in Mexico and in factories in India.[34]

ABANDONED CAMPS

The effects of isolating and segregating workers in conjunction with racialized labor hierarchies has dire consequences for some migrants. During Ramadan in 2010, I traveled to Sharjah, UAE, to take *iftar*, breaking the daytime fast Muslims observe during the month of Ramadan, with the residents of an abandoned camp. The men I ate with had what many migrants described as the "bad luck" to work for companies that had gone bankrupt or were in financial difficulties following the 2008 global economic crisis. As a result, these companies closed their operations completely or laid off large numbers of workers. Often the company owners fled the UAE in order to avoid debtor's prison, while the workers—many of whom had not been paid their wages—were left stranded in the UAE. These migrants most often worked at smaller companies that provided parts or day labor to larger multinational corporations (MNCs). With the economic turmoil of 2008, many of these smaller companies were unable to pay their bills or their employees. The low-level employees of these defunct companies continued to live at the camps, but because their employers no longer paid the bills, the residents had no water or electricity. Due to the hot weather, the residents of the camp pulled their mattresses onto the roof of their buildings to sleep at night.

Men I spoke with at the abandoned camp told me they were "stuck" or "trapped." Many believed that they could not get another job in the Emirates. Some did not have their passports because their employer had been holding them. When their employer disappeared, their passports disappeared as well. Some employees still had their passports, but they thought they would be unable to find another job because their work visas were tied to their employer. Finding another job was hopeless, they said, because in order to transfer one's visa, they would need an employer who would be willing to navigate the Emirates Ministry of Labour on their behalf.

Stuck, waiting in camps, these abandoned workers had no plane ticket home, no paycheck, and nowhere to go. Most of the men at the iftars were Hindus and Muslims from India, Pakistan, and Bangladesh. In addition, two Christian Filipino men, also residents of the abandoned camp, regularly joined the evening meal. After the Muslim men prayed, we all ate together in rows, sitting on long plastic sheets that had been laid on the ground behind a Pakistani restaurant. These were highly gendered affairs, and I never saw another woman in this area.

During these meals, I spoke with men about their past work histories, current experiences, and hopes for the future. Many expressed anger and frustration at their situation. Unable to send money to their families, work another job, or return to their homes, migrant laborers described their feelings of powerlessness, helplessness, and disenchantment with living in the Arabic-speaking Gulf. One abandoned worker, speaking in Hindustani, described his situation: "We do not have a degree; none of us can read. Why do they not give us the money they owe us? They [had] two cars and [lived] like sheikhs, but they [did] not pay us."

These men, like most others working as laborers in the Gulf, came from rural, economically depressed areas and had limited formal education. Their families went into large amounts of debt to facilitate their migration. The price of a plane ticket home for abandoned workers was well beyond the means of most families. Men living in the abandoned camps told me that they were concerned because their families in India had trouble affording daily necessities and making payments on the debt the families took on to fund migration. They also told me they were angry with the employers who had not paid them.

In order to access clean water and food, men at abandoned camps relied on men at nearby camps who were employed. Often laborers had built relationships between camps long before the companies they worked for went out of business. These relationships were developed in shared workspaces (particularly at construction projects where many corporations work), shared religious practices (praying at a mosque or celebrating a Hindu holiday like Diwali), or shared leisure activities (such as watching football [soccer] or playing cricket on Fridays, the day most workers had off). Building on these relationships, men would help each other in times of need. Employed workers often saved portions of their meals for their neighbors. This relationship was reciprocal. During the iftars supplied by the voluntary organization, men would sometimes bring an employed friend from a nearby camp who had been helping them. While the employed men were provided food by their employers, they told me the iftar meals were of better quality than the food they received regularly at their camps, and they were happy to break the Ramadan fast with samosas, curried mutton, and milk sweets. When I asked the employed workers why they shared their food with their neighbors, employed men often commented that the men who had been abandoned were *badqismat* (unlucky). In conversations with employed workers, I found they often empathized strongly with their neighbors at abandoned camps and felt that they too could potentially end up abandoned at some point.[35]

ASSISTING ABANDONED WORKERS

A voluntary association provided these residents of the abandoned camp with their evening meal during the month of Ramadan. Every night, a small, rotating group of volunteers, either Indian or Pakistani men (but never a group of Indian *and* Pakistani men), traveled from Dubai to an industrial area on the far side of Sharjah to feed these camp workers. At one of the food stalls, run by a Pakistani man, the volunteer group had arranged to provide meals for the abandoned workers. I usually traveled to the camps with middle-class South Asian men employed in sales, banking, or trading. Most were fluent in English and came from middle- and upper-class homes in South Asia.

This group of volunteers facilitated the giving of the donations that were made by wealthy South Asians, mostly women, who lived in the Emirates. These women would volunteer to pay for a camp's meals, provide water, or provide care packages for workers (most often stocked with toiletries). The voluntary organization was begun by a wealthy Pakistani woman whose husband is part owner of a lucrative manufacturing company. In her story about how she became involved in helping men at abandoned camps, she tells of an evening that she found "two boys scavenging over rubbish and fighting over handfuls of food." She stopped to ask "the boys" what was happening, and they told her of their plight. She immediately posted about this situation to her social media. Soon people volunteered to pay for a meal for these men or donate water to the camp. In the time I've known the organization, it has expanded its focus from working exclusively with abandoned workers to also providing assistance to men who are employed at low-level jobs.

Often the volunteers, much like the Indian government's approach to workers, attempt to cultivate workers as entrepreneurs, an approach that includes improving the workers' skills—for example, by offering English classes. For the men at the abandoned camps during Ramadan in 2010, volunteers regularly brought wanted ads and encouraged men to apply. When the abandoned workers shared their concerns—their passports were missing or their visas not transferable—the volunteers would dismiss these concerns and insist that the men "must try." Often as we drove home from the meals, the volunteers would disparage the men and argue with me when I said the men were abandoned through no fault of their own. Rather, the volunteers told me the residents of the abandoned camp could work but chose not to do so. They also regularly asked me if I had given any of the men money, as they did not want to "encourage" the abandoned workers "to become beggars."[36] By invoking this fear of the poor becoming beggars, middle- and upper-class Indian migrants articulated their worldview in which hard work is rewarded by continued income and less precarity. These rhetorical approaches distanced the volunteers (who saw themselves as hard workers) from the abandoned workers and also laid some of the blame for their circumstances at the feet of those who had been abandoned. Through saying workers were not trying hard enough, they individualized and depoliticized the inequalities that are a consequence of contemporary capitalism. Thus, while the wealthy volunteers found living in the Gulf a way to live their dreams, they believed laborers had failed to achieve the dream due to laborers' own, individual, lack of discipline or drive.

Eventually the voluntary organization raised enough money through individual donations to pay for the men's plane tickets home and intervened with the Pakistani, Bangladeshi, and Indian consulates to get travel permits for those who did not have passports. As the abandoned workers left the Emirates, the organization tried to give each man a small toy that he could take home to give to his children. Later that year, the Emirates Ministry of Labour asked the organization to help men who had been abandoned to fill out paperwork. The South Asian governments, despite having repatriation of abandoned workers listed as one of their missions, continues to rely on this and other organizations' fundraising to send workers home and facilitate paperwork on their end. Since 2010, the organization has grown, and it is now an informal but active intermediary for the Emirati government and South Asian governments.

From the perspective of laborers stuck at abandoned camps, there are some shortfalls to having the voluntary organization provide state services. Abandoned workers were forced to appeal to the interest of donors and, in order to elicit help from volunteers, conform to certain representations of victimhood.[37] However, neoliberal reforms do not reconfigure all individuals in the same way. While abandoned workers needed to conform to the voluntary association's standards and donor preferences in order to receive help, worker collaborations across camps highlight a form of community making that disrupts the ways corporations and states individualize and abstract labor. Appeals directly to the state and attempts to bypass the organization also highlight a sociality that pushes for state responsibility that relies on the equality of citizens and resembles more closely the tenets of liberalism than neoliberalism.

As in many other contexts globally, neoliberal reforms emphasize the role of private contracting to provide state services. In this case, this voluntary organization worked as an informal contractor for state bureaucracies, providing state services to migrant workers and mediating the state's obligation to its citizens. While often the focus is on the difference of the Gulf due to oil wealth, the abandoned camps highlight crucial aspects of contemporary neoliberal reforms. The focus on migrants as entrepreneurs and discourses that focus on preventing "beggars" serves to depoliticize worker experiences and individualize inequalities, a trend throughout neoliberalism.[38] The impact of neoliberal reforms is also seen in the role of nongovernmental organizations as new sites to make claims on the state.[39] As these discussions by members of the voluntary association show, much blame is put on individual migrants for their circumstances.

CONCLUSION

Abandoned workers are an extreme example of the challenging conditions laborers experience working in the Gulf. Many laborers are paid regularly and do not end up stuck, waiting for nongovernmental organizations' donations or government action to facilitate their repatriation. But even for those who are not abandoned, the management practices at play mean that many workers experience their time abroad as challenging. In 2009, I sat in the home of Mr. Umair in a village outside Lucknow, India. I had met his wife, son, and daughter-in-law a couple of years earlier while studying Urdu in Lucknow. Now, Mr. Umair had returned from the Gulf, and the family was eager to introduce the two of us. It was early in my research, and at the time, I thought my research question centered on how Indian Muslims' understandings of religion changed after they had lived in the Gulf.[40] As I spoke with Mr. Umair, I hoped he would share how his own religious perspectives had changed in the over thirty years he had worked in the Gulf. During our conversation, Mr. Umair's son said, with pride, that his father had worked in "every Gulf state" and "without rest" to support his family. Eager to learn more, I asked Mr. Umair if he preferred one country to another, assuming that he would discuss Saudi Arabia because it is a country with many important religious sites, including Mecca, Islam's holiest city. My assumption was reinforced by the images of Mecca that hung on the walls of Mr. Umair's home. To my surprise, Mr. Umair replied, "Countries? What countries? It is all only blowing sand."

Mr. Umair's comments were far from unique, and most laborers shut me down when I asked about religion as they insisted that all Gulf countries are the same. Workers who travel for unskilled and semiskilled positions do not often have the opportunity, money, or time to pursue religious activities beyond daily prayers while working in the Gulf. In addition, most live in camps that are geographically isolated, so very few ever ventured outside their worksites and camps. While migrants are not eager to talk with me about their religious practices, they do want to talk to me about their families and their dreams. They told me jokes to make me laugh and ghost stories to scare me (and if I looked scared, they laughed).

Workers also described their daily lives in the Gulf to me, often with frustration, but they did not make plans for collective action, despite the popularity of labor strikes with workers in India. They recognized they have little chance for collective action. Often they also have immediate economic concerns that informed their decision to migrate. These structural factors reinforce worker precarity. In these circumstances, many workers, even when unhappy with some aspect of their employment, say to me, "Kiya karo?"—an often-used expression that directly translates as, "What to do?" and is used in response to situations that are out of one's control. Even their contracts, meant to keep them secure in their jobs, had an uneven impact on the most precarious workers.

Chapter 7

THE DEMON OF UNSAFE ACTS

ALMOST A YEAR AFTER MY FIRST VISIT TO THE RIG CONSTRUCTION PROJECT IN Abu Dhabi, as I sat in the shade of a construction crane and ate lunch with a group of Indian men who were building scaffolding at the construction site, a worker fell from the rig and died. When the man fell, all work on the rig stopped. Shocked, my lunch companions hurried me into a Connex manager's office. This was a relatively uncommon time for me, as I had not spent much time with managers in their air-conditioned trailers after my first few visits. Instead, most days I sat with, observed, and interviewed South Asian and Filipino Connex employees who were what the Indian government classifies as unskilled or semiskilled workers. These men worked to build scaffolding and carry heavy loads. As I sat in the office, I worried about the unknown man's family. I was extremely upset about the death—I had spent over two years talking to Gulf migrants and their families. Some nights, I cried when I returned to my apartment after hearing men's stories or seeing their living conditions. Although there were over five thousand men working at the project site and I only knew a small fraction of the five hundred who worked for Connex, I wondered if the man was someone I knew.

At first, staff ran into and out of the office, giving managers updates on what had happened, and it was quickly established that the deceased man was from India. I then sat with managers for hours with relatively little news. After ending one phone call, Alex told me he had learned that the man was employed by one of the companies that supplied laborers to the construction project on a daily contract basis. After hours of waiting, a staff person reported to Alex and his fellow managers that the investigation was finished. According to this person, the investigation found that the worker had been wearing his safety harness improperly and that was the reason for the accident. Although no one had met the man and he did not work for Connex, an air of sadness filled the office as the management reflected on the tragic, and what they saw as a "completely unnecessary," loss of life. In the following weeks, conversations with employees, from managers to laborers, often returned to the importance of safety and knowledge while building a rig.

Worker deaths are not uncommon: on average, ten Indian workers died daily in the Gulf between 2012 and 2018.[1] When the Arabic-speaking Gulf is discussed, the precarious conditions of laborers are often attributed to exceptional practices that are unique to the region and are continued because the wealth garnered from oil rents hampers the development of liberal policies.[2] As the previous chapter described, these focuses on oil rents and khalījī traditions as the roots of illiberal labor practices obfuscate how oil companies contribute to worker precarity. In addition, methodological nationalism obfuscates how Gulf practices, like the kafala system, are deeply imbricated with neoliberal governance globally.[3] Historically, much labor history has relied on the nation-state as the "main analytic or expository frame,"[4] and such framing continues to be important to how we understand labor and corporations. Focusing on migration that crosses national borders does not negate the importance of the state, but it reminds us that nation-states are only one factor informing labor politics. Because research is often focused on the state as a primary category, the regular occurrence of accidents appears to be rare.

Oil companies' roles in shaping labor conditions are hard to find in economic or statistical analyses of labor fatalities and workplace accidents. In these studies, the metrics used to collect information on worker safety present data on accidents per country, not per industry.[5] These analyses reinforce developmentalist narratives that view ineffective state governance, not industry practices, as the cause of workplace accidents. Such assumptions concerning state policies and labor practices are called into question when we compare fatality rates in the oil and gas industry in the Gulf and globally. For example, in the United States, between 2003 and 2013, fatality rates in the oil and gas industry were seven times the national average.[6] Few comparisons, however, are drawn between local oil production sites globally. As a result, accidents are seen as localized and exceptional events.

Accidents, deaths, and environmental disasters connected to oil production, like other extractive industries, are "naturalized and normalized" as the cost of "modernity."[7] During the course of my research, I found that in the context of job sites operating under a looming threat of accidents, oil companies operationalized two ways to mitigate risk: contracting and safety standards. Safety and contracting not only work to mitigate corporate risk, but are also areas where governmental regulations, corporate practices, and worker experiences converge. This engagement with accidents during oil production muddies the geological challenges inherent in contemporary oil production and the role that oil companies' legal and disciplinary practices play in informing the conditions for accidents.

Contracting creates conditions in which workers are forced to work quickly, thereby increasing the risk of accidents. Contracting also is a way to move the workforce from place to place. In order to have a mobile workforce and mitigate corporate risk, safety standards are imposed. This chapter considers how safety is used as a way to create a disciplined, movable workforce and how safety becomes the responsibility of individuals. Because accidents are individualized, corporations mitigate their responsibility for accidents, including accidents involving individual deaths or environmental destruction. The implementation of safety standards, however, is not a simple top-down process. Workers too engage with safety standards and through things such as shared digital images reinforce the individual's role in ensuring safety. Workers' reinforcement of these safety discourses occurs despite the fact that safety regulations and the individualization of risk mean that the families of workers who die on the job have trouble receiving compensation from their employer. Human deaths become line items in corporate reports, subject to new technologies of control and, due to racial and class hierarchies, laborers are treated as disposable.[8] In the case of oil production, the disciplinary practices of contracting and safety shape how we understand and engage with disaster and the disposability of laborers. In particular, they underpin investigations into disasters and corporate legal frameworks that privilege the individualization of responsibility. The result is that risk is displaced onto the most vulnerable.

CONTRACTING AND SUBCONTRACTING

The immense resources needed to build a rig—time, money, materials, expertise, manpower—seem to beg the fragmentation of organization. The actual construction of an oil rig is contracted and subcontracted out to various companies that oversee different parts of the work. In her ethnographic work on the oil industry in Argentina, Elana Shever finds that subcontracting is a neoliberal governing technique that uses "regulatory, disciplinary, and *affective* techniques" to manage workers and encourage workers to manage themselves.[9] Similarly, in the Gulf, hiring subcontracted employees allows large companies to avoid responsibility for workers while still controlling their labor and actions. However, these are not the same contexts or processes even if their features are analogous. In Argentina, the context is privatization and loss of community co-ops. In contrast, my research sites in the Gulf were privatized and highly fractured sites well before my research began. What I find is that as these management apparatuses are implemented, even in spaces that are largely private and unregulated, there is a restructuring of work relationships in which companies are able to avoid as much risk as possible. For workers, this means that the companies are not directly responsible for workers when they are hurt or, worse, killed on the job or for negotiating or enforcing contracts with workers. This process, begun in the 1960s, has worked in conjunction with the ban on union formation to ensure that subcontracted workers are intensely vulnerable to exploitation by their employer and lack the means to address this exploitation.

Contracting between Companies

Connex and the other companies operating at the rig were working on a contract basis with one of the companies commonly referred to within the industry as "supermajors," the six largest publicly traded companies that are not state owned. Although they trade globally under different names, they are commonly known as ExxonMobil, Royal Dutch Shell, British Petroleum (BP), Chevron, ConocoPhillips, and Total S.A. The companies are the descendants of the "seven sisters": the Anglo-Persian Oil Company, Gulf Oil, Royal Dutch Shell, Standard Oil of California, Standard Oil of New Jersey, Standard Oil of New York, and Texaco.[10] These seven companies controlled the oil industry in the mid-twentieth century and, in particular, Middle Eastern oil production.

Contracting and subcontracting are integral to the history of the oil industry. With the exploration of oil in the Gulf in the first half of the twentieth century, oil concessions built on earlier contracts that established a British protectorate in much the Arabic-speaking Gulf outside of Saudi Arabia. In the places under the British protectorate, British Petroleum, a corporation that was majority owned by the British government, played a large role in oil exploration and production. These concessions gave oil companies exclusive rights to search for and develop oil and gas in the countries in question. This model of contracting between a state's land and oil companies that rented the land did not survive the decolonization process intact. In particular, the New International Economic Order and the advent of the Organization of the Petroleum Exporting Countries (OPEC) shifted relations to a more partner-based system in which the oil-producing states of the Gulf were able to gain greater control of and profit from oil productions.[11] OPEC was formed by the five founding members of Iran, Iraq, Kuwait, Saudi Arabia, and Venezuela in 1960. Qatar joined in 1961 and the UAE in 1967. In the 1970s, OPEC drew increasingly negative attention internationally as oil companies attributed the oil crisis in 1973 to political maneuvering by OPEC.[12] Following the Iranian Revolution in 1979 and the war between Iran and Iraq that began in 1980, oil prices started a steady decline until the late 1990s. Nevertheless, the sudden increase of oil prices in the 1970s "transformed a comparatively stagnant business into one of the major international growth industries of that decade."[13]

Today, the supermajors control an estimated six percent of the world's oil, in contrast to OPEC countries, which control approximately 80 percent of the world's proven oil reserves.[14] In addition to their substantial control of nonstate-owned oil, the supermajors are vertically integrated, controlling both upstream and downstream aspects of oil production. Upstream segments, including exploration and crude development, are often their largest revenue generators. Service and supply, such as the building of refineries or drills, are less lucrative. Both upstream and downstream segments are usually contracted and, often, subcontracted out, with slightly more contracting occurring in downstream oil production. While today the process of contracting labor and jobs is increasingly the norm in all economic sectors, the oil industry in the Gulf was at the forefront of this transformation. Contracts to define job parameters and oil concessions have been the bedrock to the oil industry in the Gulf from its beginning, but contracting and subcontracting became increasingly common in the 1960s and coincided with the British decision to leave the Gulf in 1971.[15]

Contracting Labor

One indicator of the increasing prevalence of contracting is seen in who employs workers in the oil industry. Of the companies that participate in the International Association of Oil and Gas Producers' safety indicators annual report, total worker-hours on projects has been increasing for at least the past thirty years. Of the increasing hours, contractors are supplying more and more labor on these projects. In 1986, 544 million hours of work were performed. Of these hours, workers employed directly by oil companies performed 306 million hours of the hours worked, or over 56 percent. The remaining labor was performed by contracted workers. In contrast, in 2013, 3.771 billion hours of labor were performed on oil and gas projects. Of these hours, workers employed by a major oil company performed 821 million hours of work, or slightly more than 21 percent. Again, the remaining work was done by contracted labor.[16] From 2015 to 2018, employees at contractors accounted on average for over 70 percent of the total working hours at oil and gas projects.[17] Contracting leads to fragmentation of the oil industry as roles on oil projects are contracted out and laborers are increasingly contracted from one company to another. It also creates crowded worksites, and in the case of the rig in Musaffah, multiple companies each built a part of the oil rig. Today contracting and safety are mobilized as disciplinary techniques that attempt to homogenize labor so that workers may be easily moved from project to project. In this process, corporations hope that commodities—in this case, oil and labor—will circulate globally with little apparent friction.[18] In the case of labor in the Gulf, I find that contracting, laws, and disciplinary practices like safety work together to create an illusion of a mobile and interchangeable workforce.

Supermajors and the biggest contractors have comparatively few laborers on their payrolls. Instead, they contract laborers from energy service providers. The first time I met Alex, he was in India hiring workers for the Connex rig construction project. The second time I met him, he was hiring workers who would be contracted out to one of the supermajors. For Alex, the process of hiring workers who would be subcontracted out was more stressful than hiring workers for his own company's projects. During our conversations, he referred to the subcontracting of workers as "selling" them; he told me, for example, that workers were regularly "sold" to other companies. In this instance, Alex was hiring pipe fitters who would be Connex employees but would be "sold" to one of the supermajor oil companies. This means that Connex would be the employer of these workers, but they would be working for a supermajor project, under the management of employees of that supermajor or a manager contracted by the supermajor from another company. Hiring these workers was more stressful, Alex told me, than hiring workers for his own project or other Connex projects because he felt these workers had to be a "better quality" when they were being sold to a supermajor.

Unlike Connex employees, there would be no "hiding" of poorly performing workers, as could be done on a Connex site. Alex said he "feels stressed" because he perceived managers at the supermajors as having unrealistic demands when it came to employees and were, in his terms, "too picky."

The language of selling labor is not limited to referring to the work of semiskilled laborers: Alex himself had been sold to other companies to work on various projects during his tenure at Connex. In my research, I found that this form of selling workers to other companies is common practice. The reason I have been given for selling workers is that some companies, and the supermajors in particular, do not like maintaining their own workforce. Many of the managers with whom I worked see it as obvious that subcontracting is preferred. Some explain to me that subcontracting allows supermajors to avoid the cost of employee benefits. Others argue that without subcontracting, the size of the workforce would be unwieldy. One employee told me, "Currently, supermajors hire hundreds of thousands of people; without subcontracting, company payrolls would have to include millions of people." From these managerial perspectives, the commodification of labor and subcontracting go hand-in-hand.

Workers are expected to be easily movable from one location to another. Basically, a good worker, according to managers, is a self-disciplining movable part. Creating disciplined workers is not the only effect of subcontracting. As a result of the practice of selling workers to other companies, workers develop networks that help them acquire future jobs. For Alex, being sold to work at other companies on short-term projects was beneficial when he was hiring workers in Mumbai.[19] This is because when he was working at other companies, he developed a greater familiarity across companies. This rooted him in a network of management and employees, most of whom are from the United States and Europe and circulate through oil projects in the Gulf and globally. As managers move between projects, they come into contact with workers from South Asia, the Philippines, and other areas of the Middle East.

Temporary Workers

The selling of workers highlights the fractured aspects of the oil industry as mini-markets are created. One impact of fractured worksites is that workers are expected to be both fast and efficient. When a company is running behind on a project, managers force workers to work overtime. In addition, companies may hire contracted day laborers to fill certain roles. Today, many companies use subcontracting as a technique to be less responsible for oil spills and as a way to avoid responsibility for labor at sites of production. Subcontracting, from a neo-liberal perspective, is a way to create mini-markets that are more efficient and better able to address their specific niche.[20] The most drastic manifestation of this can be seen with companies that simply hire men out for day work. The man who died at the rig construction project in Musaffah was this type of employee. Men employed as day laborers earn the least of all workers in the Gulf's oil industry and lack many of the benefits that workers employed by larger multinational companies receive. In the years that I have spent observing the hiring of workers for Gulf oil jobs and reading their employment contracts, I have found that companies that specialize in temporary day laborers are usually small and often do not have the standardization of holidays and overtime that large multinational companies observe.

Syed, an Indian who has worked as a manual laborer for Connex for over ten years, told me that the men who work for companies that sell temporary labor are *badqismat*, meaning unfortunate or unlucky, because their employers were not "good."[21] Alex unknowingly agreed with Syed's assessment of temporary laborers' employers and described the workers with such companies as showing up to job sites "hungry and with holes in their boots." Those who work as temporary day laborers may be contrasted with laborers hired by one multinational company but working at another one. Those latter workers are often protected by the norms that regulate international labor for large companies based in western Europe or the United States. These regulations, however, are often overseen by the industry, not by governments. In the case of oil companies, subcontracting has complicated, often negative, effects on workers, and these effects are found systemically throughout the oil and gas industry.

CONTRACTING AND SAFETY

To facilitate subcontracting and the selling of workers, industry standards are a central way to homogenize practices in a fractured workforce. Safety standards, in particular, are a set of universal practices that are invoked in workplaces globally, including at sites of oil and gas production. Companies use these standards to dictate worker action, and concern regarding safety permeated all levels—from the highest managers to manual laborers. Safety standards were discussed regularly in Abu Dhabi by managers and workers while they built the oil rig. Not only was safety actively discussed; safety practices informed the daily operations of oil companies, contractors, and workers. In particular, companies use safety to standardize practices and thereby facilitate interactions among the multiple companies at a single job site. Safety apparatuses are also used to facilitate the contracting of labor and expedite the ease with which workers are moved from project to project and among companies. However, my ethnographic research at the rig construction site and at other sites highlights how contracts and safety that attempt to standardize practices are often unsuccessful. As anthropologists have found in other parts of the world, oil industry practices are often territorialized and do not necessarily create homogenization.[22] Instead, the illusion of homogenization is created as companies subcontract and workers are forced to take on the risks that historically companies held.

Managers and corporate executives hope the ubiquity of safety standards will facilitate the movability of workers globally. Safety practices, tools, and procedures are regularly discussed at all oil projects I have visited. Once a worker has been taught safety standards, selling those workers becomes easier, and oil companies are able to move laborers, similar to machinery, from one location to the other. These practices reinforce the notion that the oil industry is separate from sites of oil production.[23] These practices also rely on workers' disciplining themselves to be safe. Much like other work ethics, safety is a disciplinary technique.[24] Approaches to safety highlight how corporate power structures mimic state governance, with emphasis on both external surveillance of worker practices and internalization of attitudes toward safety. The trend in the oil industry, as in many other contemporary workplaces, is toward replacing labor with human capital: workers are now humans who are "ensembles of entrepreneurial and investment capital."[25] The result of safety training is not necessarily fewer accidents but less organizational responsibility for the accidents that occur and greater risk for workers. Like other forms of biopower, individuals also internalize these standards and self-discipline.

The urgency of the need for additional workers on projects and the subcontracting of workers for other companies meant that there was little time for on-the-job training, so workers need to be already trained in the jobs for which they are hired. In the case of subcontracted workers, this is even more important because workers who do not meet the contracting company's expectations may be sent home. The hiring company then loses the money it spent to "bring the applicant over" in the first place—for example, the cost of plane tickets, visas, and fees paid to Indian recruiters. In addition, the hiring company will not be paid for the subcontracted worker who does not meet standards. Safety facilitates the selling of workers between companies and the hiring of subcontracted labor. Like employment contracts, which become symbolic of one's political agency and ability to consent to working conditions, safety practices are mobilized to mitigate corporate risk. As a result, risk becomes increasingly put on individual workers.

Having a good safety record often has a direct impact on a company's profit and a manager's salary, and safety performance indicators are the standard by which companies' safety records are evaluated. Fatalities and lost workday cases are all carefully recorded and then measured against the total number of hours worked in a company. The scale of this metric is huge, and the fatal incident rate is measured against every 100 million worker-hours in a company, while lost time injury is measured against every 1 million hours worked. This generalized surveillance of labor is punctuated by fatalities or lost days. Scott, a manager at Connex, explained to me the importance of safety indicators. He told me that every company has a "clock that started ticking" and would "restart" as soon as an accident or fatality was recorded. How high a company could get the clock before it reset is a matter of pride for the management, and this metric is a way companies are ranked and awarded contracts. For managers, the importance of hours without incident is reflected in managers' bonuses and their ability to negotiate additional work with their company. Finally, this clock also has an emotional aspect, reflecting to a certain extent the feelings of the managers in relation to their employees—those toward whom the managers felt a personal responsibility.

Although managers tell me the ultimate responsibility for ensuring that high-quality work is finished safely and on time is theirs, they see and describe workers as integral to this process. Managers describe this emphasis on quality work that is finished quickly and safely as "stressful," and they understand that both their current pay and their future work are directly related to quickly and safely finished work. Laborers at oil projects also tell me that this emphasis means they are often required to work "too much" overtime and to sit through safety presentations "too many times."

On one of my visits to the rig construction site near Abu Dhabi, it was clear Alex was upset. As he walked through the job site, he stopped the supervisors he oversaw, asking questions and making small corrections. This was unlike his usual, more hands-off oversight. As he turned to return to his office, I saw a wave of relief pass through the workers. Curious, I hurried after him. When I caught up with him, Alex told me he was "really upset about a near accident" and "worried about the safety of his men." This near accident had occurred the previous day at the project site.

In order to ensure safe working conditions after this, Alex planned to have daily safety checks and to begin sending memos to supervisors who spent time on the rig overseeing workers. He was going to "put pressure" on his staff—the same pressure he felt from his boss—so that there would be no safety violations.

During our conversation, Alex described the near accident as a failure by individuals to understand and properly perform safety practices. He was also concerned that an accident would ruin Connex's "clean" safety record. Attempting to explain to me why he was so upset, Alex told me, "Safety is very important, but not everyone understands this." He continued, "Because of ignorance of safety rules, lack of knowledge, or miscommunication [among workers] we had a near accident." Here, Alex describes safety as a concept that individuals must internalize and act on in order to avoid disaster. Alex is not alone in his approach to safety. Throughout the industry, when explaining the cause of an accident, reports usually center on how individuals or low-level managers failed to follow safety procedures.

The International Association of Oil and Gas Producers provides six possible categories into which the cause of accidents fall:

1. Process (conditions): Organisational: Inadequate training or competence
2. People (acts): Inattention/Lack of Awareness: Improper decision making or lack of judgment
3. Process (conditions): Organisational: Inadequate work standards/procedures
4. Process (conditions): Organisational: Inadequate supervision
5. Process (conditions): Organisational: Inadequate hazard identification or risk assessment
6. People (acts): Following procedures: Improper position (line of fire)[26]

Two of these causes clearly specify individual errors as the cause of accidents. What is striking about the other causes (those listed as organizational) is that the precipitating cause of an accident still falls on a low-level manager who is improperly adopting industry standards.

When accidents do occur, the official reasons documented for the accidents usually focus on individual errors as opposed to structural conditions, which allows corporations to displace risk from the corporation to individual employees. Thus, a focus on safety not only facilitates the selling of workers and contracting between companies; it also mitigates corporate risk. Individual accountability hides larger structural issues, including the role contracting plays in creating hurried worksites where people work long days and, they told me, fear losing their job if they do not work quickly.

THE TEMPORALITY OF CONTRACTING

Often elided in the focus on individual safety is the temporality that contracting creates. The time frame of the project and the quality of the work are ruled by contracts that set the requirements and expectations for all of the corporations working together. At each company working at the rig construction project in Abu Dhabi, a project manager spent most of his day with corporate lawyers, defining the parts of the contract for which his company was responsible. I learned more about this in 2017 when I visited Alex at another construction project in the Gulf. At that time, he had been promoted by Connex to the position of project manager. When I congratulated him on his promotion, he rolled his eyes and complained, "Now, my brain constantly hurts. I am not sure it is worth the money. I am forced to spend all day reading the tiniest little lines of a contract. Talking to a lawyer. Arguing with [construction managers] at other companies." These arguments, he told me, usually revolved around which company's fault it was that the project was behind. The stress of contracting was also present at the construction project in 2010.

At Connex, many of the employees I met built scaffolding, and some workers performed menial labor. During my research at the rig in Musaffah, managers explained to me that the pacing of building a rig was set by the completion of other contractors building their portion of the rig. For everyone working at Connex, this meant that long periods of time were spent waiting for other groups to finish their work or working forced overtime as Connex attempted to complete its contracted work within the time limit specified. For managers, this episodic temporalization felt consistently stressful, as they spent their days waiting to begin work followed by long workdays. During these periods, Connex managers also negotiated with managers at other companies concerning when their work could begin or when they expected to complete a specific job. Supervisors repeatedly told me, "Time is of the essence." Speediness, in particular, is financially lucrative as their income depends on meeting contract deadlines. This was particularly true of their bonuses, one project manager explained to me, which they could receive only if they finished their work on time. He continued to tell me that he was worried about this bonus because Connex was behind on its current phase of the project. Frustrated, he explained this was "not my fault"; the subcontractor in charge of welding was behind on that portion of the work. Once the welders finished, Connex employees were working overtime seven days a week to meet the company's contracted deadline.

In 2010 and 2011, Connex was behind on its contracted work largely due to delays by other contractors. Its management simultaneously wanted to catch up on the project in the short periods this was possible, and they were also careful to lay the blame for missed deadlines on other contractors. This was common at such projects, as companies often "waited around" and could not start a part of their contracted job until a different company first finished its contracted work. The Connex management used a stipulation in the employment contract to require employees to work overtime once it was possible for it to work on its portion of the construction. While laborers at Connex were paid hourly and reimbursed for overtime, workers responded to overtime in various ways. Some employees were delighted to earn the additional income, and many chose to work overtime regularly. Echoing a sentiment I heard from multiple migrants, Mohammed told me that he did not mind working overtime because "I come here [to Abu Dhabi] to work and save." But some workers did not want to work overtime. For example, Firhad told me he wanted a day to pray, sleep, and relax.

For many laborers with whom I spoke, waiting to work and then working over-time reminded them of the temporality of farming.[27] Ramchandra, one employee from northern India whose family owns a small farm, explained to me that in India, he would "hire himself" out to work in others' fields, and this meant there were "some days" of resting that would be followed by long, hard days of planting or harvesting. At the rig, Ramchandra told me, normal workdays would shift to long hours of pulling wires or building scaffolding. Similarly, men often describe the temporality of their employment in the Gulf as a couple of years of hard work, followed by a few months of resting at home before once again looking for a job in the Gulf and performing hard work.

WORKER ENGAGEMENTS WITH SAFETY

Through the deployment of safety, we find that the temporality of contracting and safety policies structure an employee's workday and also help structure the workforce. Here, I focus on the atomization and disciplining of subjects. This subject fashioning attempts to get migrants to discipline themselves and inhabit a middle-class subjectivity. It also assumes that migrants will begin to assess risk and take this risk on as individuals, a process that resembles efforts by recruiting agents and government bureaucrats to cultivate entrepreneurial migrants.[28]

While safety measures are implemented by managers and corporate executives, such practices are not only imposed from above. Rather, workers at job sites often engage in the neoliberal disciplining involved in safety practices. Such practices show that neoliberalism is not fixed but has a "capacity for mutation" and a "dynamic of permanent variation" lent by individuals who are the objects of neoliberal regimes and may actively reinforce such regimes.[29] Verónica Gago explains, "Neoliberalism from below is a way of accounting for the dynamic that resists exploitation and dispossession and at the same time takes on and unfolds in this anthropological space of calculation, which is, in turn, the foundation for an intensification of that exploitation and dispossession."[30] In other words, neoliberal practices are not just pushed from above by governments, international finance organizations, and corporations. Workers also engage with, strengthen, and circulate these practices, and in this section, I take up one manner in which workers engage with safety.

In September 2019, a new depiction of Durga's victory appeared on Instagram accounts of Indians I knew working in the Gulf (Figure 5). In the following days, workers in the Gulf also began to send me this image via text messaging services such as WhatsApp. The image is a play on a traditional depiction of the goddess Durga defeating the demon Mahishasura. By contrasting and contextualizing this reworking of Durga's victory, we find a way that workers situate not only the place in which they live but also the work that they do within a modernizing Hindutva project that is applicable to safety practices.

The image appeared around the holiday of Sharada Navratri, a post-monsoon Hindu festival that celebrates, for nine nights and ten days, the nine forms of the goddess Durga. Popular depictions of Durga's defeat over Mahishasura show her as a many-armed goddess; each arm holds a weapon and the goddess rides a lion (Figure 6). Under the lion lies Mahishasura, who, in traditional images, is often depicted as a buffalo or has the head of a buffalo next to his body. This story of Mahishasura's defeat is from the devotional text *Devi Mahatmya*, first recorded in the fifth or sixth century. In this story, the demon had been granted a boon by gods that he could not be killed by a man or god. Because of this boon, when Mahishasura fought the gods, the goddess Durga was the only one able to kill him.[31]

Like more traditional images of Durga's defeat of Mahishasura, the image that circulated among workers in 2019 showed the goddess with ten arms, wearing

FIGURE 5. Durga Defeats Demon of Unsafe Act.
Source: Instagram and WhatsApp.

FIGURE 6. Durga Defeats Mahishasura.

a red sari, and slaying a man with horns, meant to represent Mahishasura. In popular images, Durga holds weapons that include the trident, sword, bow, mace, and shield. In contrast, in the image circulating in 2019, Durga no longer holds weapons. Instead, she holds safety gear: ear protectors, a reflective vest, gloves, a breathing mask, and a safety harness.[32] The text on this image reads, "May this Navratri Maa Durga kill the Demon of Unsafe act within you and Give you Blessings to be safe at your work." As Durga defeats "the Demon of Unsafe act," a man wearing safety gear stands next to her, his hands clasped in devotion.

Certain features of this image work to reinforce safety as a self-disciplinary practice, as well as one that is aligned with modernity and Hinduism. First, the connection between Hinduism and contemporary oil company practices is overt in the image, as the safety gear supports. In addition, the demon Mahishasura represents the forces of chaos.[33] "Unsafe acts" also create chaos through accidents and the disruptions caused. Finally, the image promotes a self-discipline in which individuals seek to end the "unsafe act within" the body or habits of the worker. This resonates with neoliberal self-cultivation that in India's Hindutva, or Hindu nationalist, politics extends to cultivating oneself as not only an entrepreneur but also a follower of upper-caste Hindu practices.[34] Through these resonances, the goddess and the importance of her story are brought into the daily lives of Indians working in the Gulf. The image reinforces a perspective in which the tenets of Hinduism and its gods are effective and translatable into the realm of safety. The image also closely aligns with the association that Hindu nationalists make between upper-caste practices and modernity.[35] Through circulating such images on social media, a safe workplace is no longer the movable, dislocated space imagined by oil companies. Rather, Hindu practices and beliefs inform and shape engagements with practices that are often seen as modern and globally applicable. As oil companies train and enforce safety procedures, they encourage workers to self-discipline themselves to become modern, mobile labor. Workers depict these disciplinary practices within a Hindutva modernity through depictions such as Durga defeating an unsafe act.

STATE LAWS AND CORPORATE RISK

Workers internalize and advocate safety practices as their managers monitor their activities. While safety standards are internationally standardized, the day-to-day implementation of these practices is often left to the oversight of corporations. State policies and laws have facilitated an increasingly common trend in which corporations, not states, are responsible for regulating themselves. Perhaps unsurprisingly, corporations overseeing themselves means that there is often less accountability for corporations.[36] Corporations regulate themselves in multiple aspects of their operations, including safety practices. Overall, the emphasis on safety has some positive effects for workers as companies take steps to ensure that there are safer worksites and compliance with international standards. But safety, in conjunction with contracting, also allows companies to mitigate their own risk at the expense of workers. In many cases of worker subcontracting, the practice allows companies to acquire labor without training employees and without paying them fair wages. Subcontracting also allows a company to avoid negative impacts on the "accident-free" hours it reports. This is not because contracting leads to safer worksites: the general trend among contractors is that they have higher fatality rates and higher rates of lost hours due to injury than do the supermajors.[37] For example, in 2018, of the thirty-one deaths reported at oil and gas projects, twenty-nine were by employees of contractors.[38] Instead, contracting hides accidents from a company's hours. The result of contemporary employment practices is that workers have fewer rights and fewer opportunities to agitate for better working conditions, and they experience greater precarity.

In the UAE, labor laws largely favor business interests, and the families of workers have limited legal ability to sue the government. According to UAE labor law, companies must pay the families of workers who are killed or hurt to the point that they are no longer able to work. Article 149 of Labour Law No 8 of 1980 provides guidelines for compensation when workers are killed or seriously injured on a job site. The amount workers are compensated is at minimum AED 18,000 (approximately US$4,900) and the maximum is AED 35,000 (US$9,529). The calculation is twenty-four months of pay at the employee's most recent salary. Based on the hundreds of work contracts I have seen during my research, the maximum payout amount is quite low. While many manual laborers fall between the minimum and maximum payout, the two-year salaries of employees who perform jobs that require some training or experience often exceed the maximum required payout. This payout is not automatic, and the law contains stipulations as to when a company is not required to provide this money to a deceased worker's family. Article 153 of Labour Law No 8 clearly lays out that renumeration is not necessary if the worker purposefully harms himself, is under the influence of drugs or alcohol, or harms himself while committing a crime. In addition, companies do not have to compensate the worker's family "if he has willfully violated safety instructions displayed conspicuously at the place of business." Given the ubiquity of safety signage at construction sites in the Gulf, this article of the law provides companies with the ability to establish for themselves if these signs were "willfully violated." The discourse of willful violation and the assumption that safety instructions are self-evidentiary also means that states regulate corporate safety practices only to the point of ensuring proper signage at job sites. For the worker who died, the company could argue that not wearing his harness properly made the company not responsible under this article of the law.

I do not know what happened with the worker who fell from the rig and died when I visited Musaffah. I do not know his name or if his family received compensation for his death. There is a high likelihood that the family received nothing. Facebook groups and newspapers report a myriad of ways companies try to avoid compensating families when their loved ones die. For example, in 2017, a family whose male relative recently died while working in the UAE wrote to the legal advice column of *Gulf News*, an Emirati newspaper, outlining the difficulties the family faced in receiving compensation after their family member died at his job site. According to the family, the company claimed that it was not required to pay anything for the man's death because the employee had signed a contract with the company stipulating that it "will not be responsible for any injury, or death, at a company worksite." The legal advice columnist responded that such a contract was in violation of the UAE's labor law and therefore invalid. In order to collect this compensation, however, a family would need to hire a lawyer to navigate the UAE's legal system or hope that their own government interceded on their behalf. The vast majority of the families of Indian migrants are not familiar with the UAE's laws or legal system. Most Indian men working in the most precarious jobs in the Gulf come from areas of extreme poverty, and their families do not have the legal means to navigate the Emirati courts. In addition, the Indian government is slow to intervene for citizens and ask for compensation after the death or injury of a worker, if it acts at all.

THE DEEPWATER HORIZON DISASTER

My first visit to the rig construction site in Abu Dhabi was in late April 2010, just days after Deepwater Horizon's blowout in the Gulf of Mexico that resulted in the deaths of eleven crew members and an uncontrolled oil spill that took months to seal. When the well was finally sealed, 210 million gallons, or approximately

4.9 million barrels, of oil had been spilled into the Gulf of Mexico, making it the worst oil spill in American history. On that first visit to Musaffah, managers told me it was a time of "high stress" due to Deepwater Horizon's blowout. Alex explained to me that this accident seemed to have a direct impact on his work not only because of the scale of the disaster but also because the type of rig being built in Abu Dhabi was the same type as Deepwater Horizon.

In the days after the initial blowout on Deepwater Horizon, international news stories and oil industry chatroom conversations focused primarily on this spill. For Connex managers, the tragedy of Deepwater Horizon was foremost in their conversations. These managers told me that the quality of their work at Musaffah had taken on new, more pressing significance for them. This was particularly the case because the cause of the blowout and who was at fault were still being debated in the news, the industry, and legal contexts. Two project managers for another company working in Musaffah speculated aloud to me that the fault could be a badly made rig. Later that day, Alex told me that he wanted to be sure that "the quality of the work is high" in order to avoid disasters such as Deepwater Horizon. In addition to being of high quality, he told me, work also needed to be done quickly. Interjecting, another manager explained to me that Connex was "behind schedule." The manager continued, telling me that his focus was on "delivering on their end of the contract," that is, finishing their work on the rig within the time frame stipulated in the contract.

Oil company employees describe accidents on oil construction projects as harmful to human life, but also harmful to the environment and the company. An examination of the commonalities and differences in the deployment of safety standards and contracting at multiple sites demonstrates the ways in which rigs are structures that shape the relationships of workers, corporations, and states. This comparison attends to the ways in which corporations attempt to homogenize the production process and how these processes are engaged with locally. This comparison also highlights how corporate methods of risk mitigation have an uneven impact on those who are already most precarious.

Riskier procedures provide a groundwork that give rise to disaster when workers fail to attend to safety practices. Many managers in my conversations after the death of the worker in Abu Dhabi drew parallels between the Deepwater Horizon oil spill and the death of the worker. In addition to the rigs being the same type, managers also pointed out that both involved "human error," "hurried work," and "tragic results," explanations that resemble the categorizations of accidents presented by the International Association of Oil and Gas Producers, in which accidents are often the result of individual error or individual managers' poor decisions.

In the United States, the cause of the Deepwater Horizon oil spill in the Gulf of Mexico was described as a complicated intersection of lack of government oversight and corporate practices that allowed individual error to cause the accident. The National Commission's "Report to the President" highlights that the US Minerals Management Service, with oversight over this and other drilling projects, performed, at best, minimal oversight and allowed British Petroleum (BP) to set the policies and procedures it followed at the Macondo well.[39] However, despite this finding, the report then uses the International Association of Oil and Gas Producers' categories to explain the spill. Ultimately, human error and management issues were found to be responsible for the blowout on the rig. While the report addresses the challenges of deep water oil extraction, it does not consider how the greater risks of offshore sites, including higher fatal accident rates and higher rates of oil spills, are created by environmental limits that corporations attempt to overcome.[40] Instead, the authors of the report argue that company managers chose riskier procedures in order to save time.[41] The report also lays blame on individual employees. In the investigation of the events leading up to Deepwater Horizon's blowout and spill, the authors find that crew members on the rig missed some warning signs due to lack of attention and that they also actively ignored other system warnings,[42] which led to a chain of events resulting in the blowout. Crew members were unable to respond to these events properly due to the rapid progression of events, their lack of training, and their own inattention.[43] Such a focus on individual accountability and the errors of low-level management obfuscates that oil is increasingly difficult to access—oil production onshore peaked in the 1990s, and since that time, offshore oil production has rapidly grown.

Inspectors describe a series of individual errors and attempts to speed up production by low-level managers. Workers in the oil industry similarly emphasized the role of individual actions in causing the disaster. In the days following the beginning of the Deepwater Horizon spill, people employed in the oil and gas industry throughout the world began to speculate as to the cause of the disaster. At the Oil Drum, an online forum for discussions regarding oil and gas production by people working in the industry, comments by members of a chatroom often reiterated that each worker has an individual responsibility to avoid accidents. While conjecturing as to the cause of the Deepwater Horizon spill, one person, using the screen name Rockman, highlighted how accidents are caused by individuals: "In my 35 years I've never seen even one accident of any sort that was a result of 'bad luck.' Almost 100% of the time it was human error: a poor plan or a poor execution of the plan." Another, with the screen name With the Doves, supported Rockman's analysis and individualization of cause. With the Doves also alluded to how contracting may hinder safety as companies rush to finish work in the time stipulated in their contract. With the Doves wrote, "From my understanding they were rushing at the end, and took their eye off the ball. Maybe because every minute out there costs a lot of money. With that incentive, there is always a possibility that people will rush. Safety is a cultural thing. It comes down to good habits and thoughtful people." With the Doves then likened these types of safety practices to wearing a seatbelt, which they said was "a habit" they did "without thinking." This general approach to safety as a "culture" or "habit" was generally reinforced throughout the chatroom, an approach that emphasizes individual accountability and the need for individuals to discipline themselves to follow safety practices.

Emphasis on individual worker responsibility worked in conjunction with contracting practices between companies to mitigate corporate risk.[44] Contracting and subcontracting have benefits for corporate profits and help reduce corporate liability.[45] In Suzana Sawyer's analysis of an indigenous Ecuadoran movement against the American oil company Texaco and a subsequent lawsuit, she details the history and current ramifications of such corporate practices.[46] Sawyer finds that the corporate model of limited liability companies (LLC) allows large subsidiary corporations like Texaco to argue that they are not responsible for subsidiary company actions even if "the parent is the controlling holder or owns the subsidiary 100 percent."[47] This corporate structure allowed Texaco to argue that it was not responsible for the environmental damages its subsidiary caused in Ecuador in the 1990s. Texaco's structure and history have similarities to the structures of BP and Connex. Despite the fact that BP is a private limited company (Ltd.), a legal category for companies available in the United Kingdom, Canada, and Ireland, the legal structures of limited liability and private limited companies shield shareholders from personal responsibility. Much like the case with Texaco, an examination of Deepwater Horizon's spill and the legal consequences on BP after the spill demonstrate how contracting shields corporations from negative consequences and displaces the financial and environmental costs of oil spills.

Five years after spilling over 200 million gallons of oil into the Gulf of Mexico, BP settled the civil lawsuit brought by the US government and five American states located on the Gulf of Mexico for US$20.1 billion.[48] BP was the corporation most commonly connected in the news to Deepwater Horizon spill. However, after years of arbitration among stakeholders, BP was not the only company held legally and financially responsible for the spill. Rather, its "gross negligence" and the billions of dollars it had to pay in claims were spread through a network of contracted companies and also subsidized by American taxpayers. One such company is Transocean, Ltd., the corporation that owned Deepwater Horizon and leased Deepwater Horizon to British Petroleum for US$1 million per day.[49] Transocean settled with the US government for a US$211.7 million payment to the victims of the spill in 2015. Also, in 2015, Halliburton, the cement contractor for Deepwater Horizon, signed a US$1.1 billion settlement with the US government.[50] Not only did these companies settle with the government and spread the cost of the spill, but BP also received settlement money directly from its contractors at the site. For example, BP leased the Macondo well from the US government along with two other companies, and, at the time of the spill, BP held a 65 percent interest in the well. The next largest stakeholder was Anadarko Petroleum, which held a 25 percent nonoperating minority interest in the project. In October 2011, Anadarko settled all claims with BP for US$4 billion. Anadarko also transferred its 25 percent stake in the Macondo well to BP and was indemnified by BP for all costs relating to the oil spill. In addition to Anadarko, MOEX Offshore owned a 10 percent nonoperating ownership interest and agreed to pay BP US$1.07 billion in May 2011.[51] Other settlements between BP and its stakeholders include the 2011 agreement with Cameron International, the company that manufactured and sold Deepwater Horizon to Transocean in 2001, in which Cameron International agreed to a US$250 million settlement with BP to settle all claims related to Deepwater Horizon.[52]

Despite these settlements, American taxpayers continue to pay for the bulk of the oil spill. Notably, tax laws allow BP to deduct from its federal tax liability the majority of the money it paid in the final settlement.[53] This ability to deduct settlement money is not unique to this case. For example, Exxon-Mobil managed to deduct "almost all" of its $1.1 billion settlement for the 1989 *Exxon Valdez* oil spill in Prince William Sound, Alaska, because US federal tax code does not specifically prohibit corporations from making deductions based on their payment of settlements after an oil spill.[54] As a result of these tax codes and the specificities of the settlements federal agencies made with BP, BP is able to deduct US$15.3

billion from its tax liability based on the US$20.1 billion in payments made in settlements related to Deepwater Horizon.[55] This deduction does not expire: BP can apply it in perpetuity until exhausted. If we consider BP's reduced tax burden, in conjunction with its settlement with its contractors, it appears that BP had a net gain of approximately US$620 million (plus the value of Anadarko's interest in the Macondo well). This is possible given corporate structures in which contracting mitigates corporate risk.

CONCLUSION

Managers at oil projects work in an increasingly fragmented worksite with pressure to meet short deadlines created through project contracting. In order to manage workers effectively, they mobilize safety practices as they attempt to homogenize the skills of the workforce and create a standardization of worker practices. In the cases of worker death or injury, we see how contemporary contracting puts increasing risk onto individuals. This increased allocation of risk onto the most precarious occurs in conjunction with an increased emphasis on safety standards. Managers and oil company executives imagine safety standards and contracting as practices that transform workers as movable parts. While this ever-substituting realm of workers invokes images of a Fordist machine efficiency, this view of labor is a thoroughly neoliberal construct.

While events such as the death of a construction worker or an oil spill are labeled "crises," they are regular occurrences in the oil industry. Through examining the resonances between the oil spill in the Gulf of Mexico and the death of a worker in the Arabic-speaking Gulf, the consequences of corporate risk mitigation practices, particularly contracting and safety standards, become apparent. Investigations into the cause of accidents emphasize individual actions, thereby obfuscating the ways in which the oil industry creates profit, maintains control, and alludes liability. Through such processes, wealth is increasingly pooled into the hands of a few, while workers become increasingly precarious.[56] Indeed, corporations mobilize the instability of crises to create lasting policies for greater wealth production.[57] This is made possible as responsibility is diffused through the proliferation of contracts that circulate within legal spaces.[58]

As safety measures are used to displace risk, they are also mobilized in hopes of creating a self-disciplined, mobile labor pool. The circulation of images, expertise, and personnel, in conjunction with labor laws and safety practices, means that issues around safety are presented as fixed standards despite their variation in actual practice and without regard for the structural and environmental factors that increase the likelihood of accident or disaster. Workers engage with and reinforce corporate risk allocation as they approach safety as an individual responsibility and detach it from structural issues. The result is that those who are most vulnerable experience further precaritization. In the Conclusion, I examine another way laborers describe and respond to their own precarious circumstances.

Conclusion

ENDURING DEBTS

IN A VILLAGE OUTSIDE HYDERABAD, I MET RANI, A YOUNG MOTHER whose husband had died while working in the Gulf. Rani, her husband, and her mother-in-law had borrowed large amounts of money to facilitate Rani's husband's migration and used the family's farm as a guarantee on the loan. Before her husband's death, Rani used the money her husband sent from the Gulf for household expenses and to make payments on the large debt the family incurred to facilitate her husband's migration. Despite regular payments, the debt was borrowed from a local moneylender at a high interest rate, and the family still owed the majority of the debt. After her husband's death, Rani and her mother-in-law continued to work on their farm, but they were forced to borrow additional money for daily expenses. Throughout the years that I have known them, their debt has continued to grow.

Crushing debt is also accrued by men who are injured on job sites in the Gulf, a debt exacerbated because those injured do not regularly receive compensation for workplace injuries. In a village close to Rani's I met Latikha. Her husband, Darsh, had worked in the Gulf as a laborer for eight months, but his employer sent him home after an accident on the job site caused an injury that no longer allowed Darsh to work. When he returned to India, Latikha told me, the people who lent him the money "tortured him" by harassing him and asking for payment on his loan. According to Latikha, Darsh could neither work nor pay his debts, and this led him to commit suicide.

In response to the death of Rani's husband, Darsh's suicide, and other tragedies in the area that are related to Gulf migration, a man living in a village outside Hyderabad, Mr. Bashar, began a community organization that attempts to help workers and their families. He had attended a few years of school, and his family owned a small farm. Before beginning his organization, Mr. Bashar had worked almost twenty years in Bahrain and the UAE as an unskilled laborer on oil projects, where he carried heavy loads from one place to another. While he worked for what he called a "good company," he saw many Indians who had "bad" employers. When he returned home, he told me that he also saw how families faced hardships when family members died or were hurt while working abroad. In his words, "I saw so much suffering . . . so I decided to return home and dedicate my life to helping people." Now, Mr. Bashar brings men who once worked in the Gulf, the families of those who died while working in the Gulf, and their neighbors together to "put pressure" on the Indian government. He and his supporters hope the government will advocate for the better treatment of Gulf workers and pressure companies to provide compensation for families whose family members died there.

Mr. Bashar employs a two-part strategy of first raising public awareness of the issue and then using public pressure to influence government action. First, returned workers seek to draw public attention to deaths. At the same time, the organization attempts to fundraise within the deceased's community to pay for the repatriation of the deceased's remains. The deceased's family often joins in by emotionally appealing to their community and local government for the funds. The second half of Mr. Bashar's strategy focuses on creating public awareness of the issues. He does this by having local newspapers cover his rallies and, if funds allow, placing advertisements in local papers. He also circulates images of the deceased. Mr. Bashar believes the most effective images are either photos of the dead body or pictures in which the deceased's children hold a picture of their father. These images circulate on flyers, in large posters that he prints, and on social media sites; WhatsApp and Facebook are the most popular today. Using this visibility, Mr. Bashar and his associates ask, in print, social media, and rallies for the government to better protect workers. Often these requests are quite specific. For example, his group asked that a company that had mistreated workers be blacklisted and for the government to reinforce this blacklisting. In addition, the organization targets specific local state officers whom Mr. Bashar and his colleagues believe to be corrupt, and they demand that the government step in to end this corruption.

With his group, Mr. Bashar and other returned workers target local government officials, asking that they ensure the rights of citizens. Other groups, while not as active as Mr. Bashar's, are similarly composed of returned migrants who join together around a single accident that resulted in death or injury to workers who originated from the area in which the group operates. These groups seek to disrupt and challenge a system that allocates risk to individuals and instead demand that the government take a larger role in ensuring the well-being of workers and caring for workers' families in the event of injury. These strategies are not unique to returned Indian laborers. In 2016, an Indonesian community that sued an oil contractor received approximately US$1,000 per individual who died on the job site. Furthermore, in 2019, a former employee of the embassy of the Philippines told me that he felt his government has become proactive in following up on worker deaths. He connected his government's advocacy to Filipino workers using social media campaigns, particularly hashtags, to put pressure on the government to either help workers in abusive situations or act as intermediaries between workers and their employers.

Claims based on citizenship made by these community organizations are not unique to workers in the Gulf. David Bond, in his work on the US government's response to the Deepwater Horizon oil spill, found that individuals who were sickened by the spill confronted federal employees and asked for financial help, but because they did not fit into the categories created by the government for disaster relief, they were unable to access programs providing assistance.[1] In Aihwa Ong's discussion of citizenship and neoliberal governance, she finds a "perception that citizenship encoded in law is no guarantee of protection for the marginalized. In many cases, market intrusions and displacement have created areas for the activation of citizenship in demanding state delivery of resources and justice."[2] Indian migrant groups that are making claims regarding the government's need to protect their rights from government and corporate abuse are not relying on the market to bolster their voices. Rather, former migrants and their families bring their own understandings of community and responsibility to the fore.

As community organizations ask the state to intervene with corporations operating outside the territories of their own state, they critically interrogate the boundaries constructed by the state and corporations—boundaries that are used to naturalize power. Like citizenship claims made around other types of material infrastructure, claims made by community organizations highlight how people are demanding changes to governmental practices, procedures, and personnel.[3] Such claims call into question oil companies' separation from the sites of oil production and also insist on the inclusion of workers' homes when mapping the impact of oil production. The inclusion of the families of deceased workers demonstrates that while oil companies seek to present themselves as corporate citizens with moral, legal, and ethical responsibilities to the communities in which they operate, these promises are not kept.

COMMUNITY ORGANIZING IN NEOLIBERAL TIMES

Government reforms and corporate management policies displace risk onto the most vulnerable of workers, and, simultaneously, the role of states to provide assistance is minimized and social services are privatized. At times, migrants respond to these changes through forming communities. In doing so, they critique dominant discourses that celebrate the power of the market and view citizens as individual, rational actors.[4] Instead, laborers describe a personhood that is based on interconnection and social obligation. As migrants advocate for protection, they disrupt neoliberal logics and call attention to shifting state responsibilities.

The idea of difference is used to explain why individuals classified as vulnerable require permission from the government in order to migrate to the Gulf. It is also used as a reason why some workers are abandoned—they are described as exceptional or as not being properly motivated. However, in the case of Mr. Bashar, the articulation of difference becomes a politically active space where rights may be claimed. It also becomes a foundation on which solidarities may be formed.[5]

When looking at the relationships between states and corporations, citizens and laborers, assumptions arise that associate entrepreneurship, citizenship, and modernity. Government bureaucrats, recruiting agents, and volunteers helping laborers in the Gulf often invoke a healthy work ethic as a way for all Indians to participate in the middle class. Laborers, they argue, must cultivate entrepreneurship to be good representatives of India's brand. In these conversations, government officials and company owners envision migrants as rational economic actors—individuals choosing to migrate in their own best financial interest. These models ignore the historic activities and contemporary networks that influence the contours of Indian labor migration. In addition, such models obfuscate the role of oil companies in structuring state policies and omit the motivations and experiences of migrants. They also naturalize and reify contemporary labor hierarchies in which the vast majority of upper-level managers come from western Europe or

North America and most laborers come from South Asia or the Philippines. The reasons for these racial hierarchies are often explained by scarcity and surplus and, in doing so, inequalities become naturalized.

Individuals enact states and corporations as coherent entities in their everyday interactions.[6] Despite the ways in which states and corporations are made through social relations and practices, they appear to exist separately from society. This separation obfuscates the power dynamics at play and the ways in which both states and corporations generate knowledge of populations through abstraction.[7] Workers are understood as statistics and dislocated from their homes and sites of labor. Oil companies mitigate their own risks associated with accidents and worker deaths by labeling reoccurring disasters as unique crises, using contract law, and managing workers through emphasis on safety. The result is that risk is individualized and transferred to the most vulnerable. This occurs as corporations restructure areas to make them more amenable to their own interests. Critically investigating how the partnerships between states and corporations are structured and how workers engage with their worksites demonstrates how businesses act like states and vice versa, without being reducible to each other.

Such trends highlight the restructuring of the oil industry in the era of decolonization and the increased logic of neoliberalism that pervades the oil economy. The naturalization of global inequalities and the scale of the oil industry attempt to erase labor from discussions of oil, but traces remain.[8] In attending to labor and the process of labor migration, it becomes apparent the reasons for migration extend beyond economic models; the impact of colonialism and corporations on contemporary politics, the economy, and society; and the ways in which oil companies have shaped and continue to influence governance. Through these analyses, we see that inequalities are naturalized, reinforced, contested, and refused by participants in the process of migration.

Managerial practices at oil companies and colonial policies were integral to the formation of the Gulf's contemporary racialized labor hierarchies. Historically, managerial apparatuses of oil companies emerged in sites of conflict over working conditions but were also informed by the materiality of oil, neoliberal philosophies regarding development and management of markets, and the economics of oil rents.[9] These managerial apparatuses were developed in conjunction with bureaucratic practices that were used to manage migration by colonial and postcolonial states and oil companies.[10] Practices and apparatuses are not fixed; rather, by their very nature, they are continually in formation. Today, contracting and subcontracting, at both the construction site in Abu Dhabi and globally, however, create a temporality of urgency that creates a fertile space for accidents, loss of life, and damage to the environment that are exceptionalized as accidents but in fact are part of how the industry operates. Legal structures created by contracting and subcontracting, the implementation of safety practices, and perspectives on safety as an individualized disciplinary practice facilitate oil companies as they displace risk to the most precarious.

Examining the practices of participants in this migration offers us new insights into studies of capitalism and state power. Capital and the state are two closely related systems of power. Despite the ways in which they are mutually imbricated, one is not subsumed within the other.[11] These systems create and reinforce contemporary hierarchies and ultimately designate some individuals as disposable.[12] This disposability of individuals comes to the fore, in the case of Indians who migrate to the Gulf, as families struggle to eat, workers are killed on job sites, and individuals commit suicide in the face of seemingly insurmountable debts. These avoidable deaths are ignored. States and companies avoid responsibility by categorizing them as unforeseen tragedies or disasters. Deaths are counted only as numbers that are too large to comprehend and appear as footnotes in economic plans. The dead are blamed for not acting as rational actors or not properly modernizing.

Discourses rooted in Gulf traditions or the failure of Indian migrants to best optimize their capacity as laborers may give the impression that labor relations in the Gulf are particular to the area,[13] and the current complexity within the Gulf States is elided.[14] I am particularly interested in how such explanations also ignore how neoliberal policies and ideologies shape governance in the Gulf.[15] It becomes apparent in examining the role of oil companies historically and today in shaping the Gulf's racialized labor hierarchies and labor laws that the precarity of migrant laborers is directly informed by colonial capitalism and neoliberal approaches to labor.

These labor conditions are not unique; they exist globally. In his book *Brutalisme*, Achille Mbembe explicitly connects the extraction of resources, colonialism, and what he calls the brutalization of social relations, or the commodification of social relations, the subjugation and violation of bodies, and the naturalization and reification of difference.[16] Brutalism enables the necropolitical aims of the state.[17] Resource extraction has become increasingly violent and is imbricated with the armed forces and the police.[18] In such contexts, order must be maintained.

Necropolitics uses the logic of difference to order populations that are deemed dangerous.[19] In the process, racialized bodies are excluded from spaces in which they are not wanted, and this is maintained by surveillance technologies.[20] One result is that the erection of borders creates spaces that certain classes are unable to transverse.[21] Such borders are maintained through prohibitions on collective action.

Deaths of workers, abandoned camps, and other tragedies are seen as failures of an individual and are classified as exceptional in order to naturalize economic, health, and social inequalities. But by attending to the process of migration, we are able to attend to how these attempts to atomize individuals are structured and how people experience or refuse disciplinary power.[22]

THE PASTS AND FUTURES OF OIL

Individuals make sense of migration not only through protest but also through invoking poetics, including those of ghosts and dreams.[23] The oil industry in particular is a rich site to explore ghosts and dreams. Government officials often associate oil with technological futures and national security. Migrants and oil company managers describe oil as a substance that allows one to fulfill one's dreams. As one returned migrant, Mr. Sheikh, told me regarding men who want to work in the Gulf, "The villagers don't know about where they are going and the middleman [recruiting agent] sells dreams to him. Villagers only dream of going and flying in an airplane, because he has always dreamt of this." Such dreams by migrants are often at odds with the challenging work circumstances they experience in the Gulf, as well as their familial and community obligations.

Financial speculation also conjures futures in which capitalist frontiers expand for a few. When Saudi Aramco offered stock publicly in 2019, shares surged in the first two days, and the state-owned oil company reached a valuation of US$2 trillion.[24] Inequalities were already baked into the projections of Aramco's worth.[25] Few individuals are needed to run an oil rig, but the oil infrastructure, such as building the rigs, maintaining refineries, and laying pipelines, to name just a few, requires millions of workers annually. It is labor, after all, that allows oil to become a commodity. The labor and relationships needed to transform oil into a natural resource become clear in examinations of the migration process, as do the processes of dispossession and debt accumulation that create labor.

Thus, while oil promises dreams, migrant laborers and oil company managers also see oil as a specter that foreshadows future ruin. In 2018, Alex and I were both in England—he was there with his children to visit family, and I was there for a conference. When he saw on social media that I was nearby, he sent me a message, and we arranged to meet at a pub. As we drank a beer and chatted about our children, Alex sighed. "I work for the devil, no?" Quickly our conversation turned from light banter to self-reflection. As we spoke, Alex reflected on how the oil industry in which he has worked for twenty-five years is, in his view, the main driver of climate change. Prognosticating a future where the Earth is uninhabitable, he worried about the future he was building for his children. But, he continued, his pay was much higher than he could earn in other industries. Due to his financial obligations, including alimony payments to three ex-wives and child support for five children, he could not imagine how he could feasibly switch to a job in a different industry. Sighing, he expressed resignation regarding his continued role in an industry that required him to spend long periods of time away from his family, doing work that caused him constant stress, and destroying the planet.

CIRCULATION AND COMMUNITY

> The future can only be for ghosts. And the past.
> —*Jacques Derida* (1994)

Even as people live through and with pain and loss, they laugh, and they dream.[26] Sometimes these dreams are related to the consumption of commodities— workers share dreams of having enough capital to buy the accoutrements seen on TV shows or on display in malls. They sometimes describe this as "getting fat," dressing in shiny shirts, and wearing large watches. Dreams also include harder-to-articulate and less easily translatable ideas—ideas about connection, responsibility, and the future. Migrants described these in what I, as an anthropologist, categorize as poetics. Poetics emerge in such moments as the telling of ghost stories, buying gold for sisters' weddings, and describing the oil rig one is building as a temple. Additional poetics are invoked as communities are formed through circulation. As migrants, recruiting agents and their employees, government bureaucrats, and oil company managers circulate, they too build communities that invoke their own poetics. Circulation builds communities and, through relationships, creates shared values.

Other futures are imaginable and sometimes are heard in old ghost stories. In Abu Dhabi, Udesh, an Indian laborer working for Connex, and I sat staring at the skeletal outlines of the rig when he shared with me a story from his childhood. Udesh had grown up with his grandmother because his parents had passed away when he was an infant and his grandfather had died before his birth. Udesh told me what he described as "a thing he will never forget"—a story about family, community, and social obligations:

> When I was a child, I lived with my daadee [grandmother]. This was because my aunts were all married and lived with their husbands' families and my uncles all worked on ships. So I stayed with my daadee, and every day to my daadee's home came an old man to chop wood. One day, the old man did not come, but I did not think too much about it and my grandmother said nothing about it. But later that night, I was awakened because my dog—you see I had a big dog and I slept with [him] every night—was barking. And I told the dog to be quiet, but he would not hush for a long time. But then, when the dog did quiet, I heard some noise, like somebody crying, [makes crying sound], so I rushed and told my grandmother. My daadee looked, but no one was there. And then she knew. So she said, "You know that old man who chops the wood? Well, he died today, so he must be making the rounds. He must be hungry." She took some spice and mixed it with dal [lentils] and sabji [vegetables] and put it in a pot and set it on the baraamda [verandah]. And I was still scared, so I slept that night with my daadee. But after that night, the man did not come again. You see, the man and my daadee had a contract, because daadee gave him one rupee every day—it was a long time ago—for chopping the wood, and he was returning for his due.

As I listened to Udesh's story, I was struck by the relationships between community members and how one's responsibility to others, especially an employer's responsibility to an employee, is not severed even by death. While the contract between Udesh's grandmother and the man who chopped her wood was not written but formed through relationships and repetition, the appearance of the ghost, demanding that the contract terms be met, demonstrated the power of social obligations. This ghost was a reminder of Udesh's past but also a very real social actor with whom his grandmother interacted. Ghosts are social beings with their own agency, power, and, at times, danger. Ghosts also pass through the boundaries meant to keep people out and remind us of our debts that endure.

Coda

WRITING IN A PANDEMIC

AS I FINISHED THIS BOOK IN THE MIDST OF THE GLOBAL COVID-19 pandemic, it felt odd to write about migration, circulation, and community when I had not traveled in a year. South Asian migrant workers in the Gulf at that time were in extremely precarious circumstances brought on by global economic convulsions. During spring and summer 2020, I spoke with Indian laborers in the Gulf by phone and messaging to learn how the pandemic was affecting their lives.[1] At the time, oil projects had slowed or stopped due to decreased demand and the price wars between Saudi Arabia and Russia. The men I spoke with increasingly feared they would not be paid for their work and that their companies would no longer pay for their housing in camps.

These concerns are far from exaggerated, particularly given the experiences of large numbers of workers who had been abandoned following the 2008 recession. The circumstances in 2020 were more dire. With enforced isolation to contain the spread of the virus and the restrictions on movement between camps for laborers, workers felt uncertain of the future, concerned for their families' health, and worried about how they and their families would survive if they lost their jobs. They were captive to the decisions of governments and companies and had little agency to make their own choices and no good options. They feared that if they stayed in the Gulf, they risked abandonment by their employers and coronavirus infection from cramped living conditions. If they returned to India under lockdown, they feared starvation, mounting debts, joblessness, the possible loss of any small landholdings, and anti-Muslim sentiment.

Like the poor in much of the rest of the world, South Asian migrant laborers were contracting the disease and dying of it at high rates. When I spoke with Saqib, a manual laborer from Bihar, India, who was working in the UAE, he described his living situation. He was confined to a small, dorm-like room with seven other Indian men. All work at his job site had stopped, but Saqib was hopeful that he would receive his next paycheck. Another Indian laborer, Ahmed, who also worked in the UAE, explained to me that work at his factory continued, but his temperature was taken at the beginning of every shift. When he was not working at the factory, he was confined to his room. He was unsure what would happen to him if he became feverish.

I reached out to managers at a couple of companies, and they reported that they were using empty rooms at their laborers' dorms for quarantining those with symptoms. Some companies wanted their workers to leave the Gulf. In Qatar's industrial area, which had high rates of COVID-19 infection, Amnesty International reported that Nepalese workers living there were being rounded up by the police, sent to detention centers, and then deported to Nepal.

During our conversations, migrants voiced concerns that they might catch the coronavirus or be abandoned by their employers, or both. Nevertheless, almost all Indian workers with whom I spoke said that they would prefer to continue working in the Gulf as long as they were paid so they could provide for their families' daily necessities. If they returned to India, they wondered how they would earn money to feed their families. This concern was echoed by the poor in South Asia as lockdowns instituted by their governments hindered their ability to work. Some of the unemployed across South Asia held protests—from factory and construction workers in Pakistan to garment workers in Bangladesh to internal migrants living in India's biggest cities.[2] Protesters said that they would starve if their governments did not step in to feed them or subsidize their lost pay during the coronavirus lockdowns.

Migrants who had to return home to India before they were able to pay their debts would be unable to support their families and buy necessities, and their few assets, such as their small farms, would be at risk of being seized by moneylenders. Raj, who worked in Sharjah, UAE, but was on his biannual leave to his village in southern India when travel restrictions were put in place, foresaw a grim future in which he believed he would soon be "jobless and landless."

Indian migrants said they had little choice whether to remain in the Gulf or return to India, but that neither option was good. When I asked what would happen next, some replied using an Arabic phrase, *tawakkaltu ala-Allah*, indicating that they "trust in God." Others responded by asking me in Hindi, *Kya karo?* (What [am I] to do?). Both responses highlighted the extremely limited agency migrant laborers had at that time to decide their own futures.[3] Despite these circumstances, not all migrants had given up on the "dream of Dubai." One Indian migrant, Rameshwar, said in May 2020, "I came here with a plan to stay for four years. After 15 years, this feels like home and has given me the chance to build a life for my family. Of course, I will come back."[4]

Notes

INTRODUCTION

1. All names used for companies, corporations, and individuals are pseudonyms. While I try to use pseudonyms that are representative of an individual's nationality, religion, and caste, my first priority in choosing names is to ensure the anonymity of all participants. The exception is that real names are used for public figures when speaking in their official capacity.

2. Depending on one's perspective, one prefers to call this area either the Arabian Gulf or the Persian Gulf. While certainly important, the politics of naming this area fall outside the scope of this book, and I use the term *the Gulf* throughout the book.

3. In the villages to which we were traveling, the majority of people worked on small farms of less than two acres. As in India overall, the majority of farmers in these states were in debt, often to moneylenders who charge high interest rates. See Mamgain and Verick 2017; NSS 2014; PLFS 2019.

4. I capitalize *White* when it is used to reference race according to the recommendations set forward by the National Association of Black Journalists in June 2020: "NABJ also recommends that whenever a color is used to appropriately describe race then it should be capitalized, including White and Brown."

5. In India, a *pucca* house is contrasted with a *katcha* house, made of mud, thatch, or other low-quality materials. The preference is for a pucca house. Deepak did not hire Ahmed on behalf of Mancom's client on the day we met, but Ahmed continued

to look for a job in the Gulf. A few months after our first meeting, Ahmed called to tell me he found a job working as a laborer in the United Arab Emirates.

6. MEA 2018.

7. Saudi Arabia has the most noncitizen residents living there, but also the largest overall population. In 2004, foreign residents made up 27 percent of Saudi Arabia's population and, in 2008, 50 percent of the workforce. In the first decade of the twenty-first century, Qatar had the largest percentage of expatriates living and working in the state. In 2006, noncitizens were 81 percent of the population and 92 percent of the workforce. In 2007, they were approximately 80 percent of Dubai's population, and Indians were the largest expatriate community in the emirate. See Pasha 1999; Leonard 2007; Colton 2010; Winckler 2010; Castles, de Haas, and Miller 2013; McGinley 2013.

8. Other categories used by the Indian government include skilled and professional workers—a category that includes doctors, engineers, and bank managers; service workers; trade and business migrants or migrants who start their own businesses abroad; and nontechnical workers, including schoolteachers, typists, and clerks. See Rahman 2001; Rajan, Varghese, and Jayakumar 2010.

9. I use the phrase "oil industry" to refer to the extraction of oil and natural gas and all aspects of production, including the upstream search for oil and gas, the building of oil and gas refineries, and the downstream refining of oil and gas. I focus on oil and gas because of the significance of the oil industry, historically and today, for Indian migration to the Gulf; the symbolic power of oil; and the multiplicity of actors among whom oil production requires coordination.

10. I learned later that the particularly large machine components are used in natural gas pipelines. One use of the giant chains is for anchoring offshore oil rigs.

11. OPEC 2020, 7. One could fill 6,337 Olympic-sized swimming pools with 99.67 million barrels of oil and still have some left over.

12. IOGP 2020, 8.

13. Anthropologists point to scarcity as a social construct. See, for example, Sahlins 1972. For a discussion of nature and capitalism, see Fernando Coronil 1997.

14. See OPEC 2020 for current oil numbers, which are given in the discourse of "proven reserves."

15. As Timothy Mitchell's (2011, 173–199) analysis of the oil crisis in the 1970s demonstrates, this economic model of scarcity and surplus obscures the political and social factors that shape oil prices.

16. Elizabeth Ferry and Mandana Limbert (2009, 3) highlight the importance of labor (as well as time and nature) in resource production. They write, "Nature, labor,

and time converge, as people and states create and contest *resources*—objects and substances produced from 'nature' for human enrichment and use."

17. Ten lakh is 1 million. A lakh equals 100,000.

18. Indian Emigration Act 1922—Considerations of to extend its provisions to journeys by AIR and LAND—unaccompanied domestic servants, etc. NAI, MEA, Emigration, 1954. F. 17–6/54-Emi.

19. Skilled workers engaged by the Bahrein Petroleum Co., Bahrein and Revision of Form of agreement entered into between Bahrein Petroleum Co. NAI, MEA, Emigration, 1948. F. 22–8/48-Emi; Iraq's Request for helping them in their Oil Industry—Note from the Ministry of Mines and Fuel. NAI, MEA, WANA section, 1960. 6-C(34)/60WANA.

20. Letter to Ghatge from Sinclair, 14 January 1954. NAI, MEA, Emigration, 1953. F.6–6/53-Emi.

21. Tsing 2005.

22. Hanieh 2011, 2014.

23. For more on the invisibility of oil workers due to corporate structuring, see Ehsani 2018. For the impact of economic policies on labor in the Gulf, see Hanieh 2011, 2014.

24. Tsing 2015, 2016.

25. For examples of anthropological work on migration that critiques these models, see Holmes 2013; Albahari 2015; De León 2015.

26. Like Ahmed, migrants indicate that their work abroad is not fully explicable as a simple economic calculus. Indian labor migration to the Gulf may be motivated by gendered kinship obligations; positive attitudes toward migration that raise the status of those who migrate; religious narratives linking the Middle East with a supposedly purer Islam; discrimination and violence in India against Muslims, Dalits, and other minorities; and recruiting processes that may rely on workers' personal networks. See also Hansen 2001; Ali 2007; Leonard 2007; Gardner 2012; Wright 2015.

27. Regarding the scale of the oil industry, LeMenager (2014, 94) writes that this scale is "not calibrated to human values—made possible by representational sleights of hand in which racialized bodies, and labor itself, might be occluded through a mediated visibility."

28. In his book, anthropologist Syed Ali describes his detainment by police and deportation from Dubai due to his research on migrant labor. See Ali 2010, x.

29. My gender, race, and nationality influenced my research. My status as an

American White woman allowed me to work in spaces that Indian women are often discouraged from entering. In addition, being a White American conveyed a privilege that allowed me to occupy spaces that Indian migrant laborers are often barred from entering. The recruiting agents and oil company managers with whom I work are also significantly wealthier than I will ever be. For example, in contrast to my crushing student loan debt, many recruiting agents and oil company managers are able to pay for, without taking on debt, their children's Ivy League educations and own homes in multiple countries.

30. As Laura Nader (1972, 289) famously argued, "Studying 'up' as well as 'down' would lead [anthropologists] to ask many 'common sense' questions in reverse."

31. Archival work for this project was conducted at the National Archive of India, the Maharashtra State Archives, the Qatar National Archives, the UAE National Archives, the archive at the Petroleum Institute of Abu Dhabi and the British Library.

32. In his work on the Hydrami diaspora in the Indian Ocean, Engseng Ho (2006, 121–122) explores how the Indian Ocean as a region is formed by the descendants of the Prophet Muhammad. Ho follows the movements of goods and people. These circulating actors may travel on the same ships in the Indian Ocean, but they are imbricated in "social geographies of different shapes." Different social geographies, and the hierarchies contained within them, allowed for actors to begin from multiple starting points and end in a multitude of destinations.

33. There are relatively few Gulf Arabs in this book. This is not to ignore their contributions to and participation in the Gulf's oil industry. Rather, my access to research sites directly affected what nationalities and communities are present in this book. Regarding contemporary labor, Danya al-Saleh is conducting fascinating research on Qatari women working as engineers in the Gulf's oil industry. For my own historic work about strikes by Indian, Persian, and Gulf Arabs working in the oil industry, see Wright 2020a, 2021, n.d.

34. My focus on the highly localized aspects of social lives extends Farina Mir's (2010) work on *qisse*, a Punjabi literary genre. Her analysis of this literary genre during the British colonial period provides insights into how communities are imagined and maintained through a poetics of belonging that is not reducible to nationalist or communal politics.

35. Attention to the networks that shape transnational labor migration helps destabilize the central role of the nation-state in studies of labor. A focus on transnational migration illuminates how laborers build solidarities and how laborers

working outside national borders inform the policies of the nation-state. Much like studies that highlight the histories of colonialism and new nations through examining the movements of goods and people on the Indian Ocean (Metcalf 2008; Bose 2009), I argue that the migration of Indians to the oil fields of the Gulf shaped the postcolonial history of India. This engagement with networks differs from earlier anthropological engagement with social networks that used networks to get out of the bounded nature of communities. That use of networks, by J. Clyde Mitchell, Jeremy Boissevain, and J. A. Barnes, among others, took Max Gluckman's attention to situations and importantly tried to attend to both individual agency and structural forces. Unlike the metaphorical use of networks by Alfred Radcliffe-Brown (1952), the use of networks in this case was analytical. As such, networks are understood to explain relationships within and between groups but are not subsumed to structural forces. Networks, then, allowed researchers to explain the interactions they observed. In addition, the use of networks, Mitchell argued, would help anthropologists overcome the community boundedness of their research. See Mitchell 1969; Boissevain 1974; Kapferer 2006.

36. Some of the taxi drivers I met on that first visit still work in the Gulf—one drives a taxi, a few are now retired, others passed away, and others I lost touch with.

37. Poetics are speech functions that are discursively creative and represent relations; speakers use poetics to create equivalencies. See Peirce 1932; Jakobson 1960; Lempert 2008; Silverstein 2011; Bielo 2019. Poetics, as the work by Jean Comaroff and John Comaroff (1987) demonstrates, may also be used by individuals to critically interrogate their circumstances. Through the deployment of poetics, communities both represent themselves and present contrasts that shape people's understandings of their past. In the *18th Brumaire of Louis Bonaparte*, Karl Marx (1994) explains the need for social revolutionaries to draw their poetry from the future. Fernando Coronil (2019) takes up Marx's call and argues for anthro/history as a space for imagining new futures. Poetics are not only ways to create new futures; they are also useful as methodological tools. Scholars have examined the poetic tropes that inform work in fields such as history (White 1973), gender studies (Mohanty 1988, 2003), and anthropology (Trouillot 1991a, 1991b). These examinations focus on how the politics of knowledge production is situated into existing power structures through the poetic devices of metaphor, metonym, synecdoche, and irony.

38. Derrida 1994.

39. Audra Simpson's (2014, 2017) work informs my engagement with refusal as

both an object of analysis and as a method. Simpson writes, "Refusal' rather than recognition is an option for producing and maintaining alternative structures of thought, politics and traditions away from and in critical relationship to states" (2017, 19). As Franz Fanon (2004) demonstrates, this requires abandoning colonial histories, rejecting European models of development, and actively creating new futures. Achille Mbembe (2021, 224) takes up Fanon to explain how decolonization's "aim was a radical metamorphosis of relations. The ex-colonized would ... create their own time, all the while constructing the time of the world. On the loam of their traditions and their imaginaries." My thinking with and through refusal, poetics, ghosts, and dreams is also informed by Aimé Césaire's (1996a, 1996b) work on poetry and its possibilities; Édouard Glissant's (1997) work on the transformative power of "relational poetics"; Robin D. G. Kelley's (2003) insights on the imagination, dreams, and the future; and Tiana Reed's (2018) article on poetry as criticism.

40. See, Cohn 1980; Amin 1995; Cohen 1996; Stoler 2002, 2010; Murphy et al. 2011; Coronil 2019.

41. Chakrabarty 2000; Eley 2006; Palmié and Stewart 2016.

42. Mitchell 2002, 53; Tsing 2015.

PART I

1. *Saab* and *Sahib* are both Urdu words that mean mister or sir. Reflecting my gender and my age when I first met them, I call most recruiting agents "Mr.," but everyone, including recruiting agents, used *Saab* to refer to Ashraf.

2. Khalidi 2010, 83.

3. Letter from Shaikh Khaled bin Ahmad, Sharjah, to Political Resident, Persian Gulf, Bushire. 19 Jamada ath-Thaniya 1340 (17 February 1922). British Library, 189-S Of/922, *RE* (7), 773. Lord Curzon, the former viceroy of India from 1898 to 1905, spear-headed these treaties in an effort to gain control over Middle Eastern oil for Great Britain and provide a buffer between the Ottoman Empire, Russia, and British India.

4. Anscombe 1997, 44–62; Onley 2007, 2009.

5. Saleh 1991, 3; Onley 2009; Onley and Khalaf 2006.

6. Wright 2020a.

7. Wright 2021.

CHAPTER 1

1. While many of us may not regularly sign labor contracts, part of contemporary

life is clicking "I agree" to contracts we are presented with when our phones update or when we are using a myriad of online services. Most of us do not read the terms of these contracts nor do we understand them.

2. Escobar 1995; Ferguson 1994; Gupta 1995.

3. Cody 2009, 352.

4. Lowe 2015.

5. Chatterjee 1993, 224.

6. Chatterjee 1993, 159-160.

7. During most of my research, the following countries required emigration clearance: Afghanistan, Bahrain, Indonesia, Jordan, Kuwait, Lebanon, Libya, Malaysia, Oman, Qatar, Saudi Arabia, Sudan, Syria, Thailand, United Arab Emirates, and Yemen. Emigration clearance was intermittently required for Iraq.

8. The order that prohibits vulnerable women from traveling abroad for work reads, "Women below the age of 30 years may not be granted emigration clearance, who seek any kind of employment including employment as housemaids, domestic workers, hair dressers, beauticians, dancers, stage artist, laborers, general workers, etc. in any foreign country." See Government of India 1983.

9. For discussions of bureaucracy and paperwork in India, see Hull 2012; Mathur 2015.

10. Prior to 2004, the Ministry of Labour and the Ministry of External Affairs oversaw emigration. Today, the Ministry of Overseas Indian Affairs has been merged into the Ministry of External Affairs.

11. Abandoned workers are discussed in greater detail in Chapter 6.

12. For example, from 2003 to 2010, the Indian government stopped granting permission to emigrate to Iraq for work due to the war and the danger this war posed to Indian migrants. When this ban was lifted in 2010, government officials began granting clearance to "vulnerable" Indians emigrating to Iraq. In 2014, following the kidnapping of forty Indian construction workers in Mosul, Iraq, by ISIS and reports of the killing of thirty-nine of these men, travel to Iraq was once again banned. The Indian government did not formally acknowledge the deaths of these workers until 2018, when DNA testing of a mass grave outside Mosul confirmed their deaths.

13. NDTV 2011. In 2014, the minimum wage in Saudi Arabia was raised to US$320 per month, and in the UAE, the minimum wage was raised to US$409. See Nair, Menon, and Rashad 2014.

14. Rajan, Varghese, and Jayakumar 2010, 280.

15. Prime Minister's High Level Committee 2006, 287–289.

16. Prime Minister's High Level Committee 2006, 60.

17. Consul General of India, Dubai, 2016.

18. Yang 1989; Carter 1995; Bates 2000; Bose 2009; Kale 2010.

19. Metcalf 2008, 136–137, 144.

20. Wright n.d.

21. Bahadur 2013, 32; Mongia 2018.

22. Kale 2010, 6–7, 10.

23. Indian Emigration Act—Proposal for an amendment of. NAI, MEA, Emigration, 1953. 17–6/53-Emi.

24. Lowe 2015, 7, 36, 39.

25. Lowe 2015, 24.

26. Mongia 1999, 2018.

27. Mathew 2016, 54; Mongia 2018, 55.

28. Mongia 2018, 7, 16. For a longer discussion of how this affected Indian emigration to the oil fields, see Wright 2020a, 2021.

29. Countries approved for migration by unskilled workers were printed in the Gazette Notification by the Central Government after receiving approval by Parliament. Indian Emigration Act 1922—Considerations of to extend its provisions to journeys by AIR and LAND—unaccompanied domestic servants, etc. 1954. NAI, MEA, Emigration, 1954. F. 17–6/54-Emi.; "Report on the Working of the Indian Emigration Act (No. VII of 1922) for the Year 1952." NAI, MEA, Emigration, 1953. F. 17–6/54-Emi.

30. Indian Emigration Act 1922—Considerations of to extend its provisions to journeys by AIR and LAND—unaccompanied domestic servants, etc. NAI, MEA, Emigration, 1954. F. 17–6/54-Emi; See also, Emigration Act of 1922, section 02.

31. Indian Emigration Act 1922—Considerations of to extend its provisions to journeys by AIR and LAND—unaccompanied domestic servants, etc. NAI, MEA, Emigration, 1954. F. 17–6/54-Emi; Annual Report on the working of the Indian Emigration Act VII of 1922 and the Rules framed thereunder for the port of Calcutta for the year 1952. NAI, MEA, Emigration Section, 1953. F. 17–6/54-Emi; Material required by Sri Lanka Sundaram M.P. for a paper on the "Effect of Emigration." NAI, MEA, Emigration, 1954. F. 13–9/54-Emi.

32. Limitations on women's ability to emigrate relates to their precarious citizenship status. The domicile requirement for citizenship established in 1949 formalized women's statuses as citizens who were dependent on their father or husband. See Zamindar 2007; "Report on the Working of the Indian Emigration Act (No. VII of 1922) for the Year 1952." NAI, MEA, Emigration, 1953. F. 17–6/54-Emi.

33. Indian Emigration Act—Proposal for an amendment of. NAI, MEA, Emigration, 1953. 17–6/53-Emi.

34. Arendt 1958; Brown 1995; Lowe 2015.

35. Arendt 1958, 268–269, 275.

36. Arendt 1958, 272.

37. Akhil Gupta (2012, 99) argues, in a postcolonial context, that it is through the "discourses and practices of the modern nation-state" that the meaning of citizenship emerges.

38. Indian Emigration Act—Proposal for an amendment of. NAI, MEA, Emigration, 1953. 17–6/53-Emi.

39. Lok Sabha Starred Question No. 1022 for 23rd December 1955 Regarding Proposed Amendment of the Indian Emigration Act 1922. 24 November 1955. NAI, EMI, Emigration, 1955. F. 23–21/55-Emi.

40. Indian Emigration Act 1922—Proposal for Amendment of. Extract from "Important Cases," NAI, MEA, Emigration, 1953. F. 17–6/53-Emi.

41. Indian Emigration Act 1922—Considerations of to extend its provisions to journeys by AIR and LAND—unaccompanied domestic servants, etc. NAI, MEA, Emigration, 1954. F. 17–6/54-Emi.

42. Indian Emigration Act 1922—Considerations of to extend its provisions to journeys by AIR and LAND—unaccompanied domestic servants, etc. NAI, MEA, Emigration, 1954. F. 17–6/54-Emi.

43. Lanka Sundaram, "Effects of Emigration on the Economic Situation of the Population of Selected Asian Countries of Emigration (with reference to India)," 10 September 1954. NAI, MEA, Emigration, 1954. F. 13–9/54-Emi.

44. For example, when discussing the importance of independence for Indians living abroad, one bureaucrat wrote, "We conclude, that the condition of Indians seems really pitiable and naturally after the 15th August 1947 the conditions have much changed and they [emigrants] are right in asking us to intervene in the matter and look after their interests." Skilled workers engaged by the Bahrein Petroleum Co., Bahrein. NAI, MEA, Emigration, 1948. F. 22–8/48-Emi.

45. Grapevine 2015.

46. MEA 1961, 1963; Sethi, C. L. (1963). Letter from C.L. Sethi to Shri A. Dayal. [letter] NAI, MEA, New Delhi, India. Embassy of India, Kuwait. (1964). Embassy of India, Kuwait to the Ministry of External Affairs. [letter] NAI, MEA, New Delhi, India. For a discussion of the case of an Indian mother, Rubiyabai, who contacted the Indian government out of concern for her daughter, Zuleka, and how bureaucrats framed this as trafficking, see Wright 2018, 158–160.

47. This is discussed in greater detail in Chapter 4. See also Wright 2018.

48. Report on the working of the Indian Emigration Act (VII of 1922) for the year 1951. NAI, MEA, S.E.A. Section. 2/54/6551/10003.

49. Annual Report on the Working of the Indian Emigration Act VII of 1922 and the Rules Issued Thereunder during the Year Ending 31st December 1952, of the Ports of Bombay, Porbandar, Bedi Bunder and Port Okha. NAI, MEA, Emigration, 1953. F. 17–6/54-Emi.

50. Report on the Working of the Indian Emigration Act (No. VII of 1922) for the Year 1952. NAI, MEA, Emigration, 1953. F. 17–6/54-Emi; Material required by Sri Lanka Sundaram M.P. for a paper on the "Effect of Emigration," NAI, MEA, Emigration, 1954. F. 13–9/54-Emi.

51. Annual Report on the Working of the Indian Emigration Act VII of 1922 and the Rules Issued Thereunder during the Year Ending 31st December 1952, of the Ports of Bombay, Porbandar, Bedi Bunder and Port Okha. NAI, MEA, Emigration, 1953. F. 17–6/54-Emi.

52. Annual Report on the Working of the Emigration Act. NAI, MEA, Emigration, 1955. F20–2/55-Emi.

53. Skilled workers engaged by the Bahrein Petroleum Co., Bahrein. NAI, MEA, Emigration, 1948. F. 22–8/48-Emi.

54. See Graeber 2010.

55. Achille Mbembe (2017, 85–86) convincingly demonstrates that "reason" was used to deny Africans their humanity and thus legitimate slavery. After slavery was abolished, the idea of difference became central, particularly for colonial administrations, as a means of justifying and legitimating control.

56. NSS 2014, A-18-19, 120.

57. The business practices and social networks of moneylenders were outside the scope of my research, and additional anthropological research should be done in this area.

58. In addition, recruiting agents and the government blame subagents, individuals who are unregistered with the Indian government but often work with the government and recruiting agencies. This is discussed more in Chapter 3.

59. Banerjee 2010.

60. Rajan, Varghese, and Jayakumar 2010, 251–252.

61. The US dollar conversions are for 2010. This corruption could be seen as falling into three registers, much like Stephen Pierce (2016, 7–8) describes corruption in Nige-

ria: it is material insofar as it is taking extra money and delivering papers, discursive in that it invokes a moral critique, and legal insofar as the action is illegal or irregular.

62. Björkman 2015; Pierce 2016.

63. Björkman 2015, 168.

64. Banerjee 2010.

65. Government of Punjab 2008.

66. Government of India (2013, 5) defines trafficking in this way: "Whoever, for the purpose of exploitation, (a) recruits, (b) transports, (c) harbours, (d) transfers, or (e) receives, a person or persons by using threats, or using force, or any other form of coercion, or by abduction, or by practicing fraud, or deception, or by abuse of power, or by inducement, including the giving or receiving of payments or benefits, in order to achieve the consent of any person having control over the person recruited, transported, harboured, transferred or received, commits the offence of trafficking." The proposed Punjabi Prevention of Human Trafficking Act, which correlated with popular perceptions of recruiting agents, had many similarities with the United Nations definition of smuggling of migrants. In 2001, the United Nations' General Assembly passed the United Nations Convention against Transnational Organized Crime. This resolution defines smuggling of migrants as involving "the procurement for financial or other material benefit of illegal entry of a person into a State of which that person is not a national or resident." See United Nations 2000, Article 13.

67. Ayaz Qureshi (2015) demonstrates that this World Bank policy did not help the intended beneficiaries. In fact, it harmed them and created more wealth and power for elites.

68. *Times of India* 2016.

CHAPTER 2

1. Mazzarella 2003a, 36; Radhakrishnan 2011.

2. Kaur 2012.

3. Radhakrishnan 2011, 14; Khilnani 2004. See also Mazzarella 2003a, 2003b; Foster 2008, xvii; Manning 2010; MacLochlainn 2019.

4. I am indebted to Brad Weiss for his feedback on this topic.

5. David Pedersen's discussion of El Salvadoran migration to the United States examines how international organizations such as the World Bank and the United Nations describe migrants as entrepreneurs and approach migrant remittances as a way for El Salvador to develop. In the stories told about El Salvadoran migrants,

the narrative is one that describes rags-to-riches and celebrates the transnational entrepreneurial migrant. Pedersen 2013, 10–12, 174, 257–258.

6. Foucault 2010, 230.

7. Carla Freeman's work on entrepreneurship in Barbados situates entrepreneurship within the neoliberal present as "a primary site and central practice of neoliberal self-creation and labor . . . a dual project in which economic livelihoods and new subjectivities are being forged in tandem." It also entails "a vigorous entanglement of selfhood and labor for envisioning oneself and making one's self entails particular forms (and a particular intensity) of work." See Freeman 2014, 2–3.

8. I've also heard agents say the *B* in the "ABCD requirements" refers to butler, but here *B* was used to refer to *bhaiya*, or manual laborers.

9. Census of India 2011, statement 1.

10. Prime Minister's High Level Committee 2006, 18–19.

11. According to a decision regarding product labeling by the Gujarat High Court (2010), "Normally, in India, a majority of the people have accepted Hindi as a national language and many people speak Hindi and write in Devanagari script but there is nothing on record to suggest that any provision has been made or order issued declaring Hindi as a national language of the country." Such perspectives are pervasive throughout India. At one end of the political spectrum, majoritarian political sentiments conflate language, religion, and place. This conflation is often expressed through slogans such as "Hindi, Hindu, Hindustan"– one language, one religion, one culture. V. D. Savarkar (1939), the Indian nationalist who formulated the theory of Hindutva, meaning Hinduness, argued the term is meant to extend beyond religion to include "cultural, linguistic, social and political aspects as well." The slogan, "Hindi, Hindu, Hindustan" is attributed to Savarkar; see Jaffrelot 2009; Sarkar 2019. This also resonates today in debates over Hindi's place in India. The Rashtriya Swayamsevak Sangh (RSS), an Indian right-wing, paramilitary organization, currently uses the slogan widely.

12. Bear 2015.

13. Bear 2015, 15, 55.

14. See Welker 2014, 108.

15. Radharkrishnan 2011, 21.

16. Radharkrishnan 2011, 58.

17. Victor M. Rios's (2006) study of the criminalization of Latino and Black youth in the United States provides a powerful example of the power of racial ideologies within a community.

18. Hull 2010.

19. Hull 2010; Cohen 2015.

20. MOIA 2013; PLFS 2019, A-141.

21. Harvey 2018a; Graeber 2011; Hardt and Negri 2018.

CHAPTER 3

1. In Timothy Mitchell's (2011, 192–193) discussion of the oil industry, he describes how the materiality of oil frames its extraction and processing. He argues that, unlike coal, oil production locates expertise in the hands of managers and engineers: "Large firms depend on an extensive body of technical, political and economic expertise to support the discovery of new deposits." This understanding relies on the analysis of expertise that Mitchell developed in his previous work, *Rule of Experts* (2002, 291–298). There, he shows how experts delineate and define their areas of knowledge, and he points to the constitutive and violent nature of this knowledge production. He also demonstrates that nonhuman actors are not simply passive elements in the construction of an object over which expertise is developed. Mitchell (2002, 53) also looks at families, colonial administrations, mosquitoes, and laborers in order to understand what kinds of hybrid agencies, or uneasy alliances, shape "the development and expansion of capitalism." Other scholars examine expertise in the oil industry in similar ways. Andrew Barry (2013, 6), for example, focuses on expertise by examining the production of political and social knowledge by oil companies.

2. This knowledge, or what Michael Polanyi (1962) called "tacit knowledge," usually is confined to scientific knowledge.

3. Sociologist Kjeld Schmidt (2012), in his discussion of the knowledge held by employees at a company that manufactures large engines, suggests that instead of focusing on kinds of knowledge, we focus on the dialogical logics of workers.

4. My examination of the networks shaped by participants in migration and their relationships draws on work by Bruno Latour (2007). See also Law and Callon 1992.

5. This analysis builds on Engseng Ho's (2006) work on the Hydrami diaspora in the Indian Ocean in which he considers how circulation creates community.

6. See also Tsing 2005.

7. See also Elyacher 2005.

8. For example, see Witsoe 2011. For a discussion of the role of class in creating hierarchies within caste groups, see Narayan 2015.

9. Much to Arjun and Deepak's disapproval, I continued to use *aap*.

10. Politically, this form of address has been inverted by Dalit leaders to draw attention to social hierarchies and to politically mobilize Dalits. See Narayan 2015.

11. See also Anand 2017.

12. See, for example, Bear 2015; Anand 2017.

13. See, for example, Björkman 2015; Pierce 2016.

14. Anand 2017, 78, 185–186.

15. In C. Osella and F. Osella's (2012, 109) work on migration from Kerala to the Gulf, they find migrants use networks "to get done what cannot be achieved by direct approach to institutions."

16. Björkman 2015; Pierce 2016.

17. Gupta 2012.

18. Jauregui 2014, 80.

19. Lamb 2000.

20. See, for example, Chu 2010, 120; Gupta 2012.

21. Bear and Mathur 2015, 20.

22. Because the state may contract out aspects of its work to individuals, the boundaries between state and nonstate actors are blurred. See Mathur 2015, 18–20. See also Bear and Mathur 2015, 28; Gupta 1995, 2012.

23. Nasra Shah (2000) found that workers who migrate without recruiting agents earn higher salaries and state higher levels of satisfaction with their employment in the Gulf.

24. Luke Heslop and Laura Jeffery's (2020) work with migrant laborers in the Maldives finds that circulation also informs how migrants find their next jobs. As opposed to my focus here on the proximity of daily lives, their work sheds light on how such concepts as expertise and capacity are mobilized.

25. The participation of a European project manager like Alex in the interview process was not completely new, but it was uncommon. I was apprehensive as I explained my research. Most often, expatriate Indians or Arabs from oil companies came to interview workers, and these managers usually allowed me to observe their interviews. However, one multinational oil company that sent either Americans or British managers to oversee all of their hiring had expressly forbidden my presence at their interviews or any other stage of their hiring process. Due to my experience with that company, I was worried that Alex too would forbid my presence. Fortunately, my apprehension was for naught, and Alex was happy to have me shadow him during his time in Mumbai and allowed me to spend time at his work site in the UAE (as

well as other places in the Gulf, as he has moved to new locations in the years after I first met him).

26. As I watched more interviews, I learned that these networks were an important part of how many oil companies hire.

27. "Selling" labor is discussed in greater depth in Chapter 7.

28. This topic is returned to in the Conclusion.

29. Marx 1959; Graeber 2011; Hardt and Negri 2018; Harvey 2018a, 2018b.

PART 2

1. "Dubai" in this case is being used to metonymically refer to the Gulf as a whole.

2. Mueggler 2001; Palmié 2002; Lomnitz 2005.

3. Trouillot 1995, 146–147; Palmié 2002, 11; Lomnitz 2005, 260.

4. Mueggler 2001, 3; West 2005.

5. Tsing 2015, 121–128.

6. Tsing 2015, 121.

7. See Tsing 2015; Upadhya 2016.

CHAPTER 4

1. Gardner 2010; Vora and Koch 2015.

2. At home, Yogesh primarily speaks Tamil, but he is also fluent in Hindustani, and the latter is the language we use in conversations.

3. Lal 2011, 574. In some classic anthropological investigations into kinship, the nuclear family is associated with capitalism, and the assumption is that the kinship practices, such as living in joint families or giving a dowry, are traditional practices associated with earlier economic practices. See, Béteille 1965; Engels 1972 [1884]; Morgan 1997 [1868].

4. Rubin 1975, 169–177; Carsten 2004, 75.

5. Yanagisako and Collier (1987, 15) call for anthropologists to examine the "the social and cultural processes that cause men and women to appear different from each other."

6. Cohen 1999, 2011, 139.

7. Rahman 2001; Cohen 2002; Lamb 2013.

8. Bloch and Rao 2002; Kowalski 2016.

9. Kumar 1993, 116; Oldenburg 2002.

10. Trautmann 1981, 26–27, 277–285.

11. Lamb 2000; Xiang 2005.

12. Sahlins 2013, 16.

13. Schneider 1980.

14. Feeley-Harnik 1999; Carsten 2004, 114, 2011; Shryock 2013.

15. Mariner 2019.

16. Lamb 2000.

17. Trawick 1990; Daniel 1996; Busby 1997.

18. Polanyi 1957; Graeber 2009; Mathew 2016.

19. Oldenburg 2002, 148.

20. From HBM Political Agency, Trucial States, Dubai, to Sir William Luce, British Residency, Bahrain. 19 January 1966. 1181/66C RE (1):1966: 841–846). Gold smuggling is a popular trope in Hindi movies, especially in the years before the neoliberal reforms to India's economy. *Jaal* (1952) is an early representation of this smuggling, but there are more popular examples, including *Deewaar* (1975).

21. Ali 2010, 16–19.

22. This frontier, like changes to private property, is gendered, and Neha Vora (2013, 92–93) demonstrates that gold merchants celebrate Dubai's "freedoms" that are rooted in "illicit maritime masculine trade."

23. Zachariah, Prakash, and Rajan 2004.

24. Prakash, Zachariah, and Rajan 2004.

25. Mahdavi 2011, 126.

26. Lall 2009; DNA Investigations Bureau 2011.

27. In her discussion of Indian women working in call centers, Reena Patel (2010) points out that educated women working in nontraditional jobs has not led to greater gender equality in India.

28. Government of India 1956, sec. 2f.

29. For example, Anna Stirr (2017) discusses the wide variety of experiences of female performers in Dubai's nightclubs.

30. Rajwade 1938, 83.

31. Ramaswamy 2010, 9; Gupta 2002.

32. Minault 1982; Chatterjee 1989; Sangari and Vaid 1999; Metcalf 2002.

33. Zamindar 2007; Grapevine 2015.

34. Radhakrishnan 2011.

35. Ehrenreich and Russell 2002; Weeks 2011; Ahmad 2012, 23, 39–40.

36. van der Veer 2005, 278. Xiang Biao's work on Indian information technology workers in Australia demonstrates that men feel compelled to give as much dowry

as possible for their daughters' or sisters' marriages to maintain family status and free their families from the "burden" of the daughter. Xiang approaches dowry as an institution— an approach that makes clear how dowry is informed by an economic calculation and its close relationship to other social institutions, such as education. See Xiang 2005, 369–370; 2011, 33–36.

37. Pedersen 2013, 19. See also Coronil 1997; Graeber 2001, 31–32. As Karl Marx describes in his *Economic and Philosophical Manuscript of 1844* (1956), wage laborers are alienated from the product of their labor, their work, themselves, and their community.

38. Sareeta Amrute (2016, 166–70), in her study of skilled Indian migrants in Germany, argues that gifts function as one of the means by which Indian middle-class workers abroad represent their work to their families and build communities. In the case of Nepalese migration, money is particularly useful at expressing and maintaining kinship ties in a context in which sharing food or having other regular contact is absent. See Zharkevich 2019.

39. Following the work of Marilyn Strathern in Melanesia, anthropologists often argue that the value of the gift is located in social relationships of reciprocal exchange, whereas David Graeber extends Nancy D. Munn's examination of gifts to argue that value emerges in action, including how people represent the importance of their gift giving to themselves. See Strathern 1988, 143, 286; Graeber 2001, 45; Munn 1986, 127.

40. Chowdhry 2005.

41. Jeffrey 2010, 177–178.

42. Dahinden 2005; Gamburd 2008; Coe 2011a.

43. F. Osella and C. Osella 2000.

44. *Noobies* is a common slang word for "rookies." During my research, it was often used interchangeably with *kaccha limbu*, a Marathi phrase that literally means "unripe lemon."

45. For example, see Bhatt 2018.

46. Coe 2011b.

47. Zharkevich 2019.

48. Munn 1986; Keane 2003; Fehérváry 2012.

CHAPTER 5

1. In 2020, ground was broken for a Hindu temple in Abu Dhabi. It will be in traditional Indian temple architectural style and made of pink sandstone.

2. This temple terminology draws from southern Indian architectural terms. In

the north of India, *shikara* refers to the entire tower, including the superstructure of the *vimaana*.

3. My data correlate with other survey data. A study conducted in 2001 found that approximately 90 percent of the people going to the Gulf from two districts in Bihar were Muslim. However, Muslims were only 15 percent, on average, of the population in rural areas of these districts and were 19 percent and 28 percent of the population in urban areas of the districts. See Rahman 2001, 35; Hansen 2000, 2001.

4. Regarding the role of oil in the development of the economy, Timothy Mitchell (2014, 484) argues that the "future became a stable instrument for governing populations."

5. For a discussion of speculative disaster and oil, see Weszkalnys 2014.

6. Kale 2014, 31.

7. Gupta 2018.

8. Mitchell 2002, 2014.

9. Larkin 2013, 329. See also Björkman 2015; Anand 2017; Appel 2018, 49; Appel, Anand, and Gupta 2018.

10. Coronil 1997, 4.

11. Coronil 1997, 5. See also Andrew Apter's (2008) exploration of the strategic construction of the nation, culture, and tradition with oil wealth in Nigeria.

12. Coronil 1997; see also, Rogers 2012a, 2012b, 2015; Barry 2013. The poetics of infrastructure decouples infrastructure from technology and is "the means by which a state proffers these representations to its citizens and asks them to take those representations as social facts. It creates a politics of 'as if'." The key of using poetics is that we "rearrange the hierarchy of functions so that the aesthetic dimension of infrastructure (rather than its technical one) is dominant." See Larkin 2013, 335–336. Rigs also may stand metonymically for oil wealth. As Gökçe Günel's (2016) work on Masdar demonstrates, this wealth may be used to build green cities that are dreamed of as technologically advanced and a way for the Gulf States to move forward after the end of oil. Of course, there is variation in the Gulf, and in Mandana Limbert's (2010, 2016) work in Oman, she demonstrates that Omanis view rigs and oil infrastructure as a "dream time," one that will end with the end of oil.

13. Finance is also an important part of this infrastructure, and the state often operates as a facilitator of financial investment into projects. See Heslop 2020.

14. *Scheduled caste* is a term used for Dalits but is exclusive of Muslim Dalits.

15. Kaur 2015, 327–328.

16. Press Information Bureau 2016; Pradhan 2016.

17. Sundar 2019.

18. Sarkar 2019, 166.

19. This builds on Marx 1998; Hodžić 2016, 116; Hall 2017.

20. For a discussion of the state's engagements with the economy, see Mitchell 2002; Weszkalnys 2011; and Appel 2018.

21. Temples could also be viewed as infrastructure, because they provide religious organizational structure. In ethnonationalist writings, some argue that historically temples were the infrastructure of ancient India. See Srinivasan 2016.

22. Mary Hancock (2002, 21) writes that temples are "endowed with some of the same modernizing capacities attributed to museums, parks, theaters, and assembly halls." Similarly, in Pakistan, a rare Hindu temple is a place where upper-caste Hindus are able to assert their knowledge of "proper" traditions and position themselves in opposition to Hindu groups they label as "superstitious." The description of other groups as "superstitious" allows upper-caste groups to describe their practices as "educated" and "modern." See Schaflechner 2019.

23. Hancock 2002, 22.

24. Hancock 2002, 27.

25. Chatterji 2019, 399.

26. Berlant 1997.

27. Walter Benjamin (1969, 261) famously wrote, "History is the subject of a structure whose site is not homogeneous, empty time, but time filled by the presence of now." History is situated in the present and informed by visions of the future. For more on this, see Marx 1994 [1852]; de Certeau 1988 [1975]; White 1973, 1987; Derrida 1994; Trouillot 1995.

28. Asad 1993; Pandey 1999, 626.

29. Pandey 1999, 627–629.

30. Eaton 1993, 2004; Moin 2015; Sarkar 2019.

31. Ghassem-Fachandi 2012, 59.

32. Tribune 2009.

33. Specifically, the land was awarded to Ram Lalla Virajman, the divine infant form of Lord Ram. See Supreme Court of India 2019.

34. Hindustan Times 2020.

35. Bhimull 2017, 77.

36. Bhimull 2017, 50–51, 87.

37. For examples of this in other contexts, see Chu 2010; Pedersen 2013; Amrute 2016.

38. Amrute 2016, 114–118.

39. Bhatt 2018, 37–38, 42, 41.

40. Bhatt 2018, 120.

41. Ong 2016, 502.

42. Chu 2010, 6.

43. Vora 2013.

44. Molavi 2018.

45. C. Osella and F. Osella 2012, 13.

46. Molavi 2018.

47. Department of Tourism 2019.

48. Lenze 2018.

49. Akief 2017a, 2017b, 2018; al Kaashekh 2017, 2020a, 2020b.

50. Requirements to apply for citizenship include living in the UAE for at least twenty years, speaking Arabic, being a Muslim, having a good reputation and no criminal record, and having a legal means of support.

51. See also Wright 2018.

52. The linearity of development or modernity is not universally agreed on. For example, see Ferguson 1999, 252; Weiss 2017, 206.

53. Chakrabarty 2000, 11–14; see also Césaire 1972; Lowe 2015; Hall 2017.

54. Pletsch 1981, 573–574.

55. Pletsch 1981, 571.

56. See Comaroff and Comaroff 1987, 193, 205; Stoler 2008; Hodžić 2016.

57. At the time, I worried that arguing with people with whom I work (as an anthropologist) indicated I was not being an ideal social scientist. However, having known many individuals in this book for over thirteen years, I now feel it is important to both carefully listen and try to understand their words while simultaneously being reciprocal in this interaction and sharing my own experiences and worldviews—perspectives about which many of the people with whom I work frequently asked. I was more reluctant to do so at first, feeling that my job was to learn, not to share. Obviously as the few moments of debate in this book reflect, I did decide to share my own perspectives. Sharing my own experiences and perspectives has helped me learn to listen with even greater care and has opened unexpected stories.

PART 3

1. The title is a play on the popular film *Slumdog Millionaire*.

2. Labor migrants have limited access to state institutions, but this is not to say that they do not influence governance practices. See also Kanna, Le Renard, and Vora 2020.

3. Dito 2014, 97.

4. Human Rights Watch 2008, 34; Amnesty International 2013, 2014; Booth and Kelly 2016; BBC 2019.

5. See Watts 2004; Mitchell 2011. Michael Watts argues that the perspectives on resource politics must be expanded to understand the role of transnational oil companies. In Watts's research on oil production in Nigeria, he "explore[s] how oil capitalism (what I call petro-capitalism) produces, from the realities of forms of rule and political authority into which it is inserted, specific sorts of what I, following Rose, call governable space (that is a specific configuration of territory, identity and rule)." Watts 2004, 53. See also Watts 2012 for a discussion of the oil assemblage.

6. Gwenn Okruhlik's (1999) work on the impact of rentier wealth on the state, for example, shows that political outcomes are not predetermined. Although oil rents are paid directly to the state, such payments do not dictate the relationship between the state and citizens. Instead, Okruhlik argues, historical and social contexts, together with an exploration of how rents are deployed, offer a more fruitful method of analysis.

7. See, for example, Asad 2007; Butler 2009; Puar et al. 2012; Allison 2012; Lorey 2015.

8. Gardner 2010, 63–64; Longva 1999.

9. See also Kinninmont 2011, 5.

10. Longva 1997. In the Gulf, Arabness is often strongly associated with citizenship, but the relationship is far from clear-cut. This is discussed in greater detail in Gardner 2010; Limbert 2014; and Vora and Koch 2015.

11. Longva 1997. Other anthropologists have noted the significance of previous models of employment in defining the contemporary system. Specifically, the pearl trade with the role of indentured laborers or slaves in that trade was, according to Andrew Gardner (2010, 37), an "early rendition of the contemporary kafala system."

12. In anthropologist Anh Nga Longva's (1997) discussion of migration to Kuwait, she builds on the work of Abdalla S. Burja (1971) and Frederik Barth (1983) to make explicit what social customs and policies allow for the efficient running of Kuwait's intensely multicultural and multiethnic society.

13. Ahmed Kanna (2011, 72) characterizes governance in Dubai, for example, as based on two assumptions held by both the ruler and the citizens of the emirate. The first is that citizens are dependent on the ruler. The second is that only citizens are able to make claims on the state for protection.

14. Longva 1997, 100, 103–105. Christopher M. Davidson (2011, 2) describes the benefits of the sponsorship system for the rulers of the Gulf States. He finds that the kafala system has benefits for citizens, "including a sponsorship system that allows regular citizens to build rent-generating business empires on the backs of foreign workers and, less tangibly, the maintenance of a subtle social hierarchy that invariably elevates the 'locals' above Arab and Asian immigrants."

15. Mbembe 2019, 30, 35. See also Said 1979; Abu-Lughod 1991; Trouillot 1991a; Coronil 1996; Chakrabarty 2000; Mitchell 2002.

16. Report by J. B. Howes, Assistant Political Agent Bahrain. 21 December 1938. British Library [FO 1016/56], RE (8), 643–645.

17. Mahdavy 1970; Beblawi 1987.

18. For the resource curse argument, see Ross 2001, 2012. For additional critiques of the resource curse argument, see Watts 2004; Mitchell 2011; Weszkalnys 2011.

19. Luciani 1990; Hertog 2010.

20. Timothy Mitchell (2011) also questions the discourse of the resource curse. Noting that the leading industrialized countries are also some of the world's biggest oil producers, Mitchell argues that one must consider the materiality of oil; the sites where oil is extracted, refined, and shipped; the international political context; and the labor activities at oil sites.

21. Maritime Executive 2019.

22. The original Arabic reads: "Iina tahdith qanun almalakiat aleaqariat yujasid daem alqiadat alrashidat lilruwaa alhukumiat alrramiat 'iilaa tatwir alqitae alaiqtisadii fi al'imar" (Muhammed 2019).

CHAPTER 6

1. This strike did not occur at a company with which I have a relationship, and I was unable to receive more information about the strike when I contacted the management the following day.

2. Scroll India 2015.

3. See Wright n.d. Along with these two processes, there was a concurrent rise of contracting in business. Contracting has led to risk being increasingly displaced onto the most vulnerable of workers, a topic explored at length in the following chapter.

4. This perspective is indebted to Michael Watts's (2004, 2012) work on the "oil complex" and "oil assemblage."

5. Wright n.d.

6. British Petroleum was a subsidiary of the Anglo Iranian Oil Company (AIOC). In 1954, AIOC renamed itself British Petroleum (BP).

7. In addition, the company was hiring eight thousand local laborers, and Indian government representatives thought that only a few Indians would be kept at the refinery once construction was finished. Express Letter to All Passport Issuing Authorities in India, 24 November 1952. NAI, MEA, Emigration. 6637/52-Emi; Aden- Recruitment of 600 skilled workers from India. NAI, MEA, Emigration, 1953. F.23–9/52-Emi.

8. Aden-Recruitment of 600 skilled workers from India. NAI, MEA, Emigration, 1953. F.23–9/52-Emi.

9. Letter to Ghatge from Thadani, 19 March 1953. NAI, MEA, Emigration, 1953. F.23–9/52-Emi.

10. Aden-Recruitment of 600 skilled workers from India. NAI, MEA, Emigration, 1953. F.23–9/52-Emi.

11. Letter to Thadani from Ghatge, 26 March 1953; Letter to Ghatge, 26 March 1953. NAI, MEA, Emigration, 1953. F.23–9/52-Emi.

12. Aden- Recruitment of 600 skilled workers from India. NAI, MEA, Emigration, 1953. F.23–9/52-Emi.

13. Letter to the Secretary, MEA, from Thadani, 10 June 1953. NAI, MEA, Emigration, 1953. 2954/53-Emi; Letter to Indian Trade Commission from Indian Employees Committee, 4 July 1953. NAI, MEA, Emigration, 1953. F.23–9/52-Emi.; Letter to POE, Bombay, from BP, 10 June 1953. NAI, MEA, Emigration, 1953. G/16307.; Letter to the Secretary, MEA, from Thadani, 10 June 1953. NAI, MEA, Emigration, 1953. 2954/53-Emi.

14. Atabaki 2018, 191, 204.

15. Glover 2008.

16. Wright 2020a, 2021, n.d.

17. Wright 2020a.

18. Wright 2021, Wright n.d.

19. Lori 2011.

20. Agamben 1998; Mbembe 2020.

21. Vora 2014, 170. See also Gardner 2010; Hanieh 2011; Kanna 2011; Vora 2013.

22. Sulayman Khalaf (2010, 106–107) finds that among migrant laborers working in Dubai's camel racing market, many prefer to stay within the space of the market due to lack of excess wages to spend and the closeness of national communities within the market.

23. Crenshaw 1991; Puar and Rai 2002; Hall 2017.

24. Bonilla-Silva 2011; Vora 2014.

25. Gardner 2010; Vora and Koch 2015.

26. Neha Vora (2014, 176) argues that Whites from western Europe and North America also "exist within the same exploitative system as migrant laborers, although they are less duped and less exploited by the system due to their economic and cultural capital."

27. Gardner 2010; Sarmadi 2013.

28. Bristol-Rhys 2012, 81.

29. Lori 2011.

30. Buckley 2014, 146.

31. While charging workers a fee if they break their contract early is the norm today, this practice is markedly different from the worker rights the nascent Indian government advocated for in the 1950s. At that time, the Indian government responded to collective action by workers by attempting to negotiate contracts with oil companies on behalf of the workers. The government even went so far as to temporarily blacklist certain corporations because these companies charged fees to workers when the workers wanted to return to India before the end of their contract. See Letter to the Commission from the Ministry of External Affairs, 11 August 1953. NAI, MEA, Emigration. F. 23–9/52-Emi.

32. Discourses around racialized difference are one way in which the myth of race as a biological fact is perpetuated. As anthropological work clearly demonstrates, race is culturally constructed and a social categorization, not a biological reality. See Blakey 1999.

33. Vitalis 2009.

34. DasGupta 1994, 63–64; Santiago 2006.

35. Unfortunately, the experiences of these abandoned workers are not unique, and even in times of economic stability, news reports continue to circulate concerning abandoned camps. Sometimes workers are not even permitted to remain in their camp. In 2015, the news reported that twenty-three abandoned workers lived in a bus for twelve days until the Dubai Human Rights Police received a report, tracked the men down, and found them alternative accommodations. See Gokulan and Agarib 2015.

36. This fear of poor Indian beggars abroad is remarkably similar to the concerns of Indian government bureaucrats, discussed in Chapter 2, who want to improve India's brand abroad.

37. Meyers 2011.

38. Lazzarato 2009.

39. Ong 2006.

40. Thomas Blom Hansen found that, in mosques in Mumbai, many migrants felt pressure to describe the Gulf as connected to a more "pious" or "pure" form of Islam. Both recruiting agents and anthropological researchers describe the religious importance Indian Muslims attach to their work in the Gulf. However, no one wanted to talk about religion with me. For information on religion and Gulf migration, see Hansen 2000, 2001.

CHAPTER 7

1. Nayak 2018.

2. Longva 1997; Davidson 2011; Kamrava 2018.

3. Hanieh 2018.

4. Eley 2005, 2006.

5. For examples of data collection, see Hämäläinen, Takala, and Saarela 2017 or the ILO's World Statistic 2018.

6. Mason et al. 2015.

7. Kirsch 2014.

8. Mbembé 2003; Giroux 2006. For a discussion of the interactions between the state and corporations, see Mitchell 1999.

9. Shever 2012, 58, 68 (emphasis in original).

10. For a detailed discussion of the supermajors and the mergers that helped form them, see Yergin 2011.

11. Citino 2002; Likosky 2009, 3–4.

12. These popular narratives of the oil crisis importantly exclude the active role oil companies played in driving up prices. See Mitchell 2011, 173–199.

13. Anderson 1990.

14. This estimate excludes oil sands. See OPEC 2020, 22.

15. J. E. H. Boustead, Memo to H. M. Political Residency, Bahrain, 28 May 1963. RE (1963), 568. See also Wright n.d.

16. IOGP 2013, B-19, 1–5, 2–2.

17. IOGP 2019, 135.

18. Tsing 2005, 2015. In Hannah Appel's (2012, 697) work on offshore oil rigs in Equatorial Guinea, she examines how oil companies attempt to create boundaries between themselves and the locations in which they work through the fiction of the modularity of the oil rig. She describes offshore rigs as modular places that corporations anticipate will be moved to different geographic spaces. Appel defines this type

of modular capitalist project as "a bundled and repeating set of technological, social, political, and economic practices aimed at profit making that the industry works to build" anywhere it finds oil. See also Appel 2019.

19. This is also discussed in Chapter 3.

20. Ewig 2011, 102.

21. This is the same term employed workers used to describe the circumstances of abandoned workers, as noted in the previous chapter.

22. Ferguson 2005, 378.

23. See also Appel 2012, 2019.

24. For example, see Weeks 2011.

25. Brown 2015, 65–66.

26. IOGP 2013, vii.

27. See Thompson 1963; Malm 2016.

28. This is also discussed in Chapter 2.

29. Gago 2017, 5.

30. Gago 2017, 10–11.

31. As one female commentator on Instagram wrote, "The story goes that he received a boon that he couldn't be killed by any man, and didn't bother about women because, hey, what could a woman ever do to him. Oh, how magnificently he was proven wrong."

32. Unfortunately, the images I saw circulating cut off the top two items Durga holds.

33. Fuller 2004, 108.

34. Puri 2019.

35. See also Chapter 5.

36. Kirsch 2014; Welker 2014.

37. IOGP 2013, 1–5, 2–2.

38. These deaths are not for the industry as a whole. Rather, the number of deaths reported is only for workers directly employed by companies participating in International Association of Oil and Gas Producers' safety indicators annual report. IOGP 2018, 113.

39. National Commission 2011, 83–84.

40. BSEE 2018.

41. National Commission 2011, 125.

42. National Commission 2011, 119.

43. National Commission 2011, 120–122.

44. Both BP and Connex are private limited companies (Ltd.). This type of company is available in the United Kingdom, Canada, and Ireland, and it is its own legal entity. This legal type of company provides protection for the owners or shareholders, whose only liability is the capital they invested, and the company itself pays taxes. In contrast, other oil companies are limited liability companies (LLCs), which are often hybrid and combine characteristics of a corporation with those of sole proprietorship. However, they are similar to private limited companies in their shielding of shareholders from personal responsibility.

45. There are other critical aspects of the BP disaster for social science research. In particular, Michael Watts (2012) explores the Deepwater Horizon's blowout and puts greater emphasis on the role of deregulation.

46. Sawyer 2004, 2006.

47. Sawyer 2006, 32.

48. Department of Justice 2015.

49. National Commission 2011, 2.

50. SEC 2015.

51. BP 2011a; SEC 2011.

52. BP 2011b.

53. Baxandall and Surka 2015.

54. Baxandall and Surka 2015, 5.

55. Baxandall and Surka 2015, 31–32; Wood 2016.

56. For example, see Coronil 2000.

57. Hanieh 2018, 9.

58. For example, see Hull 2012, 115.

CONCLUSION

1. Bond 2013, 695.

2. Ong 2016, 503.

3. See Anand 2017, 15.

4. Rose 1996.

5. Stuart Hall uses "articulation" to mean the unity of two distinct elements. According to Hall, articulation enables us to think "how ideology empowers people, enabling them to begin to make some sense or intelligibility of their historical situation, without reducing those forms of intelligibility to their socio-economic or class location or social position." See Hall 1986, 53. In her work on Dalit feminism, Purvi Mehta (2017, 2019) clearly lays out the stakes regarding

who invokes difference, how it is invoked, and in what contexts. See also Bhabha 1994; Pandey 2010.

6. In my approach to understanding the relationship between the state, corporations, and labor, I begin with Michel Foucault's (2007) discussion of modern sovereignty. Foucault argues that juridical approaches to contract that formalized or ritualized contract theory were key to understanding sovereignty in the modern state. This discussion built on Thomas Hobbes's discussion of the social contract, in which people give up some liberty in exchange for common security. In Foucault's investigation, he points to the multiple power relations that facilitate social contracts and sovereignty. Building on this work, scholars have questioned the state's unity or coherence through examining how the state is and has historically been enacted by participants through the coordination of practices. See Brown 1995; Mitchell 1999; Trouillot 2001; Aretxaga 2003; Das and Poole 2004; Hull 2012; Welker 2014.

7. Mitchell 1999, 91.

8. Derrida 1976.

9. Vitalis 2009; Mitchell 2011.

10. Wright 2020a, 2021.

11. Mitchell 1999. Furthermore, these operate in conjunction with white supremacy, settler colonialism, and patriarchy in expressing power and shaping social relations. White supremacy and patriarchy in turn reinforce systems of violence and oppression that operate in conjunction with capitalism and contemporary governance. Discerning the differing histories of capitalism, racism, and patriarchy demonstrates that none of these are universal practices, as is often assumed, and highlights the difference between formal and real subsumption. For a longer discussion of this, see Hardt and Negri 2018. Such perspectives also allow us to decenter the Occident or Europe in one's analysis while attending to the lasting legacies of historic and contemporary colonialism and imperialism at play in the Arabian Sea. For examples of how, in other contexts and places, anthropologists have engaged with lasting colonial legacies while trying to decenter colonial perspectives, see Coronil 1996; Chakrabarty 2000; Stoler 2008; Simpson 2014; Hodžić 2016.

12. Mbembé 2003; Giroux 2006; Hall 2017.

13. The relationship between energy and culture has long been an area of exploration for anthropology. Leslie White (1949) argued that the most important factor in "cultural evolution" is energy: "Culture evolves as the amount of energy harnessed per capita per year is increased, or as the efficiency of the instrumental means of putting the energy to work is increased."

14. Kanna, Le Renard, and Vora 2020.

15. Vora 2011, 2014; Hanieh 2014; Wright n.d.

16. Mbembe 2020, 8, 52, 236.

17. Mbembe 2020, 191–193.

18. Mbembe 2019, 35.

19. Achille Mbembe (2019, 38) writes, "The permanent simulation of the state of exception justifies a 'war on terror'—a war of eradication, indefinite, absolute, that claims the right to cruelty, torture, and indefinite detention—and so a war that draws its weapons from the 'evil' it pretends to be eradicating, in a context in which the law and justice are applied in the form of endless reprisals, vengeance, and revenge."

20. Mbembe 2020, 47–48.

21. Mbembe 2020, 68. This logic applies to other sites as well. For example, Neha Vora (2019, 4) writes about how education creates and maintains "mythologies of liberalism and its others."

22. Trouillot 2001; Weiss 2004; Foucault 2007, 2010; Simpson 2014, 2017.

23. For an overview of anthropological approaches to oil, including attention to its temporality and infrastructure, see Rogers 2015.

24. Klebnikov 2019.

25. Bear 2020.

26. I owe a great debt to Chandra Bhimull for her insights and conversations with me on how to write about the complexity of individuals' lives—of how people may have extraordinarily hard lives, but also laugh and play games. I am also thankful for her suggestion to revisit Sydney Mintz's *Three Ancient Colonies*. In this book, Mintz describes that even in the worst circumstances, even when treated as "interchangeable units of labor," enslaved persons in the colonial Caribbean made meaning through, what Mintz calls, building "collective social institutions" (2010, 205, 195–201).

CODA

1. See also Wright 2020c.

2. *Arab News* 2020; Hasan 2020; Wallen 2020.

3. Many migrants also express concern that the religious discrimination they, as Muslims, regularly experience in India has become worse. A disproportionately large number of Indian migrants to the Gulf are Muslims. There have been frequent reports of violence against Muslims in India, and the coronavirus fanned further anti-Muslim violence. Social media accounts in India circulated false accusations that Indian Muslims were spreading COVID-19, and these rumors were then mobilized

to incite violence against Muslims. On April 7, 2020, for example, Hindus attacked a group of Muslim men in Jharkhand and killed one person after rumors spread that Muslims were "spitting" in order to purposefully infect Hindus with coronavirus. See Saikia 2020. For additional reporting on violence against Muslims, see Barton 2020.

4. Quoted in Sengupta 2020.

Bibliography

ARCHIVES & COLLECTIONS

British Library (cited as BL)

Gazetteer of the Persian Gulf: Oman and Central Arabia compiled by John Gordon Lorimer. Supt. Government Publishing 1908.

National Archives of India (cited as NAI)

Political Diaries of the Arab World: Persian Gulf (cited as PDAW:PG), 1904–1965, 24 vols. R. Jarman ed. Cambridge: Cambridge University Press, 1998.

Records of the Emirates (cited as RE), 1820–1960, 12 vols. P. Tuson ed. Cambridge Archival Editions, 1990.

Records of Qatar (cited as RQ), 1820–1960, 8 vols. P. Tuson, ed. Cambridge: Cambridge University Press, 1991.

GOVERNMENT DOCUMENTS

Bureau of Safety and Environmental Enforcement (BSEE). 2018. "Offshore Incident Statistics." US Government. https://www.bsee.gov/stats-facts/offshore-incident-statistics.

Consul General of India, Dubai. 2016. *Recruitment of Housemaids.* http://www.cgidubai.org/housemaid/.

Department of Justice. 2015. "U.S. and Five Gulf States Reach Historic Settlement with BP to Resolve Civil Lawsuit over Deepwater Horizon Oil Spill." October 5.

Department of Tourism, UAE. 2019. Shah Rukh Khan's Dubai: #BeMyGuest.

Government of Dubai. https://www.visitdubai.com/en/discover/shah-rukh-khan-in-dubai.

Government of India. 1921. Emigration Act of 1921.

———. 1967. Passport Act.

———. 1983. Emigration Act of 1983.

———. 2013. The Criminal Law (Amendment) Act, 2013. New Delhi: Gazette of India.

Government of Punjab. 2008. Punjab Prevention of Human Trafficking Act, 2008. (proposed)

Gujarat High Court. 2010. Suresh Kachhadia Public Interest Litigation. Filed 2009.

Ministry of External Affairs (MEA). 1951. *Annual Report 1950–51.* Government of India.

———. 1952. *Annual Report 1951–52.* Government of India.

———. 2001. *Report of the High Level Committee on the Indian Diaspora.* Government of India, December.

———. 2017. *Annual Report 2017–18.* Government of India.

———. 2018. *Annual Report 2018–19.* Government of India.

———. 2020. *Annual Report 2019–20.* Government of India.

Ministry of Overseas Indian Affairs (MOIA). 2010. *Annual Report.* Government of India.

———. 2013. *Annual Report 2012–13.* Government of India.

National Commission on the BP Deepwater Horizon Oil Spill and Offshore Drilling. 2011. "Deepwater: The Gulf Oil Disaster and the Future of Offshore Drilling." US Government, Report to the President, January.

National Commission for Enterprises in the Unorganised Sector. 2007. *Report on Conditions of Work and Promotion of Livelihoods in the Unorganised Sector.* Government of India, August.

National Crime Records Bureau. 2014. *Crime in India—2014.* New Delhi: Government of India.

———. 2015. *Crime in India—2015.* New Delhi: Government of India.

National Sample Survey Office (NSS). 2014. *Employment and Unemployment Situation in India.* NSS Report 554. New Delhi: Ministry of Statistics and Programme Implementation, Government of India.

Periodic Labour Force Survey (PLFS). 2019. *Annual Report, June 2017—June 2018.* New Delhi: Ministry of Statistics and Programme Implementation, Government of India.

Pradhan, Dharmedra. 2016. Speech by Honorable Minister of Petroleum and Natural Gas Shri Dharmendra Pradhan at the Launch Event of "Discovered Small Fields Bid Round—2016." May 25. http://www.dghindia.gov.in/assets/downloads/ms.pdf.

Press Information Bureau. 2016. "Cabinet Approves Discovered Small Fields (DSF)." Government of India.

Prime Minister's High Level Committee. 2006. "Social, Economic and Educational Status of the Muslim Community of India." Government of India, November 29.

Securities and Exchange Commission (SEC). 2011. Confidential Settlement Agreement, BP and Anadarko. US Government. https://www.sec.gov/Archives/edgar/data/773910/000119312512070408/d282676dex10xlii.htm

———. 2015. Transocean Macondo Settlement. US Government. https://www.sec.gov/Archives/edgar/data/1451505/000145150515000096/a2015macondosettlementpr.htm

Srikrishna Commission. 1998. "Justice Srikrishna Report on Mumbai Riots of 1992, 1993." February 16.

Supreme Court of India. 2019. M Siddiq (D) Thr Lrs versus Mahant Suresh Das & Ors. Civil Appeal Nos 10866–10867 of 2010. November 9.

United Arab Emirates Government (UAE). 1980. Federal Law No 8, for 1980, On Regulation of Labour Relations.

United Arab Emirates National Committee to Combat Human Trafficking. 2009. *Combatting Human Trafficking in the UAE: Annual Report, 2008–2009*. http://www.nccht.gov.ae.

United Nations, General Assembly. 2000. United Nations Convention against Transnational Organized Crime. [resolution] A/55/383.

US Department of State. 2015. *Trafficking in Persons Report 2015*. www.state.gov/j/tip.

NONGOVERNMENTAL DOCUMENTS

Amnesty International. 2013. "The Dark Side of Migration: Spotlight on Qatar's Construction Sector ahead of the World Cup." London: Amnesty International.

———. 2014. *"My Sleep Is My Break": Exploitation of Migrant Domestic Workers in Qatar.* London: Amnesty International, International Secretariat.

British Petroleum. 2011a. "BP Announces Settlement with Moex/Mitsui of Claims between the Companies Related to the Deepwater Horizon Accident." May 20. https://www.bp.com/en/global/corporate/news-and-insights/press-releases/bp-announces-settlement-with-moexmitsui-of-claims-between-the-companies-related-to-the-deepwater-horizon-accident.html.

———. 2011b. "BP Announces Settlement with Cameron International Corporation of Claims Related to the Deepwater Horizon Accident." December 15. https://www.bp.com/en/global/corporate/news-and-insights/press-releases/

bp-announces-settlement-with-cameron-international-corporation-of-claims-related-to-the-deepwater-horizon-accident.html.

Human Rights Watch. 2008. *"As If I Am Not Human": Abuses against Asian Domestic Workers in Saudi Arabia.* New York: Human Rights Watch, July.

International Labour Organization. 2018. *World Statistic.* https://www.ilo.org/global/regions/lang—en/index.htm

IMF Staff. 2008. "Benefits of Trade Liberalization." In *Global Trade Liberalization and the Developing Countries,* January.

International Association of Oil and Gas Producers (IOGP). 2013. OGP Data Series.

———. 2019. *Safety Performance Indicators—2018 Data.* Report 2018s. June.

———. 2020. *IOGP Safety Performance Indicators—2019 Data.* Report 2019s. September.

Mamgain, Rajendra P., and Sher Verick. 2017. *The State of Employment in Uttar Pradesh: Unleashing the Potential for Inclusive Growth.* International Labour Organization.

Organization of the Petroleum Exporting Countries (OPEC). 2020. *OPEC Annual Statistical Bulletin.* Vienna, Austria: OPEC. www.opec.org.

ARTICLES AND BOOKS

Agamben, Giorgio. 1998. *Homo Sacer: Sovereign Power and Bare Life.* Edited by Werner Hamacher and David E. Wellbery. Translated by Daniel Heller-Roazen. Stanford: Stanford University Press.

Ahmad, Attiya. 2012. "Beyond Labor: Foreign Residents in the Persian Gulf States." In *Migrant Labor in the Persian Gulf,* edited by Mehran Kamrava and Zahra Babar, 21–40. New York: Columbia University Press.

Akief, Muhammed. 2017a. "When You Finally Wash Your Car." March 5. https://youtu.be/Lq5kZAfQbn4.

———. 2017b. "Never Underestimate the Language Skills of People." August 19. https://youtu.be/m6Xv1bngGlE.

———. 2018. "The Sick Leave." July 21. https://youtu.be/yKujNbIhQx8.

Albahari, Maurizio. 2015. *Crimes of Peace: Mediterranean Migrations at the World's Deadliest Border.* Philadelphia: University of Pennsylvania Press.

AlKaashekh, Ahmad. 2017. "Introducing an Indian to Arab Friends." February 20. https://youtu.be/IqK6xz6FIWw.

———. 2020a. "Lamborghini Huracan Acceleration Reaction." January 25. https://youtu.be/5SZH3pMzlaA.

———. 2020b. "Work from Home Problems Part One." April 9. https://youtu.be/4dcH6nSGxV4.

al-Sayegh, Fatma. 1998. "Merchants' Role in a Changing Society: The Case of Dubai, 1900–90." *Middle Eastern Studies* 34 (1): 87–102.

Ali, Syed. 2007. "'Go West Young Man': The Culture of Migration among Muslims in Hyderabad, India." *Journal of Ethnic and Migration Studies* 33 (1): 37–58. http://doi.org/10.1080/13691830601043489.

———. 2010. *Dubai: Gilded Cage*. New Haven: Yale University Press.

Allison, Anne. 2012. "Ordinary Refugees: Social Precarity and Soul in 21st Century Japan." *Anthropological Quarterly* 85 (2): 345–370.

Amin, Shahid. 1996. *Event, Memory, Metaphor: Chauri Chaura, 1922–1992*. Delhi: Oxford University Press.

Amrute, Sareeta. 2016. *Encoding Race, Encoding Class: Indian IT Workers in Berlin*. Durham: Duke University Press.

Anand, Nikhil. 2017. *Hydraulic City: Water and the Infrastructures of Citizenship in Mumbai*. Durham: Duke University Press.

Anderson, Owen L. 1990. "The Anatomy of an Oil and Gas Drilling Contract." *Tulsa Law Review* 25 (3).

Anscombe, Frederick F. 1997. *The Ottoman Gulf: The Creation of Kuwait, Saudi Arabia, and Qatar*. New York: Columbia University Press.

Appel, Hannah. 2012. "Offshore Work: Oil, Modularity, and the How of Capitalism in Equatorial Guinea." *American Ethnologist* 39 (4): 692–709.

———. 2018. "Infrastructural Time." In *The Promise of Infrastructure*, edited by Nikhil Anand, Akhil Gupta, and Hannah Appel, 41–61. Durham: Duke University Press.

———. 2019. *The Licit Life of Capitalism: US Oil in Equatorial Guinea*. Durham: Duke University Press.

Appel, Hannah, Nikhil Anand, and Akhil Gupta. 2018. "Introduction: Temporality, Politics, and the Promise of Infrastructure." In *The Promise of Infrastructure*, edited by Nikhil Anand, Akhil Gupta, and Hannah Appel, 1–38. Durham: Duke University Press.

Apter, Andrew. 2008. *The Pan-African Nation: Oil and the Spectacle of Culture in Nigeria*. Chicago: University of Chicago Press.

Arab News. 2020. "'Starving' Bangladesh Garment Workers Protest for Pay during COVID-19 Lockdown." April 13.

Arendt, Hannah. 1958. *The Origins of Totalitarianism*. New York: Meridian Books.

Aretxaga, Begoña. 2003. "Maddening States." *Annual Review of Anthropology* 32: 393–410.

Arnold, David. 1998. "Touching the Body: Perspectives on the Indian Plague." In *Selected Subaltern Studies*, edited by R. Guha and G. C. Spivak. New York: Oxford University Press.

Asad, Talal. 1993. *Genealogies of Religion: Discipline and Reasons of Power in Christianity and Islam*. Baltimore: Johns Hopkins University Press.

———. 2007. *On Suicide Bombing*. New York: Columbia University Press.

Atabaki, Touraj. 2018. "Indian Migrant Workers in the Iranian Oil Industry, 1908–1951." In *Working for Oil: Comparative Social Histories of Labor in the Global Oil Industry*, edited by Touraj Atabaki, Elisabetta Bini, and Kaveh Ehsani, 189–226. London: Palgrave Macmillan.

Bahadur, Gaiutra. 2013. *Coolie Woman: The Odyssey of Indenture*. Chicago: University of Chicago Press.

Bakhtin, Mikhail. 1981. *The Dialogical Imagination: Four Essays*. Edited by Michael Holquist. Translated by Caryl Emerson and Michael Holquist. Austin: University of Texas Press.

Banerjee, Chandrani. 2010. "The Clay Pigeons." *Outlook India*, September 21.

Banerjee, Sikata. 2012. *Make Me a Man! Masculinity, Hinduism and Nationalism in India*. Albany, NY: SUNY Press.

Barry, Andrew. 2013. *Material Politics: Disputes along the Pipeline*. Oxford: Wiley Blackwell.

Barth, Fredrik. 1983. *Sohar: Culture and Society in an Omani Town*. Baltimore: Johns Hopkins University Press.

Barton, Naomi. 2020. "Delhi Riots." *TheWire.in*, February 25.

Bates, Crispin. 2000. "Coerced and Migrant Labourers in India." *Edinburgh Papers in South Asian Studies* 13: 2–33.

Baxandall, Phineas, and Michelle Surka. 2015. "Settling for a Lack of Accountability? Which Federal Agencies Allow Companies to Write Off Out-of-Court Settlements as Tax Deductions, and Which Are Transparent about It." U.S. Public Interest Group, Education Fund, December.

BBC Arabic. 2019. "*Qatar taedil nizam 'alkfal' lileumal al'ajanib*" (Qatar amends the sponsorship system for foreign workers). October 17. https://perma.cc/X2V3-8N96.

Bear, Laura. 2015. *Navigating Austerity: Currents of Debt along a South Asian River*. Stanford: Stanford University Press.

———. 2020. "Speculation: A Political Economy of Technologies of Imagination." *Economy and Society* 49 (1): 1–15.

Bear, Laura, and Nayanika Mathur. 2015. "Introduction: Remaking the Public Good: A New Anthropology of Bureaucracy." *Cambridge Journal of Anthropology* 33 (1): 18–34.

Beblawi, Hazem. 1987. "The Rentier State in the Arab World." In *The Rentier State*, edited by H. Beblawi and G. Luciani, 49–62. New York: Croom Helm.

Benjamin, Walter. 1969. "Theses on the Philosophy of History." In *Illuminations: Essays and Reflections*, edited by Hannah Arendt, translated by Harry Zohn, 253–264. New York: Schocken Books.

Berlant, Lauren. 1997. *The Queen of America Goes to Washington City: Essays on Sex and Citizenship.* Durham: Duke University Press.

Béteille, André. 1965. *Caste, Class, and Power: Changing Patterns of Stratification in a Tanjore Village.* Berkeley: University of California Press.

Bhabha, Homi K. 1994. *The Location of Culture.* New York: Routledge.

Bhatt, Amy. 2018. *High-Tech Housewives: Indian IT Workers, Gendered Labor, and Trans-migration.* Seattle: University of Washington Press.

Bhimull, Chandra. 2017. *Empire in the Air: Airline Travel and the African Diaspora.* New York: New York University Press.

Bielo, James S. 2019. "'Particles-to-People . . . Molecules-to-Man': Creationist Poetics in Public Debates." *Journal of Linguistic Anthropology* 29 (1): 4–26.

Björkman, Lisa. 2015. *Pipe Politics, Contested Waters: Embedded Infrastructures of Millennial Mumbai.* Durham: Duke University Press.

Blakey, Michael L. 1999. "Scientific Racism and the Biological Concept of Race." *Literature and Psychology* 45 (1/2): 29–43.

Bloch, Francis, and Vijayendra Rao. 2002. "Terror as a Bargaining Instrument." *American Economic Review* 92 (4): 1029–1043.

Boissevain, Jeremy. 1974. *Friends of Friends: Networks, Manipulators, and Coalitions.* Oxford: Basil Blackwell.

Bond, David. 2013. "Governing Disaster: The Political Life of the Environment during the BP Oil Spill." *Cultural Anthropology* 28 (4): 694–715

Bonilla-Silva, Eduardo. 2011. "The Invisible Weight of Whiteness: The Racial Grammar of Everyday Life in Contemporary America." *Ethnic and Racial Studies* 35 (2): 173–194.

Booth, Robert, and Annie Kelly. 2016. "Migrant Workers in Qatar Still at Risk Despite Reforms, Warns Amnesty." *Guardian*, December 12. https://www.theguardian.

com/global-development/2016/dec/13/migrant-workers-in-qatar-still-at-risk-de-spite-reforms-warns-amnesty.

Bose, Sugata. 2009. *A Hundred Horizons: The Indian Ocean in the Age of Global Empire.* Cambridge, MA: Harvard University Press.

Bristol-Rhys, Jane. 2012. "Socio-Spatial Boundaries in Abu Dhabi." In *Migrant Labor in the Persian Gulf,* edited by Mehran Kamrava and Zahra Babar, 59–84. New York: Columbia University Press.

Brown, Wendy. 1995. *States of Injury: Power and Freedom in Late Modernity.* Princeton: Princeton University Press.

———. 2015. *Undoing the Demos: Neoliberalism's Stealth Revolution.* Cambridge, MA: MIT Press.

Buckley, Michelle. 2014. "Construction Work, 'Bachelor' Builders and the Intersectional Politics of Urbanisation in Dubai." In *Transit States: Labour, Migration, and Citizenship in the Gulf,* edited by Abdulhadi Khalaf, Omar AlShehabi, and Adam Hanieh, 132–150. London: Pluto Books.

Burja, Abdalla S. 1971. *The Politics of Stratification: A Study of Political Change in a South Arabian Town.* Oxford: Clarendon Press.

Busby, Cecilia. 1997. "Of Marriage and Marriageability: Gender and Dravidian Kinship." *Journal of the Royal Anthropological Institute* 3 (1): 21–42.

Butler, Judith. 2009. *Frames of War: When Is Life Grievable?* New York: Verso.

Carsten, Janet. 2004. *After Kinship.* Cambridge: Cambridge University Press.

———. 2011. "Substance and Relationality: Blood in Contexts." *Annual Review of Anthropology* 40: 19–35.

Carter, Marina. 1995. *Servants, Sirdars, and Settlers: Indians in Mauritius, 1834–1874.* New Delhi: Oxford University Press.

Castles, Stephen, Hein de Haas, and Mark J. Miller. 2013. *The Age of Migration: International Population Movements in the Modern World.* London: Palgrave Macmillan.

Césaire, Aimé. 1972. *Discourse on Colonialism: A Poetics of Anticolonialism.* Translated by Joan Pinkham. New York: Monthly Review Press.

———. 1996a. "Calling the Magician: A Few Words for a Caribbean Civilization." In *Refusal of the Shadow: Surrealism and the Caribbean,* edited and translated by Krzysztof Fijalkowski and Michael Richardson, 119–122. New York: Verso.

———. 1996b. "Poetry and Knowledge." In *Refusal of the Shadow: Surrealism and the Caribbean,* edited and translated by Krzysztof Fijalkowski and Michael Richardson, 134–146. New York: Verso.

Chakrabarty, Dipesh. 2000. *Provincializing Europe: Postcolonial Thought and Historical Difference*. Princeton: Princeton University Press.

Chakravarti, Uma. 1999. "Whatever Happened to the Vedic Dasi? Orientalism, Nationalism, and a Script for the Past." In *Recasting Women: Essays in Indian Colonial History*, edited by Kumkum Sangari and Sudesh Vaid, 27–87. New Brunswick: Rutgers University Press.

Chatterjee, Partha. 1989. "The Nationalist Resolution of the Women's Question." In *Recasting Women: Essays in Colonial History*, edited by K. Sangari and S. Vaid, 233–253. New Delhi: Kali for Women.

———. 1993. *A Nation and Its Fragments: Colonial and Postcolonial Histories*. Princeton: Princeton University Press.

———. 2004. *The Politics of the Governed: Reflections on Popular Politics in Most of the World*. Delhi: Permanent Black.

Chatterji, Angana P. 2019. "Remaking the Hindu/Nation: Terror and Impunity in Uttar Pradesh." In *Majoritarian State: How Hindu Nationalism Is Changing India*, edited by Angana P. Chatterji, Thomas Blom Hansen, and Christophe Jaffrelot, 397–418. Oxford: Oxford University Press.

Chowdhry, Prem. 2005. "Crisis of Masculinity in Haryana." *Economic and Political Weekly* 40 (49): 5189–5198.

Chu, Julia Y. 2010. *Cosmologies of Credit: Transnational Mobility and the Politics of Destination in China*. Durham: Duke University Press.

Citino, Nathan J. 2002. *From Arab Nationalism to OPEC: Eisenhower, King Sa'ūd, and the Making of U.S.-Saudi Relations*. Bloomington: Indiana University Press.

Cody, Francis. 2009. "Inscribing Subjects to Citizenship: Petitions, Literary Activism, and the Performativity of Signature in Rural Tamil India." *Cultural Anthropology* 24 (3): 347–380.

———. 2013. *The Light of Knowledge: Literacy Activism and the Politics of Writing in South India*. Ithaca: Cornell University Press.

Coe, Cati. 2011a. "What Is the Impact of Transnational Migration on Family Life? Women's Comparisons of Internal and International Migration in a Small Town in Ghana." *American Ethnologist* 38 (1): 148–163.

———. 2011b. "What Is Love? The Materiality of Care in Ghanaian Transnational Families." *International Migration* 49 (6): 7–24.

Cohen, David William. 1996. "Historical Anthropology: Discerning the Rules of the Game." *Focaal* 26/27: 65–67.

Cohen, David William, and E. S. Atieno Odhiambo. 2004. *The Risks of Knowledge: Investigations into the Death of the Hon. Minister John Robert Ouko in Kenya, 1990.* Athens: Ohio University Press.

Cohen, Lawrence. 1999. "Where It Hurts: Indian Material for an Ethics of Organ Transplantation." *Daedalus* 128 (4): 135–165.

———. 2002. *No Aging in India: Alzheimer's, the Bad Family, and Other Modern Things.* New Delhi: Oxford University Press.

———. 2011. "Migrant Supplementarity: Remaking Biological Relatedness in Chinese Military and Indian Five-Star Hospitals." *Body and Society* 17 (2–3): 31–54.

Cohen, Susanne. 2015. "The New Communication Order: Management, Language, and Morality in a Multinational Corporation." *American Ethnologist* 42 (2): 324–339.

Cohn, Bernard. 1980. "History and Anthropology: The State of Play." *Comparative Studies in Society and History* 22 (2): 198–221.

Cole, Juan. 1987. "Rival Empires of Trade and Imami Shi'ism in Eastern Arabia, 1300–1800." *International Journal of Middle Eastern Studies* 19 (2): 177–203.

Colton, Nora Ann. 2010. "The International Political Economy of Gulf Migration." *Middle East Institute Viewpoints*, February.

Comaroff, Jean, and John L. Comaroff. 1987. "The Madman and the Migrant: Work and Labor in the Historical Consciousness of a South African People." *American Ethnologist* 14: 191–209.

Connell, R. W., and James W. Messerschmidt. 2005. "Hegemonic Masculinity: Rethinking the Concept." *Gender and Society* 19 (6): 829–859.

Corley, T. A. B. 1983. *A History of the Burmah Oil Company, 1886–1924.* London: Heinemann.

Coronil, Fernando. 1996. "Beyond Occidentalism: Toward Nonimperial Geohistorical Categories." *Cultural Anthropology* 11 (1): 51–87.

———. 1997. *The Magical State: Nature, Money, and Modernity in Venezuela.* Chicago: University of Chicago Press.

———. 2000. "Towards a Critique of Globalcentrism: Speculations on Capitalism's Nature." *Public Culture* 12 (2): 351–374.

———. 2019. *The Fernando Coronil Reader: The Struggle for Life Is the Matter.* Edited by Julie Skursi, Gary Wilder, Laurent Dubois, Paul Eiss, Edward Murphy, Mariana Coronil, and David Pedersen. Durham: Duke University Press.

Crenshaw, Kimberlé. 1991. "Mapping the Margins: Intersectionality, Identity Politics, and Violence against Women of Color." *Stanford Law Review* 43 (6): 1241–1299.

Dahinden, Janine. 2005. "Contesting Transnationalism? Lessons from the Study of Albanian Migration Networks from Former Yugoslavia." *Global Networks* 5 (2): 191–208.

Daniel, E. Valentine. 1996. *Charred Lullabies: Chapters in an Anthropology of Violence.* Princeton: Princeton University Press.

Das, Veena. 2004. "The Signature of the State: The Paradox of Illegibility." In *Anthropology in the Margins of the State*, edited by Veena Das and Deborah Poole, 225–252. Santa Fe: School of American Research Press.

Das, Veena, and Deborah Poole. 2004. "State and Its Margins: Comparative Ethnographies." In *Anthropology in the Margins of the State*, edited by Veena Das and Deborah Poole, 3–34. Santa Fe: School of American Research Press.

DasGupta, Ranajit. 1994. *Labour and Working Class in Eastern India.* Calcutta: K. P. Bagchi and Co.

Dasgupta, Simanti. 2014. "Sovereign Silence: Immoral Traffic (Prevention) Act and Legalizing Sex Work in Sonagachi." *PoLAR: Political and Legal Anthropology* 37 (1): 109–125.

Davidson, Christopher. 2011. *Dubai: The Vulnerability of Success.* New York: Columbia University Press.

De Certeau, Michel. 1988 [1975]. *The Writing of History.* New York: Columbia University Press.

De León, Jason. 2015. *The Land of Open Graves: Living and Dying on the Migrant Trail.* Berkeley: University of California Press.

Derrida, Jacques. 1976. *Of Grammatology.* Translated by Gayatri C. Spivak. Baltimore: John Hopkins University Press.

———. 1994. *Specters of Marx: The State of Debt, the Work of Mourning and the New International.* Translated by Peggy Kamuf. New York: Routledge.

Dito, Mohammed. 2014. "*Kafala*: Foundations of Migrant Exclusion in the GCC Labour Markets." In *Transit States: Labour, Migration, and Citizenship in the Gulf*, edited by Abdulhadi Khalaf, Omar AlShehabi, and Adam Hanieh, 79–100. London: Pluto Books.

DNA Investigations Bureau. 2011. "Bar Girls: Banned in Mumbai, Trafficked to Dubai." *Daily News and Analysis*, 1–6. http://www.dnaindia.com/mumbai/report-bar-girls-banned-in-mumbai-trafficked-to-dubai-1594036.

Eaton, Richard M. 1993. *The Rise of Islam and the Bengal Frontier, 1204–1706.* Berkeley: University of California Press.

———. 2004. *Temple Desecration and Muslim States in Medieval India.* Gurgaon, India: Hope India.

Ehrenreich, Barbara, and Arlie Russell. 2002. *Global Woman: Nannies, Maids, and Sex Workers in the New Economy.* New York: Holt.

Ehsani, Kaveh. 2018. "Disappearing the Workers: How Labor in the Oil Complex Has Been Made Invisible." In *Working for Oil: Comparative Social Histories of Labor in the Global Oil Industry*, edited by Touraj Atabaki, Elisabetta Bini, and Kaveh Ehsani, 11–34. London: Palgrave Macmillan.

Eley, Geoff. 2005. *A Crooked Line: From Cultural History to the History of Society*. Ann Arbor: University of Michigan Press.

———. 2006. "Transnational Labour History: Explorations." *Labor: Studies in Working-Class History of the Americas* 3 (1): 164–166.

Elyachar, Julia. 2005. *Markets of Dispossession: NGOS, Economic Development, and the State in Cairo*. Durham: Duke University Press.

Engels, Friedrich. 1972 [1884]. *Origin of the Family, Private Property, and the State*. New York: International Publishers.

Escobar, Arturo. 1995. *Encountering Development: The Making and Unmaking of the Third World*. Princeton: Princeton University Press.

Ewig, Christina. 2011. *Second-Wave Neoliberalism: Gender, Race, and Health Sector Reform in Peru*. University Park: Pennsylvania State University Press.

Fanon, Franz. 2004. *The Wretched of the Earth*. Translated by Richard Philcox. New York: Grove Press.

Feeley-Harnik, Gillian. 1999. "'Communities of Blood': The Natural History of Kinship in Nineteenth-Century America." *Comparative Studies in Society and History* 41 (2): 215–262.

Fehérváry, Krisztina. 2012. "From Socialist Modern to Super-Natural Organicism: Cosmological Transformations through Home Décor." *Cultural Anthropology* 27 (4): 615–640.

Ferguson, James. 1994. *The Anti-Politics Machine: Development, Depoliticization, and Bureaucratic Power in Lesotho*. Minneapolis: University of Minnesota Press.

———. 1999. *Expectations of Modernity: Myths and Meanings of Urban Life on the Zambian Copperbelt*. Berkeley: University of California Press.

———. 2005. "Seeing Like an Oil Company: Space, Security, and Global Capital in Neoliberal Africa." *American Anthropologist* 107 (3): 377–382.

Ferry, Elizabeth Emma, and Mandana E. Limbert. 2008. "Introduction." In *Timely Assets: The Politics of Resources and Their Temporalities*, edited by Elizabeth Emma Ferry and Mandana E. Limbert, 3–24. Santa Fe: School for Advanced Research Press.

Fineman, Martha. 2008. "The Vulnerable Subject: Anchoring Equality in the Human Condition." *Yale Journal of Law and Feminism* 20: 1–23.

Foster, Robert J. 2008. *Coca-Globalization: Following Soft Drinks from New York to New Guinea*. London: Palgrave Macmillan.

Foucault, Michel. 2007. *Security, Territory, Population: Lectures at the College de France, 1977–1978*. Translated by Graham Burchell. Edited by Michel Senellart. New York: Picador.

———. 2010. *The Birth of Biopolitics: Lectures at the College de France, 1977–1978*. Translated by Graham Burchell. Edited by Michel Senellart. New York: Picador.

Freeman, Carla. 2014. *Entrepreneurial Selves: Neoliberal Respectability and the Making of a Caribbean Middle Class*. Durham: Duke University Press.

Fruzzetti, Lina. 1982. *The Gift of a Virgin: Women, Marriage, and Ritual in Bengali Society*. New Brunswick, NJ: Rutgers University Press.

Fuller, C. J. 2004. *The Camphor Flame: Popular Hinduism and Society in India*, rev. and exp. ed. Princeton: Princeton University Press.

Gago, Verónica. 2017. *Neoliberalism from Below: Popular Pragmatics and Baroque Economics*. Translated by Liz Mason-Deese. Durham: Duke University Press.

Gamburd, Michele R. 2008. "Milk Teeth and Jet Planes: Kin Relations in Families of Sri Lanka's Transnational Domestic Servants." *City and Society* 20 (1): 5–31.

Gardner, Andrew. 2010. *City of Strangers: Gulf Migration and the Indian Community in Bahrain*. Ithaca: Cornell University Press.

———. 2012. "Why Do They Keep Coming? Labor Migrants in the Gulf States." In *Migrant Labor in the Persian Gulf*, edited by Mehran Kamrava and Zahra Babar, 41–58. New York: Columbia University Press.

Gettleman, Jeffrey, Sameer Yasir, Suhasini Raj, and Hari Kumar. 2020. "How Delhi's Police Turned against Muslims." *New York Times*, March 12.

Ghassem-Fachandi, Parvis. 2012. *Pogrom in Gujarat: Hindu Nationalism and Anti-Muslim Violence in India*. Princeton: Princeton University Press.

Ghosh, Amitav. 2002. *The Imam and the Indian*. New Delhi: Penguin Books India.

Giroux, Henry A. 2006. "Reading Hurricane Katrina: Race, Class, and the Biopolitics of Disposability." *College Literature* 33 (3): 171–196.

Glissant, Édouard. 1997. *Poetics of Relation*. Translated by Betsy Wing. Ann Arbor: University of Michigan Press.

Glover, William. 2008. *Making Lahore Modern: Constructing and Imagining a Colonial City*. Minneapolis: University of Minnesota Press.

Gokulan, Dhanusha, and Amira Agarib. 2015. "Workers Get Shelter after Living in Bus for 12 Days." *Khaleej Times*, December 20.

Graeber, David. 2001. *Toward an Anthropological Theory of Value: The False Coin of Our Own Dreams*. New York: Palgrave.

———. 2009. "Debt, Violence, and Impersonal Markets: Polanyian Meditations." In *Market and Society: The Great Transformation*, edited by Chris Hann and Keith Hart, 106–132. Cambridge: Cambridge University Press.

———. 2010. "Neoliberalism, or the Bureaucratization of the World." In *The Insecure American: How We Got Here and What We Should Do About It*, edited by Hugh Gusterson and Catherine Besteman, 79–96. Berkeley: University of California Press.

———. 2011. *Debt: The First 5000 Years*. New York: Melville House.

Grapevine, Rebecca. 2015. "Family Matters: Citizenship and Marriage in India, 1939–72." PhD diss, University of Michigan.

Günel, Gökçe. 2016. *Spaceship in the Desert: Energy, Climate Change, and Urban Design in Abu Dhabi*. Durham: Duke University Press.

Gupta, Akhil. 1995. "Blurred Boundaries: The Discourse of Corruption, the Culture of Politics, and the Imagined State." *American Ethnologist* 22 (2): 375–402.

———. 2012. *Red Tape: Bureaucracy, Structural Violence, and Poverty in India*. Durham: Duke University Press.

———. 2018. "The Future in Ruins: Thoughts on the Temporality of Infrastructure." In *The Promise of Infrastructure*, edited by Nikhil Anand, Akhil Gupta, and Hannah Appel, 62–79. Durham: Duke University Press.

Gupta, Charu. 2002. *Sexuality, Obscenity, Community: Women, Muslims, and the Hindu Public in Colonial India*. New York: Palgrave.

Hämäläinen, Päivi, Jukka Takala, and Kaija Leena Saarela. 2006. "Global Estimates of Occupational Accidents." *Safety Science* 44: 137–156.

Hall, Stuart. 1986. "On Postmodernism and Articulation: An Interview with Stuart Hall." Edited by Lawrence Grossberg. *Journal of Communication Inquiry* 10: 45–60.

———. 2017. *The Fateful Triangle: Race, Ethnicity, Nation*. Cambridge, MA: Harvard University Press.

Hancock, Mary E. 2002. "Modernities Remade: Hindu Temples and Their Publics in Southern India." *City and Society* 14 (1): 5–35.

Hanieh, Adam. 2011. *Capitalism and Class in the Gulf Arab States*. London: Palgrave Macmillan.

———. 2014. "Overcoming Methodological Nationalism: Spatial Perspectives on Migration to the Gulf Arab States." In *Transit States: Labour, Migration, and Citizenship in the Gulf*, edited by Abdulhadi Khalaf, Omar AlShehabi, and Adam Hanieh, 57–76. London: Pluto Books.

———. 2015. "Capital, Labor, and State: Rethinking the Political Economy of Oil in the Gulf." In *The Oxford Handbook of Contemporary Middle-Eastern and North African History*, edited by Amal Ghazal and Jens Hanssen. Oxford: Oxford University Press.

———. 2018. *Money, Markets, and Monarchies: The Gulf Cooperative Council and the Political Economy of the Contemporary Middle East.* Cambridge: Cambridge University Press.

Hansen, Thomas Blom. 2000. "Predicaments of Secularism: Muslim Identities and Politics in Mumbai." *Journal of the Royal Anthropological Institute* 6 (2): 255–272.

———. 2001. "Bridging the Gulf: Migration, Modernity and Identity among Muslims in Mumbai." In *Community, Empire and Migration: South Asians in Diaspora*, edited by Crispin Bates, 261–285. New York: Palgrave.

Hardt, Michael, and Toni Negri. 2018. "The Multiplicities within Capitalist Rule and the Articulation of Struggles." *Triple C* 16 (2): 440–448.

Harvey, David. 2018a. "Universal Alienation." *Triple C* 16 (2): 424–439.

———. 2018b. "Universal Alienation, Formal and Real Subsumption of Society under Capital: A Response to Hardt and Negri." *Triple C* 16 (2): 449–453.

Hasan, Shazia. 2020. "Workers Protest for Payment of Wages, Dues in Karachi." *Dawn*, April 19.

Hecht, Gabrielle. 2012. *Being Nuclear: Africans and the Global Uranium Trade.* Cambridge, MA: MIT Press.

Hertog, Steffen. 2010. "The Sociology of the Gulf Rentier Systems: Societies of Intermediaries." *Comparative Studies in Society and History* 52 (2): 282–318.

Heslop, Luke A. 2020. "A Journey through 'Infraspace': The Financial Architecture of Infrastructure." *Economy and Society* 49 (3): 364–381.

Heslop, Luke, and Laura Jeffery. 2020. "Roadwork: Expertise at Work in Building Roads in the Maldives." *Journal of the Royal Anthropological Institute* 26 (2): 284–301.

Hindustan Times. 2020. "Full Text of US President Donald Trump's Speech at 'Namaste Trump' Event in Ahmedabad." February 24.

Ho, Engseng. 2006. *The Graves of Tarim: Genealogy and Mobility across the Indian Ocean.* Berkeley: University of California Press.

Hodžić, Saida. 2016. *The Twilight of Cutting: African Activism and Life after NGOs.* Berkeley: University of California Press.

Holmes, Seth. 2013. *Fresh Fruit, Broken Bodies: Migrant Farm Workers in the United States.* Berkeley: University of California Press.

Hull, Matthew S. 2010. "Democratic Technologies of Speech: From WWII America to Postcolonial Delhi." *Journal of Linguistic Anthropology* 20 (2): 257–282.

———. 2012. *Government of Paper: The Materiality of Bureaucracy in Urban Pakistan.* Berkeley: University of California Press.

Jaffrelot, Christophe. 2009. "The Hindu Nationalist Reinterpretation of Pilgrimage in India: The Limits of Yatra Politics." *Nations and Nationalism* 15 (1): 1–19.

Jakobson, Roman. 1960. "Closing Statement: Linguistics and Poetics." In *Style in Language*, edited by Thomas A. Sebeok, 350–377. Cambridge, MA: MIT Press.

Jauregui, Beatrice. 2014. "Provisional Agency in India: *Jugaad* and Legitimation of Corruption." *American Ethnologist* 41 (1): 76–91.

Jeffrey, Craig. 2010. *Timepass: Youth, Culture, and the Politics of Waiting in India.* Stanford: Stanford University Press.

Kale, Madhavi. 2010. *Fragments of Empire: Capital, Slavery, and Indentured Labor in the British Caribbean.* Philadelphia: University of Pennsylvania Press.

Kale, Sunila S. 2014. *Electrifying India: Regional Political Economies of Development.* Stanford: Stanford University Press.

Kamrava, Mehran. 2018. "Oil and Institutional Stasis in the Persian Gulf." *Journal of Arabian Studies* 8 (1): 1–12.

Kanna, Ahmed. 2011. *Dubai, the City as Corporation.* Minneapolis: University of Minnesota Press.

Kanna, Ahmed, Amélie Le Renard, and Neha Vora. 2020. *Beyond Exception: New Interpretations of the Arabian Peninsula.* Ithaca: Cornell University Press.

Kapferer, Bruce. 2006. "Situations, Crisis, and the Anthropology of the Concrete: The Contribution of Max Gluckman." In *The Manchester School: Practice and Ethnographic Praxis in Anthropology*, edited by T. M. S. Evens and Don Handelman, 118–158. Oxford: Berghahn Books.

Kaur, Ravinder. 2012. "Nation's Two Bodies: Rethinking the Idea of 'New' India and Its Other." *Third World Quarterly* 33 (4): 603–621.

———. 2015. "Good Times, Brought to You by Brand Modi." *Television and New Media* 16 (4): 323–330.

Keane, Webb. 2003. "Semiotics and the Social Analysis of Material Things." *Language and Communication* 23: 409–425.

Kelley, Robin D. G. 2003. *Freedom Dreams: The Black Radical Imagination.* Boston: Beacon Press.

Khalaf, Sulayman N. 2010. "Dubai Camel Market Transnational Workers: An Ethnographic Portrait." *City and Society* 22 (1): 97–118.

Khalidi, Rashid. 2010. *Resurrecting Empire: Western Footprints and America's Perilous Path in the Middle East.* Boston: Beacon Press.

Khilnani, Sunil. 2004. *The Idea of India*. New Delhi: Penguin Books.

Kinninmont, Jane. 2011. "Bahrain." In *Power and Politics in the Persian Gulf Monarchies*, edited by Christopher Davidson, 31–62. New York: Columbia University Press.

Kirsch, Stuart. 2014. *Mining Capitalism: The Relationship between Corporations and Their Critics*. Berkeley: University of California Press.

Klebnikov, Serge. 2019. "Saudi Aramco Reaches $2 Trillion Market Value in Record IPO's Second Day of Trading." *Forbes*, December 11.

Kotiswaran, Prabha. 2012. "Vulnerability in Domestic Discourses on Trafficking: Lessons from the Indian Experience." *Feminist Legal Studies* 20 (3): 245–262.

Kowalski, Julia. 2016. "Ordering Dependence: Care, Disorder, and Kinship Ideology in North Indian Antiviolence Counseling." *American Ethnologist* 43 (1): 63–75.

Kumar, Radha. 1993. *The History of Doing: An Illustrated Account of Movements for Women's Rights and Feminism in India, 1800–1990*. New Delhi: Kali for Women.

Lal, Jayati. 2011. "(Un)Becoming Women: Indian Factory Women's Counternarratives of Gender." *Sociological Review* 59 (3): 553–78.

Lall, R. 2009. "In Dubai, Thriving Indian Clubs with a Dark Side?" *Times of India*, November 23.

Lamb, Sarah. 2000. *White Saris and Sweet Mangoes: Aging, Gender, and Body in North India*. Berkeley: University of California Press.

———. 2013. "In/Dependence, Intergenerational Uncertainty, and the Ambivalent State: Perceptions of Old Age Security in India." *Journal of South Asian Studies* 36 (1): 65–78.

Larkin, Brian. 2013. "The Politics and Poetics of Infrastructure." *Annual Review of Anthropology* 42 (1): 327–343.

———. 2018. "Promising Forms: The Political Aesthetics of Infrastructure." In *The Promise of Infrastructure*, edited by Nikhil Anand, Akhil Gupta, and Hannah Appel, 176–202. Durham: Duke University Press.

Latour, Bruno. 2007. *Reassembling the Social: An Introduction to Actor-Network-Theory*. New York: Oxford University Press.

Law, John, and Michel Callon. 1992. "The Life and Death of an Aircraft: a Network Analysis of Technical Change." In *Shaping Technology/Building Society: Studies in Sociotechnical Change*, edited by Wiebe E. Bijker and John Law, 21–52. Cambridge, MA: MIT Press, 1992.

Lazzarato, Maurizio. 2009. "Neoliberalism in Action: Inequality, Insecurity, and the Reconstitution of the Social." *Theory, Culture and Society* 26 (6): 109–133.

LeMenager, Stephanie. 2014. *Living Oil: Petroleum Culture in the American Century.* Oxford: Oxford University Press.

Lempert, Michael P. 2008. "Poetics of Stance: Text-metricality, Epistemicity, Interaction." *Language in Society* 15 (2): 171–193.

Lenze, Nele. 2018. "Networks Online and Offline: Spaces of Cultural Production in the Gulf." In *Participation Culture in the Gulf: Networks, Politics and Identity,* edited by Nele Lenze and Charlotte Schriwer. London: Routledge.

Leonard, Karen Isaksen. 2007. *Locating Home: India's Hyderabadis Abroad.* Stanford: Stanford University Press.

Likosky, Michael. 2009. "Contracting and Regulatory Issues in the Oil and Gas and Metallic Minerals Industries." *Transnational Corporations* 18 (1): 1–42.

Limbert, Mandana. 2010. *In the Time of Oil: Piety, Memory, and Social Life in an Omani Town.* Stanford: Stanford University Press.

———. 2014. "Caste, Ethnicity, and the Politics of Arabness in Southern Arabia." *Comparative Studies of South Asia, Africa and the Middle East* 34 (3): 590–598.

———. 2016. "Liquid Oman: Oil, Water, and Causality in Southern Arabia." *Journal of the Royal Anthropological Institute* 22 (1): 147–162.

Lomnitz, Claudio. 2005. *Death and the Idea of Mexico.* New York: Zone Books.

Longva, Anh Nga. 1997. *Walls Built on Sand: Migration, Exclusion, and Society in Kuwait.* Boulder, CO: Westview Press.

———. 1999. "Keeping Migrant Workers in Check: The *Kafala* System in the Gulf." *Middle East Report* 211 (Summer): 20–22.

Lorey, Isabell. 2015. *State of Insecurity: Government of the Precarious.* Translated by Aileen Derieg. New York: Verso Books.

Lori, Noora. 2011. "National Security and the Management of Migrant Labor: A Case Study of the United Arab Emirates." *Asian and Pacific Migration Journal* 20 (3–4): 315–337.

Lowe, Lisa. 2015. *The Intimacies of the Four Continents.* Durham: Duke University Press.

Luciani, Giacomo. 1990. "Allocation vs. Production States: A Theoretical Framework." In *The Arab State,* edited by Giacomo Luciani, 65-84. London: Routledge.

MachLochlainn, Scott. 2019. "Brand Displaced: Trademarking, Unmarking, and Making the Generic." *Hau: Journal of Ethnographic Theory* 9 (3): 498–513.

Mahdavi, Pardis. 2011. *Gridlock: Labor, Migration, and Human Trafficking in Dubai.* Stanford: Stanford University Press.

Mahdavy, Hossein. 1970. "The Patterns and Problems of Economic Development in

Rentier States: The Case of Iran." In *Studies in Economic History of the Middle East*, edited by M. A. Cook, 428–467. London: Oxford University Press.

Malm, Andreas. 2016. *Fossil Capital: The Rise of Steam Power and the Roots of Global Warming*. New York: Verso Books.

Manning, Paul. 2010. "The Semiotics of Brand." *Annual Review of Anthropology* 39 (1): 33–49.

Mariner, Kathryn. 2019. "Who You Are in These Pieces of Paper: Imagining Future Kinship through Auto/Biographical Adoption Documents in the United States." *Cultural Anthropology* 34 (4): 529–554.

Maritime Executive. 2019. "Labor Reforms Signal End of Kafala System in Qatar." October 19. https://www.maritime-executive.com/article/labor-reforms-signal-end-of-kafala-system-in-qatar.

Marshall, T. H. 1950. *Citizenship and Social Class*. Cambridge: Cambridge University Press.

Marx, Karl. 1959. *Economic and Philosophical Manuscripts of 1844*. Moscow: Progress Publishers.

———. 1973. *Grundrisse*. New York: Penguin Books.

———. 1994 [1852]. *The Eighteenth Brumaire of Louis Napoleon*. New York: International Publishers.

Marx, Karl, with Friedrich Engels. 1998. *The German Ideology*. Amherst, NY: Prometheus Books.

Mason, Krystal L., Kyla D. Retzer, Ryan Hill, and Jennifer M. Lincoln. 2015. "Occupational Fatalities during the Oil and Gas Boom—United States, 2003–2013." *Morbidity and Mortality Weekly Report* 64 (20): 551–554.

Mathew, Johan. 2016. *Margins of the Market: Trafficking and Capitalism across the Arabian Sea*. Berkeley: University of California Press.

Mathur, Nayanika. 2012. "Transparent-Making Documents and the Crisis of Implementation: A Rural Employment Law and Development Bureaucracy in India." *Political and Legal Anthropology Review* 35 (2): 167–185.

———. 2015. *Paper Tiger: Law, Bureaucracy, and the Developmental State in Himalayan India*. Cambridge: Cambridge University Press.

Mazzarella, William. 2003a. "'Very Bombay': Contending with the Global in an Indian Advertising Agency." *Cultural Anthropology* 18 (1): 33–71.

———. 2003b. *Shoveling Smoke: Advertising and Globalization in Contemporary India*. Durham: Duke University Press.

Mbembe, Achille. 2003. "Necropolitics." Translated by Libby Meintjes. *Public Culture* 15 (1): 11–40.

———. 2017. *Critique of Black Reason*. Translated by Laurent Dubois. Durham: Duke University Press.

———. 2019. *Necropolitics*. Translated by Steve Corcoran. Durham: Duke University Press.

———. 2020. *Brutalisme*. Paris: La Découverte.

———. 2021. *Out of the Dark Night: Essays on Decolonization*. New York: Columbia University Press.

McGinley, Shane. 2013. "Revealed: Where Gulf Expats Sent Remittance in 2012." *Arabian Business*, May 13. http://www.arabianbusiness.com/revealed-where-gulf-expats-sent-remittance-in-2012-501232.html.

Mehta, Purvi. 2017. "Dalit Feminism at Home and in the World: The Conceptual Work of 'Difference' and 'Similarity' in National and Transnational Activism." In *Women's Activism and "Second Wave" Feminism: Transnational Histories*, edited by Barbara Molony and Jennifer Nelson, 231–248. London: Bloomsbury.

———. 2019. "Dalit Feminism in Tokyo: Analogy and Affiliation in Transnational Dalit Activism." *Feminist Review* 121 (1): 24–36.

Metcalf, Barbara. 2002. *Islamic Revival in British India: Deoband, 1860–1900*. New Delhi: Oxford University Press.

Metcalf, Thomas R. 2008. *Imperial Connections: India in the Indian Ocean Arena, 1860–1920*. Berkeley: University of California Press.

Meyers, Diana Tietjens. 2011. "Two Victim Paradigms and the Problem of 'Impure' Victims." *Humanity: An International Journal of Human Rights, Humanitarianism, and Development* 2 (2): 255–275.

Minault, Gail. 1982. *The Khalifat Movement: Religion and Political Mobilization in India*. New York: Columbia University Press.

Mintz, Sidney. 2010. *Three Ancient Colonies: Caribbean Themes and Variations*. Cambridge, MA: Harvard University Press.

Mir, Farina. 2010. *The Social Space of Language: Vernacular Culture in British Colonial Punjab*. Berkeley: University of California Press.

Mitchell, J. Clyde. 1969. "The Concept and Use of Social Networks." In *Social Networks in Urban Situations*, edited by J. Clyde Mitchell, 1–50. Manchester: Manchester University Press.

Mitchell, Timothy. 1999. "Society, Economy, and the State Effect." In *State/Culture*, edited by George Steinmetz, 76–97. Ithaca, NY: Cornell University Press.

———. 2002. *Rule of Experts: Egypt, Techno-Politics, Modernity.* Berkeley: University of California Press.

———. 2011. *Carbon Democracy: Political Power in the Age of Oil.* New York: Verso.

———. 2014. "Economentality: How the Future Entered Government." *Critical Inquiry* 40 (4): 479–507.

Mohanty, Chandra Talpade. 1988. "Under Western Eyes: Feminist Scholarship and Colonial Discourses." *Feminist Review* 30 (August): 61–88.

———. 2003. "'Under Western Eyes' Revisited: Feminist Solidarity through Anticapitalist Struggles." *Signs: Journal of Women in Culture and Society* 28 (2): 499–535.

Moin, A. Azfar. 2015. "Sovereign Violence: Temple Destruction in India and Shrine Desecration in Iran and Central Asia." *Comparative Studies in Society and History* 57 (2): 467–496.

Mol, Annemarie. 2002. *The Body Multiple: Ontology in Medical Practice.* Durham: Duke University Press.

Molavi, Afshin. 2018. "Commentary: India's Most Vital Hub City Isn't in India." *Channel News Asia*, March 23. https://www.channelnewsasia.com/news/asia/india-dubai-abu-dhabi-uae-hub-city-for-non-resident-indians-10065642.

Mongia, Radhika Viyas. 1999. "Race, Nationality, Mobility: A History of the Passport." *Public Culture* 11 (3): 527–556.

———. 2018. *Indian Migration and Empire: A Genealogy of the Modern State.* Durham: Duke University Press.

Morgan, Lewis Henry. 1997 [1868]. *Systems of Consanguinity and Affinity of the Human Family.* Lincoln: University of Nebraska Press.

Mueggler, Erik. 2001. *The Age of Wild Ghosts: Memory, Violence, and Place in Southwest China.* Berkeley: University of California Press.

Muhammad, Abdul el Hey. 2019. "Abu Dhabi *tasmah lighayr almuatinin bialtamluk waltasaruf aleaqarii*." *Al Bayan*, April 18.

Munif, Abdelrahman. 1987. *Cities of Salt.* Translated by Peter Theroux. New York: Vintage.

Munn, Nancy. 1986. *The Fame of Gawa: A Symbolic Study of Value Transformation in a Massim (Papua New Guinea) Society.* Durham: Duke University Press.

Murphy, Edward L., David William Cohen, Chandra Bhimull, Fernando Coronil, Monica Patterson, and Julie Skurski, eds. 2011. *Anthrohistory: Unsettling Knowledge, Questioning Discipline.* Ann Arbor: University of Michigan Press.

Nader, Laura. 1972. "Up the Anthropologist: Perspectives Gained from Studying Up."

In *Reinventing Anthropology*, edited by Dell H. Hymes, 284–311. New York: Pantheon Books.

Naheed, Kishwar. 1985. *Aurat: khaab aur khaak kai dar-mayaan*. Lahore: Guul-Rang Publishers.

Nair, Rupam Jain, Praveen Menon, and Marwa Rashad. 2014. "India Urges Higher Pay for Millions of Gulf Workers." *Live Mint*, November 17. https://www.livemint.com/Industry/FNQ7CBS8DbBnLZZvBYSlkJ/India-urges-higher-pay-for-millions-of-Gulf-workers.html.

Nambiar, A. C. K. 1995. *The Socio-Economic Conditions of Gulf Migrants*. New Delhi: Commonwealth Publishers.

Narayan, Badri. 2015. "Democracy and Identity Politics in India: Is It a Snake or a Rope?" *Economic and Political Weekly* April 18.

Nayak, Venkatesh. 2018. "RTI Reveal." *Commonwealth Human Rights Initiative*. https://www.humanrightsinitiative.org/blog/rti-reveal-more-than-10-indian-workers-died-every-day-in-gulf-countries-in-the-last-six-years-117-deaths-for-every-us-117-remitted-

NDTV. 2011. "Minimum Wages Hiked for Indian Workers in UAE." March 16. https://www.ndtv.com/india-news/minimum-wages-hiked-for-indian-workers-in-uae-450219

Okruhlik, Gwenn. 1999. "Rentier Wealth, Unruly Law, and the Rise of Opposition: The Political Economy of Oil States." *Comparative Politics* 31 (3): 295–315.

Oldenburg, Veena Talwar. 2002. *Dowry Murder: The Imperial Origins of a Cultural Crime*. Oxford: Oxford University Press.

Ong, Aihwa. 2006. *Neoliberalism as Exception: Mutations in Citizenship and Sovereignty*. Durham: Duke University Press.

———. 2016. "Mutations in Citizenship." *Theory, Culture and Society* 23 (2–3): 499–505.

Onley, James. 2007. *The Arabian Frontier of the British Raj: Merchants, Rulers, and the British in the Nineteenth-Century Gulf*. New York: Oxford University Press.

———. 2009. "The Raj Reconsidered: British India's Informal Empire and Spheres of Influence in Asia and Africa." *Asian Affairs* 40 (1): 44–62.

Onley, James, and Sulayman Khalaf. 2006. "Shaikhly Authority in the Pre-Oil Gulf: An Historical–Anthropological Study." *History and Anthropology* 17 (3): 189–208.

Osella, Caroline, and Filippo Osella. 2012. "Migration, Networks and Connectedness across the Indian Ocean." In *Migrant Labor in the Persian Gulf*, edited by Mehran Kamrava and Zahra Babar, 21–40. New York: Columbia University Press.

Osella, Filippo, and Caroline Osella. 2000. "Migration, Money and Masculinity in Kerala." *Journal of the Royal Anthropological Institute* 6 (1): 117–33.

———. 2008. "Islamism and Social Reform in Kerala, South India." *Modern Asian Studies* 42 (2–3): 317–346.

Palmié, Stephan. 2002. *Wizards and Scientists: Explorations in Afro-Cuban Modernity and Tradition.* Durham: Duke University Press.

Palmié, Stephan, and Charles Stewart. 2016. "Towards an Anthropology of History." *Hau: Journal of Ethnographic Theory* 16 (1): 207–236.

Pandey, Gyanendra. 1999. "Can a Muslim Be an Indian?" *Comparative Studies in Society and History* 41 (4): 608–629.

———. 2010. "Politics of Difference: Reflections on Dalit and African American Struggles." *Economic and Political Weekly* 45 (19): 62–69.

Pasha, A. K. 1999. *Perspectives on India and the Gulf States.* New Delhi: Détente Publications.

Patel, Reena. 2010. *Working the Night Shift: Women in India's Call Center Industry.* Stanford: Stanford University Press.

Pedersen, David. 2013. *American Value: Migrants, Money, and Meaning in El Salvador and the United States.* Chicago: University of Chicago Press.

Peirce, Charles S. 1932. *Collected Papers of Charles Sanders Peirce: Elements of Logic.* Cambridge: Cambridge University Press.

Pierce, Steven. 2016. *Moral Economies of Corruption: State Formation and Political Culture in Nigeria.* Durham: Duke University Press.

Pletsch, Carl E. 1981. "The Three Worlds, or the Division of Social Science Labor, circa 1950–1975." *Comparative Studies in Society and History* 23 (4): 565–590.

Polanyi, Karl. 1957. *The Great Transformation: The Political and Economic Origins of Our Time.* Boston: Beacon Press.

———. 1962. *Personal Knowledge: Towards a Post-Critical Philosophy.* London: Routledge and Kegan Paul.

Postone, Moishe. 1993. "Deconstruction as Social Critique: Derrida on Marx and the New World Order." *History and Theory* 37 (3): 370–387.

Prakash, B. A., K. C. Zachariah, and S. Irudaya Rajan. 2004. "Indian Workers in UAE." *Economic and Political Weekly* 39 (22): 2227–2234.

Prakash, Gyan. 2003. *Bonded Histories: Genealogies of Labor Servitude in Colonial India.* New York: Cambridge University Press.

PTI. 2020. "It's Official," *TheWire.in*, March 8.

Puar, Jasbir K. 2007. *Terrorist Assemblages: Homonationalism in Queer Times*. Durham: Duke University Press.

Puar, Jasbir, Lauren Berlant, Judith Butler, Bojana Cvejić, Isabell Lorey, and Ana Vujanović. 2012. "Precarity Talk: a Virtual Roundtable with Lauren Berlant, Judith Butler, Bojana Cvejić, Isabell Lorey, Jasbir Puar, and Ana Vujanović." *Anthropological Quarterly* 56 (4): 163–177.

Puar, Jasbir K., and Amit Rai. 2002. "Monster, Terrorist, Fag: The War on Terrorism and the Production of Docile Patriots." *Social Text* 20 (3): 117–148.

Puri, Jyoti. 2019. "Sculpting the Saffron Body: Yoga, Hindutva, and the International Marketplace." In *Majoritarian State: How Hindu Nationalism Is Changing India*, edited by Angana P. Chatterji, Thomas Blom Hansen, and Christophe Jaffrelot, 317–331. Oxford: Oxford University Press.

Qureshi, Ayaz. 2015. "The Marketization of HIV/AIDS Governance: Public-Private Partnerships and Bureaucratic Culture in Pakistan." *Cambridge Journal of Anthropology* 33 (1): 35–48.

Radcliffe-Brown, Alfred. 1952. *Structure and Function in Primitive Society*. London: Cohen and West.

Radhakrishnan, Smitha. 2011. *Appropriately Indian: Gender and Culture in a New Transnational Class*. Durham: Duke University Press.

Rahman, Anisur. 2001. *Indian Labour Migration to the Gulf*. New Delhi: Rajat Publications.

Rajan, S. Irudaya, V. J. Varghese, and M. S. Jayakumar. 2010. "Looking beyond the Emigration Act 1983: Revisiting the Recruitment Practices in India." In *Governance and Labour Migration: Indian Migration Report 2010*, edited by S. Irudaya Rajan, 251–287. New Delhi: Routledge India.

Rajwade, L. 1938. "The Indian Mother and Her Problems." In *Our Cause: A Symposium by Indian Women*, edited by K. Nehru, 73–89. Allahabad: Kitabistan.

Ramaswamy, Sumathi. 2010. *The Goddess and the Nation: Mapping Mother India*. Durham: Duke University Press.

Reed, Tiana. 2018. "The Shape of Poetics to Come: On Taking Up the Task of Criticism." *American Quarterly* 70 (1): 139–150.

Rios, Victor M. "The Hyper-Criminalization of Black and Latino Male Youth in the Era of Mass Incarceration." *Souls: A Critical Journal of Black Politics, Culture, and Society* 8 (2): 40–54.

Rogers, Douglas. 2012a. "The Materiality of the Corporation: Oil, Gas, and Corporate Social Technologies in the Remaking of a Russian Region." *American Ethnologist* 39 (2): 284–296.

———. 2012b. *The Depths of Russia: Oil, Power, and Culture after Socialism*. Ithaca: Cornell University Press.

———. 2015. "Oil and Anthropology." *Annual Review of Anthropology* 44 (1): 365–380.

Rose, Nikolas. 1996. "Governing 'Advanced' Liberal Democracies." In *Foucault and Political Reason: Liberalism, Neo-Liberalism and Rationalities of Government*, edited by Andrew Barry, Thomas Osborne, and Nikolas Rose. Chicago: University of Chicago Press.

Ross, Michael L. 2001. "Does Oil Hinder Democracy?" *World Politics* 53 (3): 325–361.

———. 2012. *The Oil Curse: How Petroleum Wealth Shapes the Development of Nations*. Princeton, NJ: Princeton University Press.

Rubin, Gayle. 1975. "The Traffic in Women: Notes on the 'Political Economy' of Sex." In *Toward an Anthropology of Women,* edited by Rayner R. Reiter, 157–210. New York: Monthly Review Press.

Sahlins, Marshall. 1972. *Stone Age Economics*. New York: Aldine de Gruyter.

———. 2013. *What Kinship Is—and Is Not*. Chicago: University of Chicago Press.

Said, Edward. 1979. *Orientalism*. New York: Vintage Books.

Saikia, Arunabh. 2020. "The Other Virus." *Scroll.in*, April 8.

Saleh, Hassan Mohammad Abdulla. 1991. "Labor, Nationalism and Imperialism in Eastern Arabia: Britain, the Shaikhs and the Gulf Oil Workers in Bahrain, Kuwait and Qatar, 1932–1956." PhD diss., University of Michigan.

Sangari, Kumkum, and Sudesh Vaid. 1999 [1984]. "Recasting Women: An Introduction." In *Recasting Women: Essays in Colonial History*, edited by Kumkum Sangari and Sudesh Vaid, 1–26. New Delhi: Kali for Women.

Santiago, Myrna I. 2006. *The Ecology of Oil: Environment, Labor, and the Mexican Revolution, 1900–1938*. Cambridge: Cambridge University Press.

Sarkar, Tanika. 2001. *Hindu Wife, Hindu Nation: Community, Religion, and Cultural Nationalism*. Bloomington: Indiana University Press.

———. 2019. "How the Sangh Parivar Writes and Teaches History." In *Majoritarian State: How Hindu Nationalism Is Changing India*, edited by Angana P. Chatterji, Thomas Blom Hansen, and Christophe Jaffrelot, 151–173. Oxford: Oxford University Press.

Sarmadi, Behzad. 2013. "'Bachelor' in the City: Urban Transformation and Matter Out of Place in Dubai." *Journal of Arabian Studies: Arabia, the Gulf, and the Red Sea* 3 (2): 196–214.

Savarkar, V. D. 1939. "Speech to 21st Session Calcutta." In *Hindu Rashtra Darshan*. Poona: Maharashtra Prantik Hindusabha.

Sawyer, Suzana. 2004. *Crude Chronicles: Indigenous Politics, Multinational Oil, and Neoliberalism in Ecuador.* Durham: Duke University Press.

———. 2006. "Disabling Corporate Sovereignty in a Transnational Lawsuit." *PoLAR: Political and Legal Anthropology Review* 29 (1): 23–43.

Schaflechner, Jürgen. 2019. "Hinglaj Devi: Solidifying Hindu Identity at a Hindu Temple in Pakistan." *American Anthropologist* 122 (3): 528–539.

Schmidt, Kjeld. 2012. "The Trouble with 'Tacit Knowledge.'" *Computer Supported Cooperative Work* 21 (2): 163–225.

Schneider, David M. 1980. *American Kinship: A Cultural Account,* 2nd ed. Chicago: University of Chicago Press.

Scroll India. 2015. "Rare Protests by South Asian Labourers about Unpaid Wages Prompts Dubai to Mobilize Riot Police." March 10.

Seccombe, I. J., and R. I. Lawless. 1986. "Foreign Worker Dependence in the Gulf, and the International Oil Companies: 1910–50." *International Migration Review* 20 (3): 548–574.

Sengupta, Chiranjib. 2020. "Temporary Setback? Why Most Indians Won't Give Up on Their Dubai Dreams." *Outlook India*, May 25. https://www.outlookindia.com/magazine/story/world-news-temporary-setback-why-most-indians-wont-give-up-on-their-dubai-dreams/303220.

Shah, Nasra. 2000. "Relative Success of Male Workers in the Host Country, Kuwait: Does the Channel of Migration Matter?" *International Migration Review* 34 (1): 59–78.

Shever, Elana. 2012. *Resources for Reform: Oil and Neoliberalism in Argentina.* Stanford: Stanford University Press.

Shryock, Andrew. 2013. "It's This, Not That: How Marshall Sahlins Solves Kinship." *Hau* 3 (2): 271–279.

Silverstein, Michael. 2011. "What Goes Around . . . : Some Shtick from 'Tricky Dick' and the Circulation of U.S. Presidential Image." *Linguistic Anthropology* 21 (1): 54–77.

Simpson, Audra. 2014. *Mohawk Interruptus: Political Life across the Borders of Settler States.* Durham: Duke University Press.

———. 2017. "The Ruse of Consent and the Anatomy of 'Refusal': Cases from Indigenous North America and Australia." *Postcolonial Studies* 20 (1): 18–33.

Srinivasan, Rajeev. 2016. "The Temple as Infrastructure." *Swarajya Magazine*, June 18.

Stirr, Anna. 2017. "Popular Music among Nepalis in Bahrain: Nightclubs, Media, Performance, and Publics." In *Global Nepalis: Religion, Culture, and Community in a New and Old Diaspora*, edited by David N. Gellner and Sondra L. Hausner. Oxford: Oxford University Press.

Stoler, Ann Laura. 2002. *Carnal Knowledge and Imperial Power: Race and the Intimate in Colonial Rule*. Berkeley: University of California Press.

———. 2008. "Imperial Debris: Reflections on Ruin and Ruination." *Cultural Anthropology* 23 (2): 191–219.

———. 2010. *Along the Archival Grain*. Princeton: Princeton University Press.

Strathern, Marilyn. 1988. *The Gender of the Gift: Problems with Women and Problems with Society in Melanesia*. Berkeley: University of California Press.

Sundar, Nandini. 2019. "Hindutva Incorporation and Socioeconomic Exclusion: The Adivasi Dilemma." In *Majoritarian State: How Hindu Nationalism Is Changing India*, edited by Angana P. Chatterji, Thomas Blom Hansen, and Christophe Jaffrelot, 249–258. Oxford: Oxford University Press.

Thompson, E. P. 1963. *The Making of the English Working Class*. New York: Vintage Books.

Times of India. 2016. "Government to Merge Overseas Indian Affairs Ministry with MEA." January 7.

Trautmann, Thomas R. 1981. *Dravidian Kinship*. Cambridge: Cambridge University Press.

Trawick, Margaret. 1990. *Notes on Love in a Tamil Family*. Berkeley: University of California Press.

Tribune. 2009. "My Govt Is Being Defamed, Says Modi." March 9. tribuneindia. com/2002/20020310/main4.htm.

Trouillot, Michel-Rolph. 1991a. "Anthropology and the Savage Slot: The Poetics and Politics of Otherness." In *Recapturing Anthropology: Working in the Present*, edited by Richard Fox, 17–44. Santa Fe: School of American Research Advanced Seminar Series.

———. 1991b. "Anthropology as Metaphor: The Savage's Legacy and the Postmodern World." *Review* (Fernand Braudel Center) 14 (1): 29–54.

———. 1995. *Silencing the Past: Power and the Production of History*. Boston: Beacon Press.

———. 2001. "Anthropology of the State in the Age of Globalization: Close Encounters of the Deceptive Kind." *Current Anthropology* 42 (1): 125–138.

Tsing, Anna Lowenhaupt. 2005. *Friction: An Ethnography of Global Connection*. Princeton: Princeton University Press.

———. 2015. *The Mushroom at the End of the World*. Princeton: Princeton University Press.

————. 2016. "What Is Emerging? Supply Chains and the Remaking of Asia." *Professional Geographer* 68 (2): 330–337.

Upadhya, Carol. 2016 *Reengineering India: Work, Capital, and Class in an Offshore Economy*. Oxford: Oxford University Press.

van der Veer, Peter. 1994. *Religious Nationalism: Hindus and Muslims in India*. Berkeley: University of California Press.

————. 2005. "Virtual India: Indian IT Labor and the Nation-State." In *Sovereign Bodies: Citizens, Migrants, and States in the Postcolonial World*, edited by Thomas Blom Hansen and Finn Stepputat, 276–290. Princeton: Princeton University Press.

Vitalis, Robert. 2009. *America's Kingdom: Mythmaking on the Saudi Oil Frontier*. New York: Verso.

Vora, Neha. 2011. "From Golden Frontier to Global City: Shifting Forms of Belonging, `Freedom,' and Governance among Indian Businessmen in Dubai." *American Anthropologist* 113 (2): 306–318.

————. 2013. *Impossible Citizens: Dubai's Indian Diaspora*. Durham: Duke University Press.

————. 2014. "Expat/Expert Camps: Redefining 'Labour' within Gulf Migration." In *Transit States: Labour, Migration, and Citizenship in the Gulf*, edited by Abdulhadi Khalaf, Omar AlShehabi, and Adam Hanieh, 170–197. London: Pluto Books.

————. 2019. *Teach for Arabia: American Universities, Liberalism, and Transnational Qatar*. Stanford: Stanford University Press.

Vora, Neha, and Natalie Koch. 2015. "Everyday Inclusions: Rethinking Ethnocracy, Kafala, and Belonging in the Arabian Peninsula." *Studies in Ethnicity and Nationalism* 15 (3): 540–552.

Wallen, Joe. 2020. "Protests Break Out in India as Migrant Workers Stranded and Starving far from Home." *Telegraph*, April 17.

Watts, Michael. 2004. "Resource Curse? Governmentality, Oil and Power in the Niger Delta, Nigeria." *Geopolitics* 9 (1): 50–80.

————. 2012. "A Tale of Two Gulfs: Life, Death, and Dispossession along Two Oil Frontiers." *American Quarterly* 64 (3): 437–467.

Weeks, Kathi. 2011. *The Problem with Work: Feminism, Marxism, Antiwork Politics, and Postwork Imaginaries*. Durham: Duke University Press.

Weiss, Brad. 2004. "Contentious Futures: Past and Present." In *Producing African Futures: Ritual and Reproduction in a Neoliberal Age*, edited by Brad Weiss, 1–20. Boston: Brill.

————. 2017. "Getting Ahead When We're Behind: Time, Potential, and Value in

Urban Tanzania." In *African Futures: Essays on Crisis, Emergence, and Possibility*, edited by Brian Goldstone and Juan Obarrio, 199–210. Chicago: University of Chicago Press.

Welker, Marina. 2014. *Enacting the Corporation: An American Mining Firm in Post-Authoritarian Indonesia*. Berkley: University of California Press.

Werbner, Pnina. 1999. "Global Pathways: Working Class Cosmopolitans and the Creation of Transnational Networks." *Social Anthropology* 7 (1): 17–35.

West, Harry G. 2005. *Kupilikula: Governance and the Invisible Realm in Mozambique*. Chicago: University of Chicago Press.

Weszkalnys, Gisa. 2011. "Cursed Resources, or Articulations of Economic Theory in the Gulf of Guinea." *Economy and Society* 40 (3): 345–372.

———. 2014. "Anticipating Oil: The Temporal Politics of a Disaster Yet to Come." *Sociological Review* 62 (S1): 211–235.

White, Hayden. 1973. *Metahistory: The Historical Imagination in Nineteenth Century Europe*. Baltimore: Johns Hopkins University Press.

———. 1987. *The Content of the Form: Narrative Discourse and Historical Representation*. Baltimore: Johns Hopkins University Press.

White, Leslie A. 1949. *The Science of Culture*. New York: Grove Press.

Winckler, Onn. 2010. "Labor Migration to the GCC States." *Middle East Institute Viewpoints* (February): 9–12.

Witsoe, Jeffrey L. 2011. "Corruption as Power: Caste and the Political Imagination of the Postcolonial State." *American Ethnologist* 38 (1): 73–85.

Wood, Robert W. 2016. "In BP's Final $20 Billion Gulf Settlement, U.S. Taxpayers Subsidize $15.3 Billion." *Forbes*, April 6.

Wright, Andrea. 2015. "Migratory Pipelines: Labor and Oil in the Arabian Sea." PhD diss., University of Michigan.

———. 2018. "'The Immoral Traffic in Women': Regulating Indian Emigration to the Persian Gulf." In *Borders and Mobility in South Asia and Beyond*, edited by Reece Jones and Md. Azmeary Ferdoush, 145–166. Amsterdam: Amsterdam University Press.

———. 2020a. "Imperial Labor: Strikes, Security, and the Depoliticization of Oil Production." In *South Asian Migrations: A Global History: Labor, Law, and Wayward Lives*, edited by Neilesh Bose, 63–84. New York: Bloomsbury.

———. 2020b. "Making Kin from Gold: Dowry, Gender, and Indian Labor Migration." *Cultural Anthropology* 35(3): 435–461.

———. 2020c. "No Good Options for Migrant Workers in Gulf COVID-19 Lockdown." *Middle East Report Online*. April 30.

———. 2021. "From Slaves to Contract Workers: Genealogies of Consent and Security in Indian Labor Migration." *Journal of World History* 31 (2): 29-43.

———. N.d. "Producing Labor Hierarchies: An Anthropological History of Oil in the Arabian Sea." Unpublished manuscript.

Xiang Biao. 2005. "Gender, Dowry and the Migration System of Indian Information Technology Professionals." *Indian Journal of Gender Studies* 12 (2&3): 357–380.

———. 2011. *Global "Body Shopping": An Indian Labor System in the Information Technology Industry*. Princeton: Princeton University Press.

Yanagisako, Sylvia, and Jane Collier. 1987. "Toward a Unified Analysis of Gender and Kinship." In *Gender and Kinship: Essays toward a Unified Analysis*, edited by S. Yanagisako and J. Collier. Stanford: Stanford University Press.

Yang, Anand A. 1989. *The Limited Raj: Agrarian Roots in Colonial India, Saran District, 1793–1920*. Berkeley: University of California Press.

Yergin, Daniel. 2008. *The Prize: The Epic Quest for Oil, Money, and Power*. New York: Free Press.

———. 2011. *The Quest: Energy, Security, and the Remaking of the Modern World*. New York: Penguin Press.

Zachariah, K. C., B. A. Prakash, and S. I. Rajan. 2004. "Indian Workers in the UAE: Employment, Wages, and Working Conditions." *Economic and Political Weekly* 39 (22): 2227–2234.

Zamindar, Vazira Fazila-Yacoobali. 2007. *The Long Partition and the Making of Modern South Asia: Refugees, Boundaries, Histories*. New York: Columbia University Press.

Zharkevich, Ina. 2019. "Money and Blood: Remittances as a Substance of Relatedness in Transnational Families in Nepal." *American Anthropologist* 35(1): 1–13.

Index

167–68; commodification, 17, 19, 38, 166, 167; indentured, 18, 29–31, 32, 38, 221n11; marketization, 17; mobility, 17, 38, 163, 166, 167, 169, 184; scarcity and surplus, 4, 6. *See also* Contracting; Migrant workers; Oil industry workers; Workers

Labor camps, 6, 146, 147–49, 153, 155–59, 160, 224n35

Labor laws: compensation for injuries or death, 178–79; minimum wages, 27–28, 61, 207n13; modernization, 141–42; strikes prohibited, 3, 144, 145, 147, 154; unions prohibited, 164. *See also* Kafala (sponsorship) system

Labor relations, in oil industry, 6, 8, 138–40, 142, 143–47, 151–55. *See also* Strikes

Larkin, Brian, 218n12

Laws, Indian: citizenship, 101–2, 123, 208n32; on dowries, 96; on human trafficking, 100–101. *See also* Indian emigration regulations

Laws, of Gulf countries: citizenship, 127, 138–39, 220n50; commercial, 140, 142; immigration, 140; property ownership, 140, 141. *See also* Labor laws

Liberalism, philosophy and ideology, 31–33, 159, 229n21

Liberalization, 5, 41–42, 48–49, 59, 99, 103. *See also* Neoliberalism

Limbert, Mandana E., 202–3n16, 218n12

Lori, Noora, 151

Lowe, Lisa, 31–32

Managers: Arab, 21, 125, 214n25; British, 18, 60–61, 81–83, 113, 125, 131–33, 136; European and American, 60, 81, 131–33, 136, 137–38, 148, 153–54, 166–67, 190–91, 194; field research and, 7, 137–38; hiring process, 69, 70, 74–75, 81–83, 166–67,

214–15n25; networks, 82, 86, 194; perceptions of migrant workers, 59–61; project, 60–61, 81–82, 113, 167, 172

Mandirs, *see* Hindu temples

Mangoes, 15–16, 17, 19

Mariner, Kathryn A., 98

Marriages, *see* Dowries; Families

Marx, Karl, 205n37, 217n37

Masculinity, 107–9, 119

Materiality: oil, 191, 213n1, 222n20; semiotic, 90, 111

Mbembe, Achille, 192, 206n39, 210n55, 229n19

Mehta, Purvi, 227–28n5

Men, *see* Gender; Masculinity; Oil industry workers

Middle-class Indians: information technology workers, 94, 102, 104, 106, 125–26, 216–17n36; in oil industry, 126; residents and tourists in Gulf countries, 126–29, 157–58; retirement homes, 129

Migrant workers: abandoned, 27, 155–59, 190, 193, 197, 224n35; brand image of India represented by, 43–45, 46, 49, 52, 59, 61–62, 190, 224n36; challenges, 45–46; deaths, 161–63, 178–79, 187–88, 189, 192; education levels, 3, 22, 38, 42, 47–48, 62, 156; effects of pandemic, 197–99; illegal or irregular, 37, 52, 83–85; masculinity, 107–9; modernity and, 115–16, 125–26, 129–30, 133, 135–36; Muslim, 115–17, 120, 122, 124–25, 159–60, 218n3, 225n40; number in Gulf countries, 2, 10, 36–37; personal savings, 108; rights, 38, 189; spending choices, 87–88, 93, 109; wages, 27–28, 45–46; women, 28–29, 99–103. *See also* Contracts, employment; Debt; Entrepreneurial migrants; Networks;

Venezuela, 4, 118, 165

VHP, *see* Vishwa Hindu Parishad

Visas: employers as sponsors, 24, 139, 155; fees, 83, 152–53; for migrants, 25, 39, 40, 67, 71; overstaying, 83–84. *See also* Kafala (sponsorship) system

Vishwa Hindu Parishad (VHP), 123

Vitalis, Robert, 155

Voluntary associations, 6–7, 127–29, 157–58, 159

Vora, Neha, 216n22, 224n26, 229n19

Watts, Michael, 221n5, 222n4, 227n45

Weddings, *see* Dowries

White, Leslie A., 228n13

Whiteness: economic and cultural capital, 224n26; fieldwork and, 2, 10, 132, 153, 203–4n29; racist acts, 149; white privilege, 150, 203–4n29; white supremacy, 228n11. *See also* Managers; Race, racism, and racialized hierarchies

Women: citizenship, 101–2, 208n32; domestic violence and, 96; domestic workers, 29, 32, 47, 99–100; education levels, 25, 28, 102–3; emigration regulations, 25, 28–29, 32, 36, 102, 103, 207n8; entertainers, 100; femininity, 102, 112; information technology workers, 102; migrant workers, 99–103;

Muslims, 128–29; as national symbols, 101; nontraditional jobs, 216n27; recruiting agency employees, 7–8, 53; rights advocates, 103; rights dependent on husband and family, 36, 208n32; study abroad, 102; trafficking, 36, 100–101; upper- and middle-class Indians, 126–29, 157–58; as vulnerable citizens, 25, 36, 101, 102; wages, 102–3; wives of migrant workers, 110–11, 112; wives of recruiting agency employees, 88. *See also* Dowries; Gender

Workers: disposability, 163, 192; indentured, 18, 29–31, 32, 38, 221n11; precarity, 5, 62, 139, 141, 144, 151–53, 160, 162, 184–85, 192; regional stereotypes, 56; rights, 38, 139, 147, 178, 189, 224n31; social hierarchy, 73–74; solidarities, 145, 146, 149, 158–59, 190; wages in India, 22–23, 39, 45. *See also* Labor; Migrant workers; Oil industry workers

World Bank, 41, 211n67

Xiang Biao, 216–17n36

Yanagisako, Sylvia, 215n5

Zamindar, Vazira Fazila-Yacoobali, 36

Zharkevich, Ina, 111